THE MISSING GOSPEL OF MODERN CHRISTIANITY

Know, believe, and share the true message of salvation.

Trey Talley

Endorsements:

"Evangelicals love the evangel— the gospel— and they love to share it. Trouble is they don't always know the gospel and they don't always proclaim the true gospel. This clear, comprehensive, and compelling book reminds us just how good the Good News is. It will help Christians, churches, and church leaders know, love, and proclaim the true life-giving gospel of Jesus Christ. Read this book— and then go tell it on a mountain."

Stephen J. Nichols, Ph.D.
President of Reformation Bible College
Chief Academic Officer of Ligonier Ministries

"A clear and biblical guide to the doctrine of soteriology that's deeply theological and yet simple enough for lay persons in your church."

Timothy Paul Jones, Ph.D.
Professor of Apologetics and Family Ministry
The Southern Baptist Theological Seminary

"In forceful and direct terms, Talley challenges readers to think about some of the most basic and important matters of the Christian life. What is the gospel, and how should we communicate the gospel to others? Talley helps readers of all levels to come to greater clarity in understanding the gospel we are called to believe and to share with the world."

Guy Prentiss Waters, Ph.D.
James M. Baird, Jr. Professor of New Testament
Reformed Theological Seminary

"Pastor Trey Talley provides a robustly biblical articulation of the good news of God's grace to guilty sinners, through Jesus Christ. His exposition of the indispensable components of Paul's gospel from Romans shows the standard that our presentations of the gospel, whether in public preaching or in personal evangelism, must meet. Pastor Talley pulls no punches in his critique of defective and misleading approaches to evangelism; but his boldness is driven by the high stakes involved: eternal life and joy in communion with the living God, or eternal condemnation and anguish under God's just wrath. Words matter, and this book shows how crucial it is for us to choose our words well as we speak on behalf of the God of holiness and mercy, into the lives of people who desperately need to be reconciled to him, through the only mediator between God and humans, Christ Jesus, son of God and son of David."

Dennis E. Johnson, Ph.D.
Professor Emeritus of Practical Theology
Westminster Seminary California

The Missing Gospel of Modern Christianity:
Know, believe, and share the true message of salvation.

Copyright 2019 Trey Talley

Kindle Publishing

All rights reserved.

ISBN: 978-1-0816-7760-2

"Scripture quotations are from The ESV® Bible
(The Holy Bible, English Standard Version®), copyright © 2001
by Crossway, a publishing ministry of Good News Publishers.
Used by permission. All rights reserved."

DEDICATIONS AND ACKNOWLEDGEMENTS

In honor of Dr. R. C. Sproul (1939-2017) and Ligonier Ministries whose teaching has greatly impacted both my life and my beliefs.

Special thanks to my loving and supporting wife, Felisha, whose steady patience has allowed me to write this book.

Tapanga, Tradley, and Titan, may you continue to stand firm in the faith of which you have been taught.

Special thanks to all of those who make up our wonderful church, The Church At Pecan Creek. May God continue to use us to make the gospel known.

CONTENTS

INTRODUCTION: Are you struggling to find the right words to share the gospel?...............1

PART I: WHAT IS THE GOSPEL?

1. The Messenger: An Apostle Of Jesus Christ. 9
2. The Message: Good News From God.................14
3. Component #1: Jesus Is The Fulfillment Of Prophecy. 22
4. Component #2: Jesus Is God. 34
5. Component #3: Jesus Is Human.................48
6. Component #4: Jesus Died For Sins. 61
7. Component #5: Jesus Rose From The Dead. 84
8. Component #6: Jesus Is Christ................91
9. Component #7: Jesus Is Lord...................98
10. Component #8: Salvation Is By Grace Alone........104
    Conclusion To PART I: 114

PART II: CONSEQUENCES OF CHANGING GOD'S GOSPEL.

11. Are Professing Christians Proclaiming The Gospel Correctly? 119
12. Are All Gospels *The* Gospel? 124
13. Is The Wrong Gospel Creating False Christians?..........138
14. Are Your Fellow Church Members Saved? 147
    Conclusion To PART II: 152

PART III: POPULAR, YET UNBIBLICAL, WORDS USED TO SPEAK OF SALVATION.

15. An Evaluation Of Current Evangelistic Techniques And Questions. 157
16. Do You Have A Relationship With God?............................. 162
17. Have You Made A Decision For Christ?............................. 175
18. Would You Like To Ask Jesus Into Your Heart?................ 179
19. Jesus Is Knocking. Will You Let Him In? 185
20. Instructing A Person To Tell Jesus To Come Into His Life..... 189
21. Do You Want To Become A Christian?................................ 191
22. Have You Invited (Or Accepted) Jesus to Be Your Personal Savior? 193
23. Have You Said The Sinner's Prayer?................................. 198
24. Do You Know That God Loves You? 205
25. God Loves You And Has A Great Plan For Your Life. 210
26. Do You Have A Personal Testimony?................................ 213
27. Do You Want To Go To Heaven?...................................... 216
28. Come To The Front! 219
29. Lifestyle Evangelism. 228
    Conclusion To PART III: 232

PART IV: UNPOPULAR, YET BIBLICAL, WORDS USED TO SPEAK OF SALVATION.

30. Don't Be Afraid To Use Biblical Words. 237
31. Believed. 239
32. Repented. 247
33. Saved. 255
34. Justified. 261
35. Atoned. 267
36. Redeemed. 272
    Conclusion To PART IV: 276

FINAL THOUGHTS 279
BIBLIOGRAPHY 285

INTRODUCTION

When professing Christians are asked about their salvation, their mind often goes to a time when they walked an aisle at church, raised a hand, made a decision, said the sinner's prayer, were baptized or joined a church. While such activities are often relied upon as proof of salvation, the truth of the matter is that such activities are no guarantee of salvation. For instance, it is possible that a person could walk an aisle at church, raise a hand, make a decision, say the sinner's prayer, be baptized, join a church and still be just as unsaved as a person who had done none of these things. Can people claim to be Christians, yet still be on their way to hell? The answer is, "Yes." So, if these things do not provide the surety of salvation, then what does? This leads to some critical questions, such as "How can a person be saved?", "How do you know if you are actually saved?", and "How do I check on the salvation of others?"

The Apostle Paul writes that the gospel "is the power of God unto salvation for everyone who believes…"[1] In other words, belief in the gospel is essential for a person to be saved. Whether a person has walked an aisle, filled out a card, raised a hand, said the sinner's prayer, asked Jesus into their heart, or even whether or not he or she was baptized, is not the key to determine if one is genuinely saved. The key issue is belief, and the key belief must be the gospel. This means that belief in the gospel is not a secondary

---

[1] Romans 1:16: All Bible references are from *The Holy Bible: English Standard Version Containing the Old and New Testaments: ESV.* (Wheaton, IL: Crossway, 2007)

or tertiary matter when it comes to determining one's salvation, it is primary. Since believing in the gospel is required for salvation, it is of utmost importance to know what the Apostle Paul had in mind when he used the word "gospel."

So, what is the gospel? Many have heard the word "gospel" and can put together the six letters that make up the word. However, it is not enough to just know the word, say the word, or spell the word correctly; we must know the message that the word *gospel* represents. More than just a word, the gospel is a message that is packed with the truth of God about His Savior. However, the details of the gospel message are becoming less and less known even by professing Christians. As the trusted theologian, Graeme Goldsworthy has written:

> It is a matter for some concern that some books and study courses on evangelism seem to assume that every Christian is clear about what the gospel is, and that what is needed most is help in the techniques of explaining the gospel to unbelievers. Experience suggests that this assumption is poorly based and that there is a great deal of confusion among believers about what the gospel is.[2]

This confusion over the gospel is expected among those who do not even profess to be Christians, but as Goldsworthy has written, there are many professing Christians that are also confused about the gospel. Such "confusion" about the gospel is no small matter since it is the essential belief for one to be saved. But sadly, there are many professing Christians who take the liberty to change, and even replace, the gospel message with a message of their own. Usually, this is done somewhat unintentionally by taking too much information away from the gospel, or by adding too much non-gospel information to the gospel. Even though such false communication about the gospel may be inadvertent, it creates a tremendous problem for Christianity. J. I. Packer writes,

---

[2] Graeme Goldsworthy, *Preaching the Whole Bible as Christian Scripture: The Application of Biblical Theology to Expository Preaching* (Grand Rapids, MI: W.B. Eerdmans, 2000), 81.

"The result of these omissions is that part of the biblical gospel is now preached as if it were the whole of that gospel; and a half-truth masquerading as the whole truth becomes a complete untruth."[3] Of all people, Christians, should *not* be the ones that are confused about the gospel or taking liberty with the gospel. We should be the ones who know it, believe it, proclaim it, and are adamant about preserving it. As R. C. Sproul has written, "This Gospel is the only Gospel: there is no other; and to change its substance is to pervert and indeed destroy it."[4]

Changing God's message of salvation has dire consequences.[5] The result is the creation of manmade false gospels being believed and proclaimed as the one true gospel from God. Such changed gospels are not from God, and do not carry the "power of God for salvation." If the wrong gospel is being presented, no matter how adamant a professing Christian is in sharing it, and no matter how sincerely someone believes in it, if it is the wrong gospel, then there is no salvation. Instead of saving, false gospels have the opposite effect.[6] As one of the most influential Christian writers of the twentieth century, A.W. Pink, wrote:

> The 'Gospel' which is now being proclaimed is, in nine cases out of every ten, but a perversion of the Truth, and tens of thousands, assured they are bound for Heaven, are now hastening to Hell, as fast as time can take them. Things are far, far worse in Christendom than even the 'pessimist' and the 'alarmist' suppose.[7]

What a dire summation of the state of professing Christians' ability to articulate the gospel correctly. According to Pink, the

---

[3] J. I. Packer, introduction, in *The Death of Death in the Death of Christ*, by John Owen (Edinburgh: Banner of Truth Trust, 1983), http://www.the-highway.com/Death.html.
[4] R. C. Sproul, *Getting the Gospel Right: The Tie That Binds Evangelicals Together* (Grand Rapids, MI: Baker Books, 1999), 100.
[5] Galatians 1:6-9
[6] Romans 1:16
[7] Arthur W. Pink, *Studies on Saving Faith* (Memphis, TN: Bottom of The Hill Publishing, 2011), 12.

vast majority of people claiming to be Christians are actually *not* Christians. These pseudo-Christians have heard and believed a gospel, but it is the wrong gospel, and it lacks the power of God to save them. What is more shocking is that professing Christians are the primary makers and propagators of the false gospels which lead people into false conversions and a false assurance of their salvation.

Of all people, why would professing Christians want to alter the message of salvation? Most likely, they do not miscommunicate the gospel out of an evil desire to mislead others. Instead, the miscommunication appears to occur due to a general lack of knowledge about the gospel message they claim to know and proclaim. This lack of gospel knowledge then leads to the communication of a gospel which is inadequate or even distorted. Despite their good intentions, if professing Christians do not know and understand the gospel, then any attempt to convey the gospel to others will be insufficient.

It is here where we find the source of the confusing, inadequate, and incorrect gospels that well-meaning Christians often proclaim; they just don't know the gospel well enough to communicate it to others correctly. Good gospel *communication* requires a good *knowledge* of the gospel. If an individual does not personally know the gospel, then how can he or she share the gospel correctly with others? Knowing and understanding the gospel personally should produce clearer gospel communication. However, when the knowledge and understanding of the gospel are poor, it is a given, that one's communication of it to others will be as well.

With so many professing Christians proclaiming different versions of the gospel, it appears that the gospel is unintentionally being redefined to mean anything that a person wants it to mean. Far from being a set message delivered by God, for us to hear, believe, and repeat to others, there is now great liberty taken with the message. Such liberty has substantially clouded the definition of the gospel and, in many cases, created a gospel that is not even close to the original.

Recently, I asked a group of Christians at a local collegiate Bible Study; "What is the gospel?" Sadly, as I expected, the answers they gave significantly varied. One said, "It is a way of life." Another said, "It is asking Jesus in your heart." Another said, "The gospel is all of God's Word." Still, another man began to explain that the gospel was God getting him through a painful divorce that he had just gone through. And another said, "The gospel is about doing what is right in life." So, which of the students got the answer right, or is there even such thing as a right answer? In a room, full of professing Christian students there was not even a near agreement on the gospel, but even more concerning is that not one student seemed to be troubled by the differing definitions that were given.

Similarly, the other day, a man knocked on my office door and introduced himself as an assistant to a well-known evangelist that was coming to Dallas to put on a massive evangelistic crusade at the convention center. The assistant was canvassing the area and distributing fliers to help increase attendance. As I spoke with him, I discovered that he had been on staff with this popular evangelist for five years. He spoke at length about the details of the massive evangelistic crusade and how they were hoping for 10,000 people to be saved. "Wow, that is a lot of salvations!", I said. Then I asked the man, who apparently knew all about evangelism, "Well, if you don't mind me asking, what is the gospel?" He replied, "What do you mean?" "Well," I said, "you work for an evangelist, you are helping with an evangelistic crusade, and you are expecting 10,000 to be saved at the event. So, what is the gospel that will be presented at the convention center so that 10,000 people can be saved?" A seemingly easy question for a man who has worked for a major evangelistic organization for five years. However, the question sent him scrambling for an answer. And what he did next seemed to be a bizarre mental exercise of saying everything and anything Christian that he could possibly think of in his attempt to define the gospel. Unfortunately, he never landed on anything close to a biblical definition of the gospel. After quite some time of rambling, he finally stopped. Exhaustedly he replied, "Wow, I really needed that! It has been a long time since I've had to think about the gospel."

How could this be? I would like to say the problem of defining the gospel found with the group of college students and the staff member for the big-name evangelist were rare, but the more I ask professing Christians to define the gospel, the more I realize just how prevalent the problem of clear gospel proclamation has become.

Can the content of the gospel message be whatever we determine it to be? Can each Christian make up his or her own gospel? While our relativistic culture would undoubtedly say, "Yes!" We, as Christians must say, "No!" As those who are to represent the Word of God correctly, we must understand that we do not have the right to create our own individual gospel message and call it, *the* gospel. The gospel is a far more precise message than many Christians are willing to admit. The gospel is a message that has been determined by God that we are to believe, and proclaim to others, as is and unaltered. We should not treat any important message with such subjectivism and especially a message from God Himself that involves eternal salvation.

With that said, let me ask you, "What is the gospel?" Really, think about it for a moment. How will you answer this question regarding the foundational belief of the Christian faith? What will you say? What words will you choose to speak about salvation? For many professing Christians, such a question would cause much anxiety and even panic, but this need not be the case. The gospel can be known. We as Christians just need to do a better job of studying the gospel that God has made abundantly clear in His Word.

Would you like to know and understand the gospel better? Do you want to be able to speak about the gospel to others correctly, without confusion? Would you like to be confident that the gospel that you are sharing is *the* gospel that is the "power of God for salvation?" In the following pages, we will explore each phrase of the gospel message that was given to the Apostle Paul to gain a better understanding of what he regarded as "the gospel of God." By knowing the information of the gospel message better, you will be better equipped to communicate salvation to others in a way that is biblical, Christ-honoring, and God-glorifying.

PART I:

WHAT IS THE GOSPEL?

Chapter 1

THE MESSENGER: AN APOSTLE OF JESUS CHRIST.

Paul, a servant of Christ Jesus, called to be an apostle, set apart for the gospel of God, which he promised beforehand through his prophets in the holy Scriptures, concerning his Son, who was descended from David according to the flesh and was declared to be the Son of God in power according to the Spirit of holiness by his resurrection from the dead, Jesus Christ our Lord, through whom we have received grace . . . (Rom. 1:1-5)

Before we get to the actual study of the gospel, let us begin first with a look at the person who is stating this gospel summary. In the opening sentence of his letter to the Romans, Paul let them know that he was "called to be an apostle."[8] The word "apostle" simply means "one who is sent." Paul used the word "apostle" to convey that he had been sent, but not sent by just anyone, but by Jesus Christ. In other words, Paul had the authority to speak on God's behalf because he had been uniquely called, commissioned, and sent by Jesus Christ. Similar to his introduction of himself in Romans is his reminder to the Galatians of who he is, ". . . an apostle—not from men nor through man, but through Jesus Christ and

---

[8] Romans 1:1

God the Father, who raised him from the dead."[9] In other words, Paul did not nominate himself to this position, nor did he rely on a group of people to tell him that he was an apostle. Paul's calling and his message were directly from God. Paul's role as an Apostle was a rare and unique calling, as Martin Lloyd Jones wrote in *The Cross*:

> If you and I want to know what the message of the Christian church is, surely the thing for us to do is to go back to the beginning. How did the Christian church begin? What was the message? Here are men called apostles. These were the men who founded the Christian church. They all said that they were not preaching their own ideas, but that they had been given the message by the Lord Jesus Christ. Therefore, if we want to know what the Christian message is, we must go back and consider the Apostle's message.[10]

The early church understood that even though Christ had ascended back into heaven, He had given the Apostles authority to establish the church through their teaching. This fact can be seen from the earliest Apostolic message delivered by Peter on the Day of Pentecost, "So those who received his word were baptized, and there were added that day about three thousand souls. And they devoted themselves to the apostles' teaching..."[11] Not only did the Apostle Peter proclaim the gospel that they were saved by, but the people then devoted themselves to being taught by the Apostles.

Paul, in his letter to the Ephesians, also associates the Apostles with Old Testament Prophets as men who were expressly authorized to speak for God. Just as God had authorized the prophets of long ago, He was now using the Apostles to build His church. Paul writes, "but you are fellow citizens with the saints and members of the household of God, built on the foundation of the apostles

---

[9] Galatians 1:1
[10] Martyn Lloyd-Jones and Christopher Catherwood, *The Cross: God's Way of Salvation* (Westchester, IL: Crossway Books, 1986), 19.
[11] Acts 2:41-42

and prophets, Christ Jesus himself being the cornerstone."[12] It is with such apostolic authority that Paul writes the Romans. He is one who has been sent and authorized by Christ to represent the teaching that the church is to be founded upon. This is important to remember, especially as we get into Paul's teaching of the gospel. We can trust that the gospel that he claims can save, actually does save because he is an Apostle of Christ.

To understand how Paul became an "apostle set apart for the gospel of God," it is good to go back to the book of Acts to refresh our memories of his calling by God, and to what God had called him.[13] Initially, Paul was a man who was determined to destroy Christianity. He had been given special authority by the high priest to arrest anyone that was a Christian. However, as Paul was on his way to the city of Damascus to capture Christians, he had a life-changing encounter with the resurrected and ascended Jesus Christ.

The other twelve Apostles were all men who had been with Jesus from the time of His baptism to His resurrection, and who had been eye-witnesses to the ministry of Jesus.[14] However, Paul was chosen to be an Apostle long after the Twelve. The encounter with Jesus on the road to Damascus had left Paul blind, but God sent a believer named Ananias to Paul to return his sight and to tell him that he had been chosen by God to be an Apostle. As Luke records:

> Now there was a disciple at Damascus named Ananias. The Lord said to him in a vision, 'Ananias.' And he said, 'Here I am, Lord.' And the Lord said to him, 'Rise and go to the street called Straight, and at the house of Judas look for a man of Tarsus named Saul, for behold, he is praying, and he has seen in a vision a man named Ananias come in and lay his hands on him so that he might regain his sight.' But Ananias answered, 'Lord, I

---
[12] Ephesians 2:19-20
[13] Romans 1:1
[14] Acts 1:21-22

> have heard from many about this man, how much evil he has done to your saints at Jerusalem. And here he has authority from the chief priests to bind all who call on your name.' But the Lord said to him, 'Go, for he is a chosen instrument of mine to carry my name before the Gentiles and kings and the children of Israel. (Acts 9:10-15)

Paul was a man who hated Jesus Christ and who was doing everything he could do to stop the spread of Christianity. However, he was saved and chosen by Jesus Christ to be His representative. Paul's transformation was so radical, his calling so clear, and his message so important, that he immediately began operating as an Apostle, one sent from God.

> And immediately he proclaimed Jesus in the synagogues, saying of Christ that, 'He is the Son of God.' And all who heard him were amazed and said, 'Is not this the man who made havoc in Jerusalem of those who called upon this name? And has he not come here for this purpose, to bring them bound before the chief priests?' But Saul increased all the more in strength, and confounded the Jews who lived in Damascus by proving that Jesus was the Christ. (Acts 9:20-22)

Take special notice of the message that Paul proclaimed. He let them know that Jesus is the Son of God and that Jesus is the Christ. Even at Paul's first proclamation of the gospel, he understood that saving faith is linked intrinsically to the correct view of Jesus. It is not enough for his hearers to know that Jesus was a man who had lived and died, but they must see that Jesus is the Son of God and that He is the long-awaited prophesied Christ. It is here in Damascus, where we begin to see Paul first operating as an Apostle of Jesus Christ.

Summary: Paul had been chosen, equipped, and sent by the risen Jesus Christ with apostolic authority to proclaim a message. This was a message from God, that according to Jesus' own words, had the power to "open their eyes, so that they may turn from darkness to light and from the power of Satan to God, that they may receive forgiveness of sins and a place among those who are sanctified by faith in me."[15] And it is with such apostolic authority that Paul writes his letter to the Romans, in which he will clearly articulate the gospel message that he received from God, which must be believed in for one to be saved.

---

[15] Acts 26:18

Chapter 2

THE MESSAGE: GOOD NEWS FROM GOD.

Paul, a servant of Christ Jesus, called to be an apostle, **set apart for the gospel of God,** which he promised beforehand through his prophets in the holy Scriptures, concerning his Son, who was descended from David according to the flesh and was declared to be the Son of God in power according to the Spirit of holiness by his resurrection from the dead, Jesus Christ our Lord, through whom we have received grace . . . (Rom. 1:1-5)

Paul was set apart by Jesus Christ Himself to carry the message of the gospel, that he received from God, to the people. This message will prove to be a message that is so vital that believing it or not believing it would result in whether a person is saved from the wrath of God, or not. As J. I. Packer writes of Paul, the message which he had received, and Paul's command to deliver the message to others:

> His royal Master had given him a message to proclaim; his whole business, therefore, was to deliver that message with exact and studious faithfulness, adding nothing, altering nothing, and omitting nothing. And he was to deliver it, not as another of man's bright ideas, needing to be beautified with cosmetics and high heels of

fashionable learning in order to make people look at it, but as a word from God, spoken in Christ's name carrying Christ's authority, and to be authenticated in the hearers by the convincing power of Christ's Spirit. . . I came Paul is saying, not to give you my own ideas about anything, but simply to deliver God's message.[16]

Paul had supernaturally received a message from God, and now his purpose in life was to be a messenger of the most significant news ever given to mankind. This would be the first of many times that Paul would repeat the saving message of Jesus Christ.

CONSIDER THE SOURCE.

If information is only as reliable as the one providing it, then Paul had received his information from the most reliable source possible, God. The God who created the universe, the only God, had given Paul a message. It is essential to understand that Paul did not create the gospel. It was a message that originated from God Himself. In writing on the importance of understanding the source of the gospel, R. C. Sproul has written:

> In the opening words of his Letter to the Romans, Paul speaks of himself as one called to declare 'the gospel of God' (Romans 1:1). The word here indicates possession. That is the gospel Paul is called to proclaim is not merely good news about God. Rather the gospel is God's possession. It is his property. In this regard, the original owner and author of the gospel is God himself.[17]

The source of Paul's message is God, and this fact must not be taken lightly, and neither should the content of the message.

---

[16] J. I. Packer, *Evangelism and the Sovereignty of God* (Downers Grove, IL: IVP Books, 2012), 47.
[17] Sproul, *Getting the Gospel Right*, 110.

"GOSPEL," MORE THAN A WORD.

The word "gospel' comes from the Greek term *euangellion*, and literally means "good news." When translated into Latin, the Greek term becomes a word that may sound a bit more familiar, *evangel*. Perhaps you have heard of evangelicals? But who or what, are evangelicals? Following what we know of the word *evangel*, evangelicals would be the people who *believe* this good news from God. Or, perhaps you have been engaged in evangelism. In other words, you were the one *telling* the good news of God to others.

In ancient times, the word *gospel* was a term that was tied to a good announcement that came from royalty. Such gospel could be an announcement about the birth of a prince, or perhaps a declaration of a great victory over another nation. In other words, the word "gospel" was shorthand to describe a broader message that was good and originated from a high authority.

Now, you might be wondering why I am spending so much time clarifying the word, *gospel*, but in our day professing *evangelicals*, as well as many *evangelists*, and some who practice *evangelism* seem to have lost the *evangel* that they are supposedly proclaiming. You see, many professing Christians know the *word* gospel, but they do not know the *message* of the gospel. God does command us to "repent and believe in the gospel," but He is not commanding us to just believe in one single word.[18]

Hearing that the *word* gospel is, in and of itself, insufficient to announce the *message* of the gospel might come across as a heretical statement at first. So, let's think this through for a moment. Can a person believe in the "gospel" and be saved? Of course, they can. Right? Truly, this is where it can get a bit tricky. In all actuality, the answer could be "Yes," or the answer could be "No." Don't worry; I am not turning into a relativist, the point is that the joining together of six letters of the alphabet g-o-s-p-e-l, and then believing in that word is not what Paul calls the "power of God

---

[18] Mark 1:1

unto salvation."[19] Just knowing the word "gospel" is not adequate for salvation to occur. The gospel is a message which is made up of many words, which in turn, make up multiple key phrases, which combine to form the message of the gospel.

PEANUT BUTTER JELLY SANDWICH AND THE GOSPEL.

What does a peanut butter jelly sandwich have to do with the gospel? Let's find out. A peanut butter and jelly sandwich has exact ingredients that cannot be added to or subtracted from, or the sandwich is no longer a true PB&J. So, what does it take to make a peanut butter and jelly sandwich? It is not a trick question. Think about the ingredients for half a second, and the odds are that you have arrived at the right answer. Obviously, to make a peanut butter and jelly sandwich, you must have three ingredients: peanut butter, jelly, and bread.

Now, what if you were at my house one day, it was between meals, and I said, "I am making a peanut butter and jelly sandwich. Would you like me to make you one as well?" That offer sounds good to you, so you reply with a, "Yes, please." In your mind, you have a good idea of what I am about to serve you. Nevertheless, what if I only put jelly between two pieces of bread, left out peanut butter, and served it to you? You would immediately realize that even though I said that it was a peanut butter and jelly sandwich, that in reality, it was not, because the peanut butter was missing. On the other hand, what if I served you a gooey glob of peanut butter and a glob of jelly on a plate and called that a peanut butter and jelly sandwich? Well, once again, this would not be a PB&J sandwich. Why? Because a critical ingredient—the bread—was missing.

Likewise, as we study the gospel, we will find that there are vital ingredients, or components, to this good news from God that we must hear and believe to be saved. This means that if you

---

[19] Romans 1:16

have had a gospel communicated to you, which was missing key components, then it was actually *not* the gospel. Obviously, this is far worse than receiving a PB&J sandwich that was missing jelly. And on the other side of our PB&J analogy, if you are the one proclaiming a gospel which is missing vital components, then you are no longer proclaiming the gospel through which God has promised to save.

Unfortunately, this type of thing happens quite often. For instance, what if a gospel is proclaimed, but the deity of Jesus is never mentioned? Is that the same, complete, gospel that Paul received, or is it a different and incomplete gospel in which a vital component has been left out? For another example, what if a Christian, desiring to share the gospel, does so without ever mentioning the fact that Jesus rose from the dead? Is that the original gospel, or once again has a vital component been removed? Such mistakes in the communication of the gospel are quite common. Instead of proclaiming the gospel in its entirety, people often remove essential components of the message and reduce it down to a quick soundbite, such as: "Just ask Jesus into your heart, and you'll be saved." Or, "God has a great plan for your life if you'll just let Him in." Such statements are missing vital information and are not even similar to the message that Paul received from God. In the end, the modern trend to shorten the gospel into a brief statement removes critical components, making it a different gospel that is no longer the gospel of God.[20]

Now, let's go the other direction with this PB&J sandwich analogy. What if instead of taking ingredients out, I add extra ingredients to the PB&J sandwich? This time, I go back to the kitchen and make sure that I put all the right ingredients into the sandwich. However, instead of only combining bread, peanut butter, and jelly, I also add in mustard and ketchup. Within the first bite, you know that this is not the traditional peanut butter jelly sandwich you were expecting. I then object and say, "No, you said it had to have all three ingredients, and I made sure that all three were put together as you desired." You would, of course, object

---

[20] Galatians 1: 6-10

and say, "Yes, but you added something that was not supposed to be there and ruined the whole thing." So, I take it back, start over, and this time combine bread, peanut butter, jelly, relish, soy sauce, and a sardine for good measure. Obviously, this combination of ingredients does not constitute a PB&J sandwich.

I do apologize for the simple nature of comparing a PB&J sandwich to the gospel, but it does serve well as an easily imagined visual aid that helps to show the relation of how both the PB&J sandwich and the gospel require specific ingredients. The gospel is a set message that has been delivered by God, recorded by man, and must be believed in for salvation. If we take the liberty to subtract or add information to it as we see fit, then it is highly possible that what we call the gospel is no longer the original gospel of God that brings about salvation. This is a severe problem that modern Christians face. Unfortunately, many have grown so accustomed to the multitude of recipes for the gospel, that few seem to be able to recall the original recipe for the authentic gospel message. This is no small matter. In fact, it is perilous, because far worse than having a PB&J sandwich that taste like sardines, if we mutilate the gospel, the consequences can be eternal.[21]

WHAT ARE THE COMPONENTS OF THE GOSPEL?

Many Christians labor to reinvent the gospel wheel when there is just no need to do so. We are not allowed to fashion the gospel into a different message which we believe will work better than the gospel of God. The gospel should not be altered into a message that we think people might more easily receive. The gospel is God's, and it is the message which God has purposed to bring salvation. However, Christians often, inadvertently, assume that they can put their own spin on the gospel, reinvent the wheel, and make their own version of the gospel work a little better than God's. Whether intentionally or unintentionally any reinventing of God's gospel is ludicrous. The gospel is a message for believing and repeating, but not for amending and recreating. As Paul

---

[21] Galatians 1:8

writes in 2 Corinthians, "Since we have the same spirit of faith according to what has been written, 'I believed, and so I spoke,' we also believe, and so we also speak."[22] The message is set, and we must continue to present the authentic gospel with all of its components—omitting nothing and adding nothing—to a world that is perishing without it.

As we begin to look at the components of the "gospel of God" that were given to Paul, we must remember that information must be conveyed for salvation to occur, yet salvation is not just a matter of gaining an academic knowledge about certain truths of the Bible. Salvation is a supernatural act of God to bring to life what is spiritually dead. However, God works through authentic gospel proclamation to bring people to salvation. As Paul reiterated to the Ephesians, "In him you also, when you heard the word of truth, the gospel of your salvation, and believed in him, were sealed with the promised Holy Spirit."[23] God saved the Ephesians, but it was the message of the gospel that God used to bring them to salvation. Regarding the power of the gospel, R. C. Sproul writes:

> The power of the gospel is not found simply in the words that express it. The message is powerful because the word is accompanied by the working of the Holy Spirit, who himself is the power of God. It is as if the gospel were a weapon in the hands of God, gaining its efficacy from the power of God himself... The Holy Spirit works in and by the preaching of the gospel.[24]

The gospel message is exceptionally unique in that God has ordained it as *the* message to bring people to repentance and belief in Jesus Christ.

Summary: The Apostle Paul had been given a specific message from God, and it was this particular message that he referred to as

---

[22] 2 Corinthians 4:13
[23] Ephesians 1:13
[24] Sproul, *Getting the Gospel Right,* 115.

the gospel. It was a message that he was to proclaim so that people could believe for their own salvation. It was also a message that those who believed were to continue to repeat to others so that they too could be saved. As Paul writes later in Romans:

> How then will they call on him in whom they have not believed? And how are they to believe in him of whom they have never heard? And how are they to hear without someone preaching? And how are they to preach unless they are sent? As it is written, "How beautiful are the feet of those who preach the good news!"[25]

There should be no doubt in the Christians mind that the message of the gospel was to remain the same. The gospel that Paul received, he preached, and the gospel that he preached, others were to continue to repeat to others. No one was authorized to change God's gospel by taking from it or adding to it. The gospel that was given to Paul, from God, was never meant to be up to individual manipulation. The same goes for modern Christians as well. We need to understand that the gospel is a specific message with exact components and that it is not a Christian's job to add to it or subtract from the gospel. We are to proclaim it as God has given it.

---

[25] Romans 10:14-15

Chapter 3

COMPONENT #1: JESUS IS THE FULFILLMENT OF PROPHECY.

Paul, a servant of Christ Jesus, called to be an apostle, set apart for the gospel of God, **which he promised beforehand through his prophets in the holy Scriptures,** concerning his Son, who was descended from David according to the flesh and was declared to be the Son of God in power according to the Spirit of holiness by his resurrection from the dead, Jesus Christ our Lord, through whom we have received grace . . . (Rom. 1:1-5)

Paul immediately let his readers know that the good news from God that he was about to proclaim to them, was not his own creation, nor was it something disconnected from God's previous revelation to the prophets. He informed them that his message of good news was the fulfillment of the good news that God had promised long ago through His prophets. The many references of the prophets to the coming salvation through the Messiah were now realized in the person and work of Jesus the Christ. What the prophets wrote long ago, and what Paul was writing to the Romans currently, was all connected and part of the same message of salvation from God.

Since the fulfillment of prophecy is how Paul began his gospel summary to the Romans, then we should strive to understand the significant role that the prophets played in God's revelation. As we have seen, Apostles were uniquely called and authorized by God to represent Him. In a very similar manner, God used prophets to be His mouthpiece before the time of the Apostles. Though separated by hundreds or even thousands of years, God worked through both the Prophets and the Apostles to reveal Himself to mankind.[26] Prophets were people that God specifically called to be a mouthpiece to His people. God chose men like, Moses, Elijah, Elisha, Isaiah, Jeremiah, Ezekiel, and others to be His prophets. God would give them divine revelation, and they would then, in turn, speak to people for God. Sometimes a prophet's declaration from God was a specific message for the people in his day and was to be heeded immediately; other times, the prophet would announce events that were to happen in the distant future.

Have you ever wondered how the prophets could speak about events in the future with absolute precision? It is because God was revealing this information to them. Their prophecies were not mere predictions but were treated as future facts that were announced ahead of time to them by God. Only God knows all things completely, including the future, and only a person that God reveals this kind of divine revelation to could speak about events that were going to happen in the future.

This meant that not just anyone and everyone was a prophet. Prophets were few and far between, and it was not like anyone could just choose to be one on their own. Prophets were called by God, as we see with the calling of the prophet Jeremiah, God said, "Before I formed you in the womb I knew you, and before you were born I consecrated you; I appointed you a prophet to the nations…and whatever I command you, you shall speak… Behold, I have put words in your mouth."[27] A Prophet, like an Apostle, could not just appoint himself to the position. God did the calling, and God gave them the prophecies.

---

[26] Ephesians 2:20
[27] Jeremiah 1:5,7,9

Notice the directions given in Deuteronomy regarding how the people could know if a prophet was indeed from God or not.

> I will raise up for them a prophet like you from among their brothers. Moreover, I will put my words in his mouth, and he shall speak to them all that I command him. In addition, whoever will not listen to my words that he shall speak in my name, I myself will require it of him. But the prophet who presumes to speak a word in my name that I have not commanded him to speak, or who speaks in the name of other gods, that same prophet shall die.' And if you say in your heart, 'How may we know the word that the LORD has not spoken?' — when a prophet speaks in the name of the LORD, if the word does not come to pass or come true, that is a word that the LORD has not spoken; the prophet has spoken it presumptuously. You need not be afraid of him. (Deut. 18:18-22)

If a prophet was from God, then whatever he prophesied in God's name came true. God knows the future perfectly, and there is nothing that has happened or will happen that God does not already know about fully. He is truly omniscient (all-knowing) and does not acquire new information. God knows everything perfectly before anything even comes to be.[28] He is also the only one who has such knowledge. Therefore, fulfilled prophecy, not only validated a prophet as genuine, but it also further proved that there is only one *real* God. Look at God's challenge to the false gods in the book of Isaiah.

> Set forth your case, says the LORD;
> bring your proofs, says the King of Jacob.
> Let them bring them, and tell us
> what is to happen.
> Tell us the former things, what they are,
> that we may consider them,

---

[28] Psalm 139:1-4, 15-16, Isaiah 46:9-10

> that we may know their outcome;
> or declare to us the things to come.
> Tell us what is to come hereafter,
> that we may know that you are gods;
> do good, or do harm,
> that we may be dismayed and terrified.
> Behold, you are nothing,
> and your work is less than nothing;
> an abomination is he who chooses you. (Is. 41:21-24)

God's test of the false prophets was to see if they could prophesy and accurately foretell the future. Which of course, they could not, because they were not God's prophets, and such information could only come from God. Only the One, true, omniscient, immutable, and omnipotent (all-powerful) God can announce future events and cause them to come to fruition.

Some prophets spoke of events that were to happen in a relatively short time, even in just a day or two. And just as they had prophesied, it would come to pass. We see this in the prophesies Moses received about the plagues that Egypt encountered. Moses would give details of a catastrophic event that would happen the next day, and the event would happen just as Moses had foretold it. Why did Moses tell Pharaoh of the coming plague or even the removal of the plague ahead of time? It was to show that Moses was a prophet of the One true God. We see this in the encounter of Pharaoh asking Moses to take away the plague of frogs the next day.

> And he said, "Tomorrow." Moses said, "Be it as you say, so that you may know that there is no one like the LORD our God. The frogs shall go away from you and your houses and your servants and your people. They shall be left only in the Nile." So Moses and Aaron went out from Pharaoh, and Moses cried to the LORD about the frogs, as he had agreed with Pharaoh. And the LORD did according to the word of Moses. The frogs died out in the houses, the courtyards, and the fields. (Ex. 8:10-13)

However, some prophecies were not intended to be fulfilled the next day, or the next week, but hundreds or even thousands of years later. This is the case with Isaiah's prophecies concerning the coming Christ, which also have to do with the gospel. The book of Isaiah was written around 700 years before Christ, yet Isaiah wrote much about the future Messiah. Jesus even quoted one of Isaiah's prophecies as He began his ministry and then proclaimed that He was fulfilling the prophecy right then and there.

> And he came to Nazareth, where he had been brought up. And as was his custom, he went to the synagogue on the Sabbath day, and he stood up to read. And the scroll of the prophet Isaiah was given to him. He unrolled the scroll and found the place where it was written,
>
> > 'The Spirit of the Lord is upon me,
> > because he has anointed me
> > to proclaim good news to the poor.
> > He has sent me to proclaim liberty to the captives
> > and recovering of sight to the blind,
> > to set at liberty those who are oppressed,
> > to proclaim the year of the Lord's favor.'
>
> And he rolled up the scroll and gave it back to the attendant and sat down. And the eyes of all in the synagogue were fixed on him. And he began to say to them, 'Today this Scripture has been fulfilled in your hearing.' (Luke 4:16-21)

Jesus used this prophecy to let his hearers know that He was the one that Isaiah had prophesied about. The one that God said He would send was now in their presence, and this was in fulfillment of the prophecy given hundreds of years earlier.

PROPHECY WAS IMPORTANT TO PAUL.

The gospel is the culmination of the Messianic prophecies being fulfilled in Jesus Christ. The Messiah, who was prophesied to come, had now come and accomplished salvation. This is what Paul meant when he wrote of the gospel that was, "Promised beforehand through his prophets in the holy Scriptures."[29] Paul let the Romans know that this was not some brand-new story, but that it was the fulfillment of an old story, one which God's prophets had been announcing various details of for ages. Their multitude of prophecies had now culminated into the ultimate revelation from God, the good news of salvation by the Messiah, Jesus Christ the Son of God.[30]

Paul made a similar point regarding Messianic prophecy and its time of fulfillment when he wrote, "But when the fullness of time had come, God sent forth his Son, born of woman, born under the law, to redeem those who were under the law, so that we might receive adoption as sons."[31] Not only had the time come for the Messianic prophecies to come to pass, but by mentioning that Jesus was born of a woman, even seems to bring together the earliest announcement of the good news found in the first book of the Bible. After the sin of Adam and Eve, God announced to Satan, "I will put enmity between you and the woman, and between your offspring and her offspring; he shall bruise your head, and you shall bruise his heel."[32] God sent Adam and Eve out of His presence, but He gave them a promise, concerning the good news, that someday One would eventually come who would bring about the defeat of Satan, and that the one who would defeat him would be her offspring. Regarding this first good news announcement and promise, Alistair Begg and Sinclair Ferguson, in their book *Name above all Names* write:

---

[29] Romans 1:2
[30] Mark 1:1
[31] Galatians 4:4-5
[32] Genesis 3:15

Genesis 3:15 has long been referred to as the 'Protoevangelium,' the first announcement of the good news of the gospel. It contains the earliest promise of Christ's coming—a prophecy that his appearance will be the climax of an extended conflict.[33]

Though this was the first promise of God regarding the good news of the one who was to come and destroy the works of Satan, it was only the first of many. From that time on, God spoke through His prophets to give additional details regarding this good news of His promise to send a Savior. Paul's point in writing, "set apart for the gospel of God, which he promised beforehand through his prophets in the holy Scriptures," was to alert the reader that this is *the* good news. The good news that God announced would one day come has come. The One of whom God had declared, and of whom God spoke through His prophets about, has fulfilled the prophecies, and the good news of salvation is found in Him.

The Scriptures were designed by God to not only teach about His plan of salvation in general, but to also give specific prophetic identifiers of the coming Messiah. We see Scriptures being used in such a way early in John's Gospel by Philip who was one of the first to announce the identity of the Messiah, when he said, "We have found him of whom Moses in the Law and also the prophets wrote, Jesus of Nazareth, the son of Joseph."[34] Philip enthusiastically made this announcement to his brother Nathaniel. This was no small matter, the Messiah of who's coming Moses and all of the prophets had prophesied about, had now arrived.

PROPHECY WAS IMPORTANT TO JESUS.

Jesus Himself taught the importance of the Old Testament Messianic prophecies and made sure that people understood that He was fulfilling them. Jesus told the Pharisees, "You search the

---

[33] Alistair Begg and Sinclair B. Ferguson, *Name above All Names* (Wheaton, IL: Crossway, 2013), 20.
[34] John 1:45

Scriptures because you think that in them you have eternal life; and it is they that bear witness about me."[35] Following His resurrection, Jesus made His fulfillment of prophecy abundantly clear to some of His disciples on the road to Emmaus. The disciples were grief-stricken over the recent crucifixion, death, and apparent end of their leader. However, the resurrected Jesus appeared and enlightened them by pointing out the Messianic prophecies that He had fulfilled. Jesus said:

> 'O foolish ones, and slow of heart to believe all that the prophets have spoken! Was it not necessary that the Christ should suffer these things and enter into his glory?' And beginning with Moses and all the Prophets, he interpreted to them in all the Scriptures the things concerning himself . . . (Luke 24:25-27)

Jesus literally called them "foolish." They were ignorant of all that the prophets had spoken. If they had truly understood the prophecies, then they would have realized that everything that had happened to Jesus was according to the revelation that God had previously given through His prophets. What did Jesus do to comfort these distraught disciples, He took them from foolish to wise by teaching them about prophecy. Sometime later, Jesus appeared to the other Disciples to comfort and strengthen them in the same way; by informing them that He had fulfilled the Messianic prophecies.

> Then he said to them, 'These are my words that I spoke to you while I was still with you, that everything written about me in the Law of Moses and the Prophets and the Psalms must be fulfilled,' Then he opened their minds to understand the Scriptures, and said to them, 'Thus it is written, that the Christ should suffer and on the third day rise from the dead, and that repentance and forgiveness of sins should be proclaimed in his name to all nations, beginning from Jerusalem.' (Luke 24:44-47)

---

[35] John 5:39

Jesus had died and risen from the dead, but it was His fulfillment of prophecy that He used to teach these disciples as to His identity as the Christ.

The importance of His fulfillment of the Messianic prophecies is difficult for modern Christians, that are unfamiliar with Scripture, to fully appreciate. But for Jesus, it was imperative that His Disciples understand this point. Consider this, of all things Jesus could have taught the disciples about in this post-resurrection moment; He wanted them to fully realize that everything had precisely happened as God had foretold through His prophets.

PROPHECY WAS IMPORTANT TO THE APOSTLES.

Similarly, the book of Acts has several gospel presentations given by the Apostles that have the same purpose in mind. The Apostles intentionally connected the dots of fulfilled prophecy to reveal to their audience that the Christ had come, and His name is Jesus. This is an integral part of their gospel proclamation.

For example, the first sermon ever uttered by an Apostle after the ascension of Christ was primarily about fulfilled prophecy. Jesus had lived, died, risen, ascended to heaven, had just dramatically sent the Holy Spirit, a huge crowd gathers, and Peter began by talking about *prophecy*? Why? Because fulfilled prophecy was part of the gospel and that his audience needed to hear about it. It is apparent that God fully approved the gospel that was being preached that day, as He saved three thousand who believed the gospel just as Peter had presented it, which included much about Jesus fulfilling Old Testament prophecies.

Peter did not treat the historical connection of Jesus to the prophets lightly. He did not consider it boring information that was insignificant to evangelism. Quite the opposite, he viewed this connection as critical in the clarification of the person of Jesus. All we have to do is look at Peter's next sermon in Solomon's Portico to see that his teaching on Jesus' fulfillment of prophecy was common to his gospel proclamations:

But what God foretold by the mouth of all the prophets, that his Christ would suffer, he thus fulfilled. Repent therefore, and turn back, that your sins may be blotted out, that times of refreshing may come from the presence of the Lord, and that he may send the Christ appointed for you, Jesus, whom heaven must receive until the time for restoring all the things about which God spoke by the mouth of his holy prophets long ago. Moses said, 'The Lord God will raise up for you a prophet like me from your brothers. You shall listen to him in whatever he tells you. And it shall be that every soul who does not listen to that prophet shall be destroyed from the people.' And all the prophets who have spoken, from Samuel and those who came after him, also proclaimed these days. (Acts 3:18-24)

Peter gave them the big picture of the salvation that had come; by telling them of the salvation that God had promised. He let them know that this was not something new, but that this was the fulfillment of something old. This was the salvation and the Savior that God had been announcing through His prophets for ages. The time was now, salvation had come, and the Savior is, Jesus. Did God honor Peter's gospel proclamation in Solomon's Portico? Yes. Once again, God honored the clear gospel proclamation of Peter, which included fulfilled prophecy, by saving thousands of people that day as well. "But many of those who had heard the word believed, and the number of the men came to about five thousand."[36]

Peter did not only use fulfilled Messianic prophecy to evangelize the Jews, but he used it with the Gentiles as well. This can be seen from his witness to the Gentiles in the home of the Roman Centurion Cornelius. As Peter was witnessing, he told them that God had,

---

[36] Acts 4:4

> ... commanded us to preach to the people and to testify that he is the one appointed by God to be judge of the living and the dead. To him all the prophets bear witness that everyone who believes in him receives forgiveness of sins through his name. (Acts 10:42)

Again, we see that the prophets were definitely a component of the gospel that Peter preached to both Jews and Gentiles.

It was common for Peter to preach this way; in fact, it appears to be the norm for him to do so. Not only do his sermons contain many examples of fulfilled prophecy as part of the gospel, but his writings in First and Second Peter do as well.

> Concerning this salvation, the prophets who prophesied about the grace that was to be yours searched and inquired carefully, inquiring what person or time the Spirit of Christ in them was indicating when he predicted the sufferings of Christ and the subsequent glories. It was revealed to them that they were serving not themselves but you, in the things that have now been announced to you through those who preached the good news to you by the Holy Spirit sent from heaven, things into which angels long to look. (1 Peter 1:10-12)

The great salvation of which the prophets had spoken and into which the angels longed to look had now come, and that it had happened just as the prophets had foretold that it would. Also, Peter pointed out that the prophets were "serving not themselves but you." These prophets still benefit us today by enabling us to connect the dots of God's revelation easily through His prophets to the fulfillment of them in Jesus.

Summary: When was the last time you heard the gospel communicated with a connection to prophecy? Is the gospel that is commonly presented today shown to be connected to God's historical plan of salvation? Or, is it detached and isolated from the Old Testament? The promises of God and their fulfillment in Jesus the

Christ were fundamental to the gospel proclamation of both Jesus and His Apostles.

If it were crucial to their communication of the gospel, then it would certainly seem that we should keep prophecy in our gospel proclamation as well. We must not think that we, as modern Christians, have come up with a new and improved way to proclaim the gospel by leaving out fulfilled prophecy from the gospel message. Instead, we should see the importance of prophecy to the gospel, and to appreciate its value as Peter did when he wrote, "And we have the prophetic word more fully confirmed, to which you will do well to pay attention as to a lamp shining in a dark place..."[37] Just because the Messianic prophecies have now been fulfilled by Jesus, does not mean that we are no longer supposed to pay attention to them. Instead, the more we look into them, and understand them, the brighter God's truth becomes. Such an understanding is essential for seasoned believers, as well as people who are hearing about Jesus for the very first time. As we look over how Jesus and the Apostles shared the gospel, we quickly see that prophecy was important for clear communication. If it was important to their gospel, then it should be important to ours as well, since after all, there is only one gospel.

---

[37] 2 Peter 1:19

Chapter 4

COMPONENT #2: JESUS IS GOD.

> Paul, a servant of Christ Jesus, called to be an apostle, set apart for the gospel of God, which he promised beforehand through his prophets in the holy Scriptures, **concerning his Son,** who was descended from David according to the flesh and was declared to be the Son of God in power according to the Spirit of holiness by his resurrection from the dead, Jesus Christ our Lord, through whom we have received grace . . . (Rom. 1:1-5)

In this short phrase, "concerning his Son" we have the epicenter of the gospel. The message which had been given to the Apostle Paul by God, and which the prophets had prophesied about for thousands of years, had now come to be fully known. What was it about? Who or what is the subject matter of the message? The message is all about the Son of God. The good news from God, the gospel, is centered on the person and work of the second person of the Godhead, who became flesh. He, the Son of God, is the epicenter of the gospel message. As Martin Luther wrote, "The Content, or Object of the Gospel, or as some put it, the Subject, is Jesus Christ the Son of God."[38]

---

[38] Martin Luther, *Commentary on Romans*, ed. John Theodore Mueller (Grand Rapids, MI: Kregel Classics, 1976), 35.

Is the fact that Jesus Christ is God, emphasized enough in gospel communication today? If this component is left out, which is the centerpiece of the gospel, then whatever the message being communicated is, one thing is for sure, it is not the gospel. Can a person be saved if they believe that Jesus was just an excellent teacher, just a prophet, or a really nice person? Of course not! If the gospel of God's main ingredient—Jesus is God—has been removed, then you have a gospel that is not like the original because it is one that is no longer "concerning his Son."[39] This problem is not a new one, this component of the gospel was greatly opposed even while Jesus was actively preaching and teaching during His earthly ministry, as we see from multiple encounters between Jesus and the Jewish leaders. Take this one for example:

> And this was why the Jews were persecuting Jesus, because he was doing these things on the Sabbath. But Jesus answered them, 'My Father is working until now, and I am working.' This was why the Jews were seeking all the more to kill him, because not only was he breaking the Sabbath, but he was even calling God his own Father, making himself equal with God. (John 5:16-18)

The Jews wanted to kill Jesus because He was claiming to be equal in deity to God the Father. However, even with the threat of death, Jesus never capitulated. Throughout His ministry, He continued to proclaim that God the Father and He, the Son of God, have the same work, authority, and honor.[40]

Jesus was not just a man, He was, and is God. Every time He explained this fact of the gospel, His enemies tried to kill Him. As we see here in a dialogue that takes place between Jesus and the Pharisees recorded in the tenth chapter of John:

> 'I and the Father are one.' The Jews picked up stones again to stone him. Jesus answered them, 'I have shown you many good works from the Father; for which of

---

[39] Romans 1:3
[40] John 5:19-23

them are you going to stone me?' The Jews answered him, 'It is not for a good work that we are going to stone you but for blasphemy, because you, being a man, make yourself God.' Jesus answered them, 'Is it not written in your Law, 'I said, you are gods'? If he called them gods to whom the word of God came—and Scripture cannot be broken—do you say of him whom the Father consecrated and sent into the world, 'You are blaspheming,' because I said, 'I am the Son of God'? If I am not doing the works of my Father, then do not believe me; but if I do them, even though you do not believe me, believe the works, that you may know and understand that the Father is in me and I am in the Father.' (John 10:30-38)

The Pharisees knew what Jesus was saying. They knew full well that Jesus was claiming equality with the Father. As a matter of fact, they understood this so well that they wanted to kill him on the spot. However, as controversial as this claim was, Jesus would not allow such a vital component of His identity, and of the gospel message, to be overlooked or communicated lightly. The deity of Jesus was of utmost importance to His description of Himself to others, even when He knew that the hearers would hate Him for declaring it.

MANY PEOPLE HATED THIS COMPONENT, AND MANY PEOPLE STILL DO.

The deity of Jesus is the central doctrine to the Christian faith, and therefore, it is the most attacked doctrine of the Christian faith. If you teach people that Jesus was a good man, a great teacher, or a wise man, virtually no one will get upset with your message, but see what happens when you tell them that, "Jesus is God." It is a component of the gospel that is exceptionally divisive by its nature. Nevertheless, that does not mean that we should leave it out.

We must remind ourselves that even though this doctrine was divisive to those Jesus was speaking to, He still clearly proclaimed it. And it was because of this that His audience hated Him, and on more than one occasion tried to kill Him.

> 'Your father Abraham rejoiced that he would see my day. He saw it and was glad.' So the Jews said to him, 'You are not yet fifty years old, and have you seen Abraham?' Jesus said to them, 'Truly, truly, I say to you, before Abraham was, I am.' So they picked up stones to throw at him, but Jesus hid himself and went out of the temple. (John 8:56-59)

The Jews were so furious about what Jesus said about Himself that they desired to immediately stone Him to death. What did Jesus say to create such a harsh reaction? Was He claiming to be extremely old, older even than Abraham? Or was there something more?

Claiming to be over a thousand years old might make His hearers believe that He was insane, but claiming to be extremely old should not have caused the Jews to want to kill Him on the spot. There is actually more to the story that we need to see. The reason they wanted to kill Jesus was that He distinctly claimed to be God by referring to Himself as "I am."[41] Although the "I am" statement may seem ambiguous or confusing to modern Bible readers, it was clear to the Jews who heard Jesus that day. Jesus had taken the name of God, which had been revealed to Moses in the book of Exodus, and applied it to Himself.

> Then Moses said to God, "If I come to the people of Israel and say to them, 'The God of your fathers has sent me to you,' and they ask me, 'What is his name?' what shall I say to them?" God said to Moses, "I am who I am." And he said, "Say this to the people of Israel, 'I am has sent me to you." (Ex. 3:13-14)

God commanded Moses to tell the Israelites, "I am" has sent you. This name is more than just a few letters strung together

---

[41] John 8:58

to make a sound that a person is to be called, it is packed with meaning. It describes who God is and puts Him in a category that is beyond all others. God says of Himself, "I am who I am." In other words, His nature cannot be declared in words, cannot be conceived of by human thought. The "I am" statement says of God that He exists as nothing else does: necessarily, eternally, unchangeable, and with all power in and of Himself.

The Pharisees were well acquainted with the Exodus story, and they understood the meaning of Jesus' "I AM" statement about Himself. God's name was regarded as holy, highly esteemed, and even protected, so protected that "whoever blasphemes the name of the Lord shall surely be put to death."[42] The Pharisees completely understood what Jesus was saying, and that is why they wanted to kill Him. They believed that Jesus had committed the ultimate blasphemy by claiming to be God. However, Jesus had not committed blasphemy, because His statement was true.

THE GOSPEL WRITERS BOLDLY PROCLAIMED THAT JESUS IS GOD.

Jesus is clearly presented as God in all four Gospels. His deity is taught in various locations throughout and particularly in the opening of each one. The fact that all four Gospel writers believed the deity of Christ so vital that they intentionally included it at the beginning of their gospel accounts should make us aware that this is an essential component of the gospel. For example, look at a few of the opening verses from The Gospel of Matthew:

> But as he considered these things, behold, an angel of the Lord appeared to him in a dream, saying, 'Joseph, son of David, do not fear to take Mary as your wife, for that which is conceived in her is from the Holy Spirit. She will bear a son, and you shall call his name Jesus, for he will save his people from their sins.' All this took place to fulfill what the Lord had spoken by the prophet:

---

[42] Leviticus 24:16

'Behold, the virgin shall conceive and bear a son, and they shall call his name Immanuel (which means, God with us).' (Matt. 1:20-23)

There is a lot of information packed into these three verses, that is meant to show that not only the birth of Jesus but that the person of Jesus is unique among all mankind. First, Joseph learned that no man was involved in the making of the child that was in Mary's womb. Instead, Mary's Son was from the Holy Spirit. Secondly, the angel announced that the Child is the One that will "save his people from their sins." Last, but certainly not least, the angel then connected his announcement to a messianic prophecy from the book of Isaiah that spoke of the virgin birth and the fact that the virgin's son would be God, "Immanuel" (which means God with us)." God, the sovereign creator of the universe, was going to put on flesh and dwell among humanity.

The Gospel of Mark's opening sentence declared the deity of Christ. Mark began his Gospel account by writing, "The beginning of the gospel of Jesus Christ, the Son of God."[43] From the first words, Mark was clear about the focus of his Gospel. He wanted his readers to understand that Jesus was both the Christ and the Son of God. This information was essential to his message.

Next, Mark substantiated his opening statement by pointing to Jesus as the one that John the Baptist had come to announce.[44] Mark also records that even God the Father declared that Jesus is the Son of God. God made this announcement following Jesus' baptism by John, "And when he came up out of the water, immediately he saw the heavens being torn open and the Spirit descending on him like a dove. In addition, a voice came from heaven, 'You are my beloved Son; with you I am well pleased.'"[45] Mark stated that Jesus is the Son of God in the first sentence of his Gospel and then elaborated on this point throughout the remainder of his

---

[43] Mark 1:1
[44] Mark 1:2-8
[45] Mark 1:10-11

gospel because the identity of Jesus as God was a vital fact of the gospel.

Luke began his gospel record by giving the account of Gabriel's visit to Zechariah and Elizabeth regarding their son, who was to be the herald that was to precede the Messiah. He then further identifies the Messiah by recording the interaction between Mary and Gabriel:

> And behold, you will conceive in your womb and bear a son, and you shall call his name Jesus. He will be great and will be called the Son of the Most High. And the Lord God will give to him the throne of his father David, and he will reign over the house of Jacob forever, and of his kingdom there will be no end. (Luke 1:31-33)

The good news from Gabriel is clear: Mary will conceive a son, but not just any son, "The Son of the Most High!"

In writing the Gospel of John, the Apostle John skipped the preliminaries of genealogy, John the Baptist, and the birth narrative of Jesus and organized his gospel in such a way as to establish the deity of Jesus at the beginning, and to go forward from there. However, he begins not with the birth of Christ, but with the existence of the Son of God from all eternity:

> In the beginning was the Word, and the Word was with God, and the Word was God. He was in the beginning with God. All things were made through him, and without him was not anything made that was made. . . And the Word became flesh and dwelt among us, and we have seen his glory, glory as of the only Son from the Father, full of grace and truth. (John 1:1-3,14)

Jesus did not begin life when Mary conceived Him. He had existed even before He was born of Mary, as the eternal Son of God, and John wanted to make sure that this fact was understood. John made a point, from the very first words of his gospel account to state the identity of Jesus as both God and man. He wanted all who came into contact with his record to know that the One who was with

God (the Father) from the beginning is God (the Son) and that this incarnation of God with man is Jesus.

Before one can even get out of the first chapter of John, the same point is reiterated, only this time from the mouth of John the Baptist, "And I have seen and have borne witness that this is the Son of God."[46] Then, just a few verses later, John records Nathanael's early confession as to the identity of Jesus, "Nathanael answered him, "Rabbi, you are the Son of God! You are the King of Israel!"[47] Here again, we see that John, like the other Gospel writers, was not vague about Jesus being God. He provides several critical statements in the opening chapter of his gospel that boldly declare the deity of Jesus.

All four of the Gospel writers made sure that they openly communicated that Jesus was God. Why? Because the deity of Jesus Christ is of utmost importance to the gospel. It is the crux of the matter. There is no doubt that the Gospels, are in accord with Paul's opening statement to the Romans that "the gospel of God," is "concerning His Son."[48] To leave this critical information out of the gospel was just unthinkable to all of these men.

JESUS TEACHES HIS DISCIPLES THAT HE IS GOD.

Jesus, of course, knew how important it was for people to know Him for who He truly was, and this was especially true when it came to His disciples. He would soon depart, and the disciples would be tasked with proclaiming the one and only true gospel to the world. So one day, when Jesus was alone with His Disciples, He asked them, "Who do people say that the Son of Man is?' And they said, 'Some say John the Baptist, others say Elijah, and others Jeremiah or one of the prophets."[49]

---

[46] John 1:34
[47] John 1:49
[48] Romans 1:3
[49] Matthew 16:13-14

The disciples then gave Jesus a listing of the various titles or names that people were calling Jesus. The disciples then informed Jesus that the word on the street was quite positive. Unlike the Pharisees who basically called Jesus, "Satan."[50] These people at least acknowledged that He had to be a prophet, and maybe even one of the great prophets of all returned from the dead. They knew Jesus was a miracle-working prophet from God but was this sufficient? Had they answered with enough truth?

THE ANSWER WAS IN THE QUESTION.

The disciples had given Jesus all the various opinions of the people as to His identity, but Jesus had already given the right answer to his question within the question which He had just asked them. Let's look at that question one more time, Jesus asked, "Who do people say that the Son of Man is?" He gave them the answer, or at least an excellent clue, by using the title "Son of Man" to describe Himself. Why does He do this? What does the "Son of man" even mean? Is Jesus just saying that He is merely a man like we are, or is there something more being said? The fact of the matter is that this title was previously used by the Old Testament prophet Daniel to describe the One whom he saw in a vision that was equal to God.

> I saw in the night visions, and behold, with the clouds of heaven there came one like a son of man, and he came to the Ancient of Days and was presented before him. And to him was given dominion and glory and a kingdom, that all peoples, nations, and languages should serve him; his dominion is an everlasting dominion, which shall not pass away, and his kingdom one that shall not be destroyed. (Dan. 7:13-14)

Daniel saw the "son of man" coming before God the Father as no mere mortal man could do: as an equal. How could this be?

---

[50] Matthew 12:24

No one can see God and live.[51] Sin separates humanity from God, but here we have a man coming before God the Father (the Ancient of days) and not only coming before Him but also receiving all dominion from Him. This was a difficult passage to understand fully, but by using the exact title of the one in Daniel's vision, Jesus was revealing that He is the "son of man" that was seen by Daniel in the vision. The one like a "son of man" but also equal to God was the God-man, Jesus Christ.

The enemies of Jesus knew what the words "Son of Man" meant. After they had arrested Jesus, they tried to catch Him in a verbal trap that could justify putting Him to death. They finally get what they need when Jesus says that He is the "Son of Man." They understood that Jesus was claiming to be God and demanded that He be put to death.

> However, Jesus remained silent. And the high priest said to him, 'I adjure you by the living God, tell us if you are the Christ, the Son of God.' Jesus said to him, 'You have said so. But I tell you, from now on you will see the Son of Man seated at the right hand of Power and coming on the clouds of heaven.' Then the high priest tore his robes and said, 'He has uttered blasphemy. What further witnesses do we need? You have now heard his blasphemy. What is your judgment?' They answered, 'He deserves death.' (Matt. 26:63-66)

How important was the right identification of Jesus to His own teaching and preaching? It was so important that He was willing to die for its truth. Even in the face of death, He did not deny that He was God but fully professed it for even His enemies to hear.

PETER ANSWERS CORRECTLY.

Many people could see Jesus with their own eyes, but they refused to see Him for all that He truly was. The people had many

---

[51] Exodus 33:20; John 1:18

opinions, but their views were all insufficient. Jesus was far more than a prophet. After the disciples gave Jesus the many opinions of others, Jesus turned to the disciples to hear who they believed Him to be:

> He said to them, 'But who do you say that I am?' Simon Peter replied, 'You are the Christ, the Son of the living God.' And Jesus answered him, 'Blessed are you, Simon Bar-Jonah! For flesh and blood has not revealed this to you, but my Father who is in heaven.' (Matt. 16:15-17)

Peter said that Jesus was the "Son of the living God!" Peter realized that the person sitting with them was not just a man, but He was also God in the flesh. Did Jesus accept this divine title, or did He chastise Peter for too lofty of an accolade? Not only did He accept the title of "Christ" and "the Son of the living God," but Jesus then acknowledged that the source of this revelation to Peter was none other than God the Father. Peter was given the eyes to see past the flesh of the one born of a woman, to see the One who is the Son of God.

WHO DO PEOPLE SAY THAT JESUS IS TODAY?

People still like to claim that Jesus was merely a historical figure, a good man, a good teacher, or even a prophet. However, any answer that does not include the fact that *Jesus is God* is insufficient. People may say the name "Jesus," but have a completely wrong or incomplete definition in their mind that is attached to that name.

Think about it, even some false religions admit that they believe in a historical Jesus, but their definition is radically different than that which Jesus used to define Himself. For example, the Jehovah's Witnesses believe in a person named Jesus; however, they teach that Jesus was not the Son of God, but was a created being, an angel, who became man and lived a sinless life.[52] They feel that Jesus is

---

[52] The Watchtower Bible and Tract Society, "Who Is Jesus Christ? Is Jesus God or God's Son? | Bible Teach," in *What Does the Bible Really Teach?*, accessed April 24, 2017, https://www.jw.org/en/publications/books/bible-teach/who-is-jesus-christ/.

important, morally pure, supernatural, and even angelic. But they utterly refuse to believe in a Jesus who is God.[53] What does this mean for those who believe in such a Jesus? Can they adhere to such a radically false definition of Jesus, and still be saved? No, because they have rejected the real Jesus, and have therefore rejected the real gospel that "is the power of God for salvation."[54] By removing the deity of Jesus from the gospel, Jehovah Witnesses have removed a vital component of the gospel and have created a false definition of Jesus and a false gospel that cannot save anyone.[55]

For another example, consider The Church of Jesus Christ of Latter-Day Saints, also known as Mormons. Surely, they must believe in Jesus, after all the word, *Jesus* is even in the name of their church. However, it takes more than spelling His name right, it takes right belief. Mormons believe that Jesus was a perfect man who never sinned. They believe that Jesus was important, was a great teacher, a wonderful person, and even give him the status of being the first spirit created by the God of this planet.[56] But, they utterly deny that Jesus is fully God. Do they have the right gospel? Have they believed in the real Jesus? The answer is, once again, "No."[57] They might have spelled the name right, but they rejected the real Jesus and in turn, believed in a make-believe Jesus of Joseph Smith's vivid imagination.[58]

---

[53] Watch Tower Staff, *Reasoning from the Scriptures* (New York: Watchtower Bible and Tract Society of New York, 1985), 306.

[54] Romans 1:16

[55] For an apologetic comparison of Jehovah's Witness doctrine to Christianity see: Matt Slick, "Jehovah's Witness' Beliefs," CARM Christian Apologetics & Research Ministry, September 22, 2016, Points 5-7, accessed November 15, 2016, https://carm.org/jehovahs-witnesses-beliefs.

[56] Joseph F. Smith, *Family Home Evening Manual* (Salt Lake City, UT: Church of Jesus Christ of Latter-day Saints, 1972), 125-126.

[57] Brigham Young, *Journal of Discourses by Brigham Young... His Two Counsellors, the Twelve Apostles and Others*, vol. 3 (Liverpool: Orson Pratt, 1856), 247.

[58] For an apologetic comparison of LDS doctrine to Christianity see: Matt Slick, "Mormon Beliefs, Are They Christian?," CARM Christian Apologetics & Research Ministry, October 10, 2016, Mormon Beliefs documented, accessed November 15, 2016, https://carm.org/mormon-beliefs

The identity of Jesus as both God and man was, and is, so important that Jesus told the Pharisees, who would not accept His deity, "that you would die in your sins, for unless you believe that I am he you will die in your sins."[59] Jesus let them know that they would die in, or with, their sins unless they believed that He was God. To die in, or with, your sins is exactly as it sounds. It means that a man's sins are with him at death and will remain with him as he faces God in judgment. This meant that their continued rejection of Jesus as God would result in their sins not being forgiven because they had rejected a vital component of the gospel. Whether it was the Pharisees of Jesus' day, the Jehovah Witnesses and Mormons of our day, or people who simply reject the deity of Christ, those who remove the component of "Jesus is God" have created an imaginary Jesus.

Professing Christians, are usually quick to acknowledge that other religions and cults have a different Jesus than the One revealed in the Bible. However, Christians must be diligent not to make a similar mistake as that of the other religions and cults, by creating a Jesus other than the One revealed in Scripture, a Jesus who is both man and God. Such an error can quickly happen when Christians are not diligent in adequately defining Jesus in their communication of the gospel to others. Though even the most scholarly of us will seldom present every detail of the gospel perfectly, we should at least strive to do so, and especially when it comes to something as important as Jesus being God in the flesh.

Summary: The core of the gospel is the fact that *Jesus is God*. This component of the gospel was of utmost importance to Paul, Peter, the Gospel writers, and to Jesus Himself for clear gospel proclamation. But what about us, do we value the importance of this component of the gospel as they did? It can be tempting to leave this component out of the gospel because, admittedly, it can be divisive, but if we remove the core of God's message about salvation, then we have mutilated the gospel in such a way that it

---

[59] John 8:24-25

is no longer the gospel that Scripture calls people to believe in for salvation.

Jesus did not allow people creative license for people to define Him however they chose. He clearly taught that salvation was tied to acceptance of Him for who He truly was, God in the flesh. And the same goes for people today, if people choose to deny this key component of the gospel, then their belief is in a Jesus who is just a figment of their imagination and has no connection to reality, for a Jesus who was only a man never existed, therefore, would have no power to save anyone. The gospel that we are commanded by God to believe in for our salvation, and to proclaim to others to believe in for their salvation, must have at its core, a message that centers around the fact that *Jesus is God*, "for in him the whole fullness of deity dwells bodily."[60]

---

[60] Colossians 2:9

Chapter 5

COMPONENT #3: JESUS IS HUMAN.

Paul, a servant of Christ Jesus, called to be an apostle, set apart for the gospel of God, which he promised beforehand through his prophets in the holy Scriptures, concerning his Son, **who was descended from David according to the flesh** and was declared to be the Son of God in power according to the Spirit of holiness by his resurrection from the dead, Jesus Christ our Lord, through whom we have received grace ... (Rom. 1:1-5)

The Savior must be human. This fact may seem elementary and unneeded; however, it is a vital part of the gospel message. There is no doubt that the Bible clearly teaches that Jesus is God, but now we explore another critical component of the gospel message, the humanity of Christ.

After Adam and Eve had sinned, God announced judgments over Satan, Adam, and Eve, and to the world as well, yet He also gave the first promise of a Savior that would destroy Satan. God said, "I will put enmity between you and the woman, and between your offspring and her offspring; he shall bruise your head, and you shall bruise his heel."[61] In other words, the Savior would not just appear directly from heaven and defeat Satan. Instead, He was

---

[61] Genesis 3:15

to be born of a woman and therefore be human. It is this Messianic prophecy from God that Paul draws from to make his point to the Romans that Jesus "was descended from David according to the flesh." It is also a point that he elaborated on often, in his letter to the Galatians where he writes, "But when the fullness of time had come, God sent forth his Son, born of woman."[62]

At the very beginning of the book of John, he makes sure that his readers understand that Jesus is God and that He is also a man. He writes, "In the beginning was the Word, and the Word was with God, and the Word was God… And the Word became flesh and dwelt among us."[63] This is the doctrine that we often refer to as the "incarnation." Mary conceiving Jesus within her womb was not the beginning of the Son of God. That moment was the unification of two natures; the deity of Christ and the humanity of Christ. The One who "was God" from all eternity, without a human body, acquired human nature.

Think about it, Jesus is truly God, and Jesus is truly man. This aspect of the person of Jesus can be perplexing, as we have nothing on earth to compare it. However, just because it is difficult to comprehend in its totality, does not mean that we remove the dual nature of Christ. As we have covered already, we must strive to maintain the gospel in its original form or else it becomes a different message.

REMOVING THE HUMANITY OF JESUS IS AN OLD DISTORTION.

There is great danger in removing the humanity of Jesus from the person of Jesus. This is a lesson that we can learn from the past to help us to prevent the same mistake from happening today. In A.D. 361, the removal of this gospel component was titled Apollinarianism, so named because of its founder Apollinarius. He so elevated the deity of Christ, that he removed the humanity of Jesus. What is interesting is that Apollinarius may not have had

---

[62] Galatians 4:4
[63] John 1:1,14

evil intentions in mind when he removed the humanity of Christ, but the reality was that his teaching was still biblically incorrect. As the great theologian Louis Berkhof has written:

> His chief interest was to secure the unity of the person in Christ, without sacrificing His real deity; and also to guard the sinlessness of Christ. But he did so at the expense of the complete humanity of the Savior, and consequently his position was condemned... [64]

The teaching of Apollinarius was deemed unbiblical, heretical, and rejected by the Council of Constantinople in A.D. 381. It was labeled heretical because it did not correctly describe who Jesus truly was as presented in the context of Scripture. Apollinarius changed the object of belief from Jesus, who was *both* God and man to a Jesus, that was *only* God. This heresy may not seem all that bad on the surface, but if we alter the components of the gospel, especially regarding the person of Jesus, then we no longer have the original "gospel of God" or the real Jesus Christ. Instead, we are left with a gospel made up by a man, and any altering of God's gospel is extremely dangerous. As apologist Matt Slick writes:

> This heresy denies the true and complete humanity in the person of Jesus which in turn can jeopardize the value of the atonement, since Jesus is declared to be both God and man to atone. Jesus needed to be divine in order to offer a pure and holy sacrifice of sufficient value to The Father, and He needed to be a man in order to die for men.[65]

Apollinarius's teaching was considered heresy because it presented a Jesus that was not human, but only God. Regarding the importance of fighting for the right belief of Christ being

---

[64] Louis Berkhof, *Systematic Theology* (Grand Rapids, MI: W.B. Eerdmans Pub., 1996), 307.

[65] Matt Slick, "Apollinarianism," CARM Christian Apologetics & Research Ministry, accessed April 24, 2017, https://carm.org/.

fully man and fully God, Professor and church historian, Stephen Nichols writes:

> The early church was right in spending so much time and effort on the doctrine of Christ. They were right to contend that Christ is the God-man, very God of very God and at the same time truly human with flesh and blood. They were right to contend that Christ is two natures conjoined in one person without division, separation, confusion, or mixture, to use the language of the Chalcedonian Creed. They were also right to contend that the gospel collapses without this belief.[66]

As shown, removing the humanity of Jesus is not a new method of changing the gospel. Even before Apollinarius, the Apostle John had to refute this false teaching during his day. False teachers had removed the humanity of Jesus by denying His incarnation and instead taught that Jesus only *appeared* to be human.[67] This was of no small matter and stirred John to contend for the faith. He wrote, "Beloved, do not believe every spirit, but test the spirits to see whether they are from God, for many false prophets have gone out into the world. By this, you know the Spirit of God: every spirit that confesses that Jesus Christ has come in the flesh is from God."[68] John puts the positive confession of Jesus Christ's humanity as a test for sound doctrine. Those who did not agree should instantly be known as false prophets, people who were misrepresenting God. John further warned of this false teaching about Christ when he wrote, "for many deceivers have gone out into the world, those who do not confess the coming of Jesus Christ in the flesh. Such a one is the deceiver and the antichrist."[69] Regarding this controversy, theologian Simon Kistemaker writes:

---

[66] Stephen J. Nichols, *For Us and for Our Salvation: The Doctrine of Christ in the Early Church* (Wheaton, IL: Crossway Books, 2007), 15.
[67] R. C. Sproul, ed., *The Reformation Study Bible: English Standard Version* (Orlando, FL: Reformation Trust, 2015), 2262.
[68] 1 John 4:1-2
[69] 2 John 1:7

John gives his readers a formula for determining whether a spirit comes from God or from the devil: The Christian recognizes the Spirit of God in anyone who openly confesses that Jesus Christ is both human and divine, and that Jesus Christ, who is the Son of God, 'has come in the flesh.' Here we have the established principle for testing whether a particular teaching comes from the Holy Spirit.[70]

Kistemaker goes on to warn:

Although John addresses the church of the first century, nothing has changed since that time. Today we have numerous teachers and preachers who deny that Jesus Christ is human and divine. They are not from God, says John. In fact, he labels the spirit of such denial 'the spirit of the antichrist.'[71]

As you can see, removing the humanity of Jesus was no small matter. Those who did so were referred to as "anti-Christ." Yet, both in John's day and in ours there are those who claim to be Christians who have removed this vital component from the gospel that they believe in, and the gospel that they proclaim and call others to believe in. Professing Christians need to understand and declare that *Jesus is God*, but part of the gospel is that *Jesus is human* as well.

THE MESSIAH HAD TO BE DESCENDED FROM DAVID.

The Messiah was not going to be born to just anyone, but the Messianic promise had been given to a specific family tree. This

---

[70] William Hendriksen and Simon Kistemaker, "1 John," in *New Testament Commentary*, vol. James, Epistles of John, Peter, and Jude (Grand Rapids, MI: Baker Book House, 2007), 325.

[71] William Hendriksen and Simon Kistemaker, "1 John," in *New Testament Commentary*, vol. James, Epistles of John, Peter, and Jude (Grand Rapids, MI: Baker Book House, 2007), 326.

particular genealogy was one of the God-ordained ways that people were to know the identity of the Messiah. Over the years, God had added to His original pronouncement of the humanity of the coming Messiah by speaking through various prophets, to announce the exact family line from which the Messiah must descend. In summary, He was to be human and must come from the lineage of Abraham, Isaac, Jacob, Judah, Jesse, and King David.

To better understand Paul's point in his gospel summary to the Romans, when he wrote, "who was descended from David according to the flesh," it is good to reflect on these Old Testament prophecies to see their importance in the identification of the Messiah as Jesus of Nazareth.

ABRAHAM:

After God had made His promise to Eve, He announced to Abraham that it would be from his lineage that the Messiah was to continue.

> And the angel of the LORD called to Abraham a second time from heaven and said, 'By myself I have sworn, declares the LORD, because you have done this and have not withheld your son, your only son, I will surely bless you, and I will surely multiply your offspring as the stars of heaven and as the sand that is on the seashore. And your offspring shall possess the gate of his enemies, and in your offspring shall all the nations of the earth be blessed, because you have obeyed my voice.' (Gen. 22:15-18)

From this prophecy, we see that God had chosen Abraham as the one from whose lineage the Messiah would come. From Abraham would come a particular offspring/seed that would defeat the enemy and be a blessing to all the nations. The Apostle Peter would later reference this prophecy of Abraham to prove that Jesus was the Messiah; by showing that Jesus was the one that God had said would come from Abraham. After he healed the lame man, Peter explained to the audience not only by whose power the man was healed, but he also revealed the ancestry of Jesus to show that He is the Savior that God had promised.

> You are the sons of the prophets and of the covenant that God made with your fathers, saying to Abraham, 'And in your offspring shall all the families of the earth be blessed.' God, having raised up his servant, sent him to you first, to bless you by turning every one of you from wickedness. (Acts 3:25-26)

Paul referred to the same passage about Abraham's offspring when he explained the gospel to the Galatians. He wrote, "Now the promises were made to Abraham and to his offspring. It does not say, 'And to offsprings,' referring to many, but referring to one, 'And to your offspring,' who is Christ."[72] Paul's point is that the promise God had made to Abraham has been fulfilled by Abraham's offspring: Jesus.

ISAAC:

After God had promised Abraham that the Messiah would come from his direct line, God later chose Abraham's son Isaac to perpetuate the Messianic lineage. Abraham's son Ishmael was not selected to carry that line.

> God said, 'No, but Sarah your wife shall bear you a son, and you shall call his name Isaac. I will establish my covenant with him as an everlasting covenant for his offspring after him. As for Ishmael, I have heard you; behold, I have blessed him and will make him fruitful and multiply him greatly. He shall father twelve princes, and I will make him into a great nation. But I will establish my covenant with Isaac, whom Sarah shall bear to you at this time next year.' (Gen. 17:19-21)

---

[72] Galatians 3:16

JACOB:

Isaac later married and had two sons of his own: Jacob and Esau. However, once again, God removed any speculation and declared that it was through Jacob that the Messiah would come. Here is part of that conversation between Jacob and God.

> And behold, the LORD stood above it and said, "I am the LORD, the God of Abraham your father and the God of Isaac. The land on which you lie I will give to you and to your offspring. Your offspring shall be like the dust of the earth, and you shall spread abroad to the west and to the east and to the north and to the south, and in you and your offspring shall all the families of the earth be blessed. (Gen. 28:13-14)

JUDAH:

Jacob married and had twelve sons. The line of the promised Messiah seemed uncertain. Which son would the Messiah come from? However, on his deathbed, Jacob prophesied that the line of the Messiah would continue through his son Judah.

> The scepter shall not depart from Judah, nor the ruler's staff from between his feet, until tribute comes to him; and to him shall be the obedience of the peoples. (Gen. 49:10)

This is a significant narrowing down of the Messianic line. By this announcement, God had eliminated the possibility of the Messiah coming from any of the other eleven sons and made it clear that the Messiah would one day rise from the lineage of Judah.

JESSE:

The line of the Messiah through Abraham continued throughout the time of Israel's bondage in Egypt and the subsequent exodus. God was faithful to maintain the line as He had promised. Each person throughout the line was essential to the story, but for the sake of time, we move to the father of King David.

> The LORD said to Samuel, 'How long will you grieve over Saul, since I have rejected him from being king over Israel? Fill your horn with oil, and go. I will send you to Jesse the Bethlehemite, for I have provided for myself a king among his sons.' And Samuel said, 'How can I go? If Saul hears it, he will kill me.' And the LORD said, 'Take a heifer with you and say, 'I have come to sacrifice to the LORD.' And invite Jesse to the sacrifice, and I will show you what you shall do. And you shall anoint for me him whom I declare to you.' (1 Sam. 16:1-3)

Samuel went to the house of Jesse to anoint the next king; however, God let him know that it was not the first-born son or even the other sons that Jesse brought forth, but God had chosen the youngest son, David.

> Then Samuel said to Jesse, 'Are all your sons here?' And he said, 'There remains yet the youngest, but behold, he is keeping the sheep.' And Samuel said to Jesse, 'Send and get him, for we will not sit down till he comes here.' And he sent and brought him in. Now he was ruddy and had beautiful eyes and was handsome. And the LORD said, 'Arise, anoint him, for this is he.' Then Samuel took the horn of oil and anointed him in the midst of his brothers. And the Spirit of the LORD rushed upon David from that day forward. And Samuel rose up and went to Ramah. (1 Sam. 16:11-13)

Isaiah the prophet would later expound on the connection of Jesse to the coming Messiah with this prophecy:

> There shall come forth a shoot from the stump of Jesse,
> and a branch from his roots shall bear fruit.
> And the Spirit of the LORD shall rest upon him,
> the Spirit of wisdom and understanding,

the Spirit of counsel and might,
the Spirit of knowledge and the fear of the LORD.
And his delight shall be in the fear of the LORD.
He shall not judge by what his eyes see,
or decide disputes by what his ears hear,
but with righteousness he shall judge the poor,
and decide with equity for the meek of the earth;
and he shall strike the earth with the rod of his mouth,
and with the breath of his lips he shall kill the wicked.
Righteousness shall be the belt of his waist,
and faithfulness the belt of his loins…

In that day the root of Jesse, who shall stand as a signal for the peoples—of him shall the nations inquire, and his resting place shall be glorious. (Is. 11:1-5, 11)

DAVID:

The final revelation concerning the human lineage of the Messiah was that He would come from the line of King David.

> 'When your days are fulfilled and you lie down with your fathers, I will raise up your offspring after you, who shall come from your body, and I will establish his kingdom. He shall build a house for my name, and I will establish the throne of his kingdom forever. I will be to him a father, and he shall be to me a son. When he commits iniquity, I will discipline him with the rod of men, with the stripes of the sons of men, but my steadfast love will not depart from him, as I took it from Saul, whom I put away from before you. And your house and your kingdom shall be made sure forever before me. Your throne shall be established forever.' In accordance with all these words, and in accordance with all this vision, Nathan spoke to David. (2 Sam. 7:12-17)[73]

---

[73] See also: Isaiah 9:6-7

While this prophecy does have to do with David's son Solomon, the statement "your kingdom shall be made sure forever before me," speaks of no mere earthly temporal king. This prophecy speaks of another son that would come and reign forever. This is none other than Jesus Christ. As theologians, Keil and Delitzsch comment:

> For it is not merely in its earthly form, as a building of wood and stone, that the temple is referred to, but also and chiefly in its essential characteristic, as the place of the manifestation and presence of God in the midst of His people. The earthly form is perishable, the essence eternal. This essence was the dwelling of God in the midst of His people, which did not cease with the destruction of Jerusalem, but culminated in the appearance of Jesus Christ, in whom Jehovah came to His people, and, as God the Word, made human nature His dwelling-place in the glory of the only begotten Son of the Father; so that Christ could say to the Jews, 'Destroy this temple, and in three days I will build it up again (John 2:19)'[74]

THE NEW TESTAMENT BEGINS WITH THE HUMAN LINEAGE OF JESUS.

Given the mandatory lineage of the Messiah, it is no wonder that the opening words of the New Testament are Matthew's record of Jesus' fulfillment of the exact bloodline of which the Messiah must come. Not only was Jesus qualified to be the Messiah in every other way, but even in His flesh, He meets the qualifications predetermined by God's prophetic word. Though quite lengthy, perhaps you can see why it was important for Matthew to take the

---

[74] Carl Friedrich Keil and Franz Delitzsch, *Commentary on the Old Testament*, vol. 2, Joshua, Judges, Ruth, 1 and 2 Samuel (Peabody, MA: Hendrickson Publishers, 2011), 600.

time to prove that Jesus is connected to Abraham, Isaac, Jacob, Judah, Jesse, and David. Matthew records:

The book of the genealogy of Jesus Christ, the son of David, the son of Abraham.

> Abraham was the father of Isaac, and Isaac the father of Jacob, and Jacob the father of Judah and his brothers, and Judah the father of Perez and Zerah by Tamar, and Perez the father of Hezron, and Hezron the father of Ram, and Ram the father of Amminadab, and Amminadab the father of Nahshon, and Nahshon the father of Salmon, and Salmon the father of Boaz by Rahab, and Boaz the father of Obed by Ruth, and Obed the father of Jesse, and Jesse the father of David the king…
>
> …and Jacob the father of Joseph the husband of Mary, of whom Jesus was born, who is called Christ. (Matt. 1:1-6, 16)

While some might consider this list of Jesus' human relatives boring, the genealogy is necessary to show that Jesus was qualified to be the Messiah.

The Apostle Paul makes the same point in his opening words of his letter to the Romans, by writing that Jesus was "descended from David."[75] This is a much more reduced manner compared to Matthew's listing of ancestors. However, the point is the same; it is important for his readers to know that Jesus is qualified to be the Savior, due in part because He comes from the line of David. When Paul summarizes the lineage of Christ as "descended from David," he is not only proclaiming the true human nature of Jesus but also that Jesus had come from the Messianic line that God had announced over time through His prophets.

Summary: Should you present the entire lineage of Jesus every time you witness? While that may not be a bad idea, it does not

---

[75] Romans 1:3

seem to be necessary, nor was it the point Paul made when he wrote, "Who was descended from David according to the flesh."[76] However, Paul was at the least pointing out the fact that Jesus was truly human, and that His humanity had fulfilled the predetermined lineage of which the flesh of the Messiah must come.

Do you make sure that you include the identity of Jesus as both God and man when you communicate the gospel? Would you have been classified as an Apollinarian if you were alive in A.D. 381? If you only speak of His deity, that Jesus is God, but fail to mention that He has come in the flesh, then the gospel that you are professing would align well with Apollinarius, and with the false teachers that John wrote against. We must realize that a gospel devoid of Christ's humanity is not the gospel that God delivered to Paul. Understandably, it is difficult, if not impossible, to exhaustively communicate how Jesus was at the same time fully God and fully man. However, we cannot just choose the more comfortable components of the "gospel of God"[77] when we witness. We cannot add to the gospel, and we cannot take away from it, and yet still call it the "gospel of God." Clearly, the humanity and the deity of Jesus was important to the Old Testament prophets, Christ Himself, and to the ones that He had trained to be His primary witnesses, the Apostles.

The dual nature of Christ is unique to Him, in that no one else on earth is, or ever will be, at the same time truly God and truly man; however, this is the person of Jesus the Son of God who was born of the flesh. And it is this uniqueness that makes Jesus, the God-man, perfectly equipped to be the perfect representative of humanity, who lives a holy life and dies in our place.[78]

---

[76] Romans 1:3
[77] Romans 1:1
[78] Hodge, A.A. *Outlines of Theology*, "How can it be shown that the doctrine of the incarnation is a fundamental doctrine of the gospel." (London: Banner of Truth Trust, 1972), p. 385

Chapter 6

COMPONENT #4: JESUS DIED FOR SINS.

Paul, a servant of Jesus, called to be an apostle, set apart for the gospel of God, which he promised beforehand through his prophets in the holy Scriptures, concerning his Son, who was descended from David according to the flesh and was declared to be the Son of God in power according to the Spirit of holiness by his resurrection from the **dead**, Jesus Christ our Lord, through whom we have received grace . . . (Rom. 1:1-5)

JESUS DIED.

Before we get to the resurrection of Jesus, it is crucial to understand the death of Jesus and the purpose of His death. The Apostle Paul included Jesus' death as not only a historical fact but also as a component of the message of the gospel that he had received. While we often take the death of Jesus for granted and assume that everyone knows and understands it, this is simply not the case. Many people in the world are confused about the death of Jesus Christ, and many Christians are failing to explain it to them.

Even, His own Disciples did not understand why Jesus had to die and were utterly shocked when He was crucified. Though the Disciples were stupefied by the death of Jesus, they shouldn't have been.[79] The death of the Messiah had been clearly prophesied and typified in the Old Testament.[80] Jesus, the Messiah Himself, even foretold His death and the details of His death to the Disciples so they would know about it ahead of time. Jesus was not ambiguous about the fact that He was going to be put to death, as we see in this passage from Mark, "And he began to teach them that the Son of Man must suffer many things and be rejected by the elders and the chief priests and the scribes and be killed, and after three days rise again."[81]

The death of Jesus is an essential fact of the gospel message, which is included in all four of the gospels. Each gospel writer made sure to include, not only the glorious details about the life of Jesus but also the facts surrounding His death. Take, for example, the writing of the Apostle John:

> When Jesus had received the sour wine, he said, "It is finished," and he bowed his head and gave up his spirit. Since it was the day of Preparation, and so that the bodies would not remain on the cross on the Sabbath (for that Sabbath was a high day), the Jews asked Pilate that their legs might be broken and that they might be taken away. So the soldiers came and broke the legs of the first, and of the other who had been crucified with him. But when they came to Jesus and saw that he was already dead, they did not break his legs. But one of the soldiers pierced his side with a spear, and at once there came out blood and water. He who saw it has borne witness—his testimony is true, and he knows that he is telling the truth—that you also may believe. (John 19:30-35)

As you read over John's record of the death of Jesus, it is clear that John desired to make sure that his readers clearly understood that Jesus was thoroughly dead. John had not just heard the details of Jesus' death from others, but he was an eye-witness of

---

[79] John 24:21-27
[80] Psalm 22, Isaiah 53, Acts 2:23;3:18;4:28
[81] Mark 8:31

it. John also recorded that the Roman soldiers, who were sent to speed up the deaths of the three men, knew for sure that Jesus was already dead. The soldiers saw no need to speed up the death of Jesus by breaking his legs because Jesus was already dead. John even emphasizes not only the actual death of Jesus but the purpose of his recording the details of the His death "that you also may believe." A right belief in Jesus includes the truth about His death.

The death of Jesus is also a standard component of the evangelistic sermons and writings recorded in the New Testament. The Apostle Peter even included this fact of the gospel in his first evangelistic sermon on the Day of Pentecost. It had only been fifty days since Jesus died, and apparently, most of the people present for Peter's gospel proclamation were fully aware that Jesus had been put to death. However, Peter still believed it necessary to state the obvious, "this Jesus, delivered up according to the definite plan and foreknowledge of God, you crucified and killed by the hands of lawless men."[82] Yes, he is exposing their sinfulness by emphasizing that they put Jesus to death, but he is also stating information that is vital to the gospel: the death of Jesus.

The Apostle Paul also treated the death of Christ as a fundamental truth of the gospel that needed to be emphasized. Notice the importance Paul placed on the death of Jesus when he evangelized the Corinthians, "And I, when I came to you, brothers, did not come proclaiming to you the testimony of God with lofty speech or wisdom. For I decided to know nothing among you except Jesus Christ and him crucified."[83] It is not that "Christ and him crucified" was literally the only information that Paul knew about Jesus, but it does show that the death of Jesus was a core component of Paul's gospel message.

The point is that the death of Jesus was commonly understood to be an essential part of the gospel message. His death was foretold by the prophets, included in all four gospel accounts, and it was also included in the evangelistic sermons and writings of the Apostles. So, what does this mean for us and our communication

---

[82] Acts 2:22-23
[83] 1 Corintians 2:1-2

of the gospel? It means that the death of Jesus should be equally common to our communication of the gospel as well, for without His death, there can be no resurrection.

JESUS DIED FOR OUR SINS.

Even though we have established the fact that Jesus really did die, we need to also wrap our minds around why Jesus died. What makes the good news beneficial to us is not that Jesus merely died, but that Jesus died for our sins. It is one thing to understand the fact that Jesus died, but as believers, we must be able to express why it was necessary for Jesus to die and what was accomplished by His death. The purpose of Jesus' death was of major significance to the Apostle Paul, as seen in his letter to the Corinthians. He writes, "For I delivered to you as of first importance what I also received: that Christ died for our sins..."[84] Was Paul saying that none of the other details about Jesus Christ mattered? No, but he was using extreme shorthand to show the focal beneficiary point of the gospel is that Jesus died in place of sinners. Regarding this passage, R. C. Sproul writes:

> Paul was saying that in all of his teaching, in all of his preaching, in all of his missionary activity, the central point of importance was the cross. In effect, this teacher was saying to his students, 'You might forget other things that I teach you, but don't ever forget the cross, because it was on the cross, through the cross, and by the cross that our Savior performed His work of redemption and gathered His people for eternity.'[85]

Obviously, the Apostle Paul, as Sproul stated, believed the cross was "the central point of importance." What happened on the cross was the death of a man, but a death that accomplished more than any other man's death ever could.

---

[84] 1 Corinthians 15:3
[85] R. C. Sproul, *The Truth of the Cross* (Lake Mary, FL: Reformation Trust Pub., 2007), 5.

Although Paul does not go into great detail about what the death of Jesus accomplished in the opening of his letter to the Romans, he does go on to expound on the subject a great deal throughout the letter. We will be examining some such passages shortly, but to gain a fuller understanding of the need of the Messiah to die for our sins, it serves us well to first glean from some prophecies and typologies of the Old Testament.

THE DEATH OF THE PASSOVER LAMB.

A great typological example of the purpose of Christ' death is found in the historical account of the people of Israel being set free from the bondage of Egyptian slavery. God had already sent nine plagues upon Egypt to punish the Pharoah; however, the Pharaoh would not relent. Finally, God announced that He would achieve His purpose of setting His people free by one final act of wrath. During the night, God was going to come through the land of Egypt, and bring death to the firstborn son in every household. But God also provided a method of salvation. God would allow the substitutionary death of a lamb to appease His wrath.

> Then they shall take some of the blood and put it on the two doorposts and the lintel of the houses in which they eat it. … It is the LORD's Passover. For I will pass through the land of Egypt that night, and I will strike all the firstborn in the land of Egypt, both man and beast; and on all the gods of Egypt I will execute judgments: I am the LORD. The blood shall be a sign for you, on the houses where you are. And when I see the blood, I will pass over you, and no plague will befall you to destroy you, when I strike the land of Egypt. This day shall be for you a memorial day, and you shall keep it as a feast to the LORD; throughout your generations, as a statute forever, you shall keep it as a feast.
>
> All the people of Israel did just as the LORD commanded Moses and Aaron. And on that very day the

LORD brought the people of Israel out of the land of Egypt by their hosts. (Exodus 12:7,11-14, 50-51)

God's wrath was going to come through the land of the Egyptians and the Israelites. If the blood of the lamb were on the door of the home, no one inside would die. The blood meant that a substitutionary death had occurred, which saved the firstborn of that household from receiving the wrath of God. In other words, death was required in every home, it would be the firstborn's death or the death of a lamb. God had provided only one way of salvation, and that salvation was by the death of a lamb.

That night everything happened precisely as God said it would. Each home that was not protected by the death of the lamb suffered the death of the firstborn. However, God's wrath and judgment passed over every single home that had sacrificed a lamb. God's judgment and His salvation were 100% effective. The next day the Egyptians were so distraught by all of the death that had occurred in their homes that the Pharaoh released Israel from slavery to go and worship God.

This was such an important event, that God commanded the Israelites to reset their calendars according to the Passover. He also commanded them to have an annual time of sacrifice and feast to commemorate the day that the Lord's wrath passed them over. As God had commanded, the Jewish people continued to celebrate the Passover Feast for over 1200 years. However, on the night before the crucifixion of Jesus Christ, God put an end to the annual Passover Feast and sacrifice. That evening, Jesus and the disciples were partaking of the prescribed annual Passover Feast when unexpectedly, Jesus made a shocking announcement to His disciples. Jesus revealed that He was the sacrifice (the Passover Lamb) that was about to die for their sins. Matthew writes:

> Now as they were eating, Jesus took bread, and after blessing it broke it and gave it to the disciples, and said, "Take, eat; this is my body." And he took a cup, and when he had given thanks he gave it to them, saying, "Drink of it, all of you, for this is my blood of the cov-

enant, which is poured out for many for the forgiveness of sins. I tell you I will not drink again of this fruit of the vine until that day when I drink it new with you in my Father's kingdom." (Matt. 26:26-29)

Shockingly, Jesus radically altered the focus of the God-ordained feast. Jesus revealed that the annual celebration of the Passover was about to be once and for all fulfilled by the sacrifice of Himself. He was the Lamb that would fully atone for the sins of His people. His blood was going to be shed, not on the wooden doorway of homes to protect the firstborn, but God's Lamb and Firstborn Son was going to shed His blood on the wooden cross. The next day Jesus would become the sacrifice that would allow God's wrath to pass over the sins of all for whom Jesus died.

The Apostle Paul frequently used the language of substitutionary sacrifice to describe the purpose of the death of Jesus, and in his letter to the Corinthians, Paul made an extremely concise statement that should remove any doubt of what Jesus had accomplished in His death. Paul wrote, "For Christ, our Passover lamb, has been sacrificed."[86] Paul was clearly bringing attention to the death of Jesus and the death of the Passover lambs of Exodus. The sacrifice of Jesus Christ was the sacrifice that ended the need for further Passover Lambs to be sacrificed for the death of Jesus fully appeased the wrath of God.

The Apostle Peter also drew from the language of the Passover event of choosing a lamb "without blemish" to describe what Jesus had accomplished by His death. Peter writes, "knowing that you were ransomed ..., not with perishable things such as silver or gold, but with the precious blood of Christ, like that of a lamb without blemish or spot."[87] Peter certainly understood and taught that Jesus was the supreme sinless sacrifice that took the wrath of God to ransom us from the bondage of our sins.

As we see the substitutionary death of the Passover Lamb of Exodus and the Passover Lamb of Jesus Christ becoming increas-

---

[86] 1 Corinthians 5:7
[87] Exodus 12:5; 1 Peter 1:18-19

ingly clear, we must also bring attention to the words that John the Baptist used to announce Jesus to the masses. Remember, John the Baptist was the prophet that was sent by God to proclaim the arrival of the Messiah.[88] However, John did not announce Jesus to the people by directly calling Him "Messiah." Instead, John saw Jesus coming and proclaimed to the crowd, "Behold, the Lamb of God, who takes away the sin of the world!"[89] Of all the titles that John could have chosen from, he purposefully, and under the prophetic direction of God, referred to Jesus as "the Lamb of God." John was intentionally using language which described the purpose of the Passover Lamb. The Lamb, which God had provided, was going to fulfill what the previous Passover Lambs had only foreshadowed.

As you see, this type of comparison abounds in the writing of the New Testament. As the theologian, T.D. Alexander emphasizes,

> The Passover features prominently in the NT understanding of the death of Jesus Christ. According to Matthew, Mark, and Luke, the Last Supper, which was subsequently to be commemorated as the Lord's Supper, was a Passover meal. By highlighting Jesus' unbroken bones John alludes to the fact that the death of Jesus resembles that of the Passover sacrifice. Undoubtedly, NT writers interpret the death of Jesus as bringing about a new exodus that entails people being freed from the power of Satan and ransomed from the domain of death.[90]

So why did Jesus die? He died in our place to appease the wrath of God. The lessons that were taught on an annual basis for over 1200 years found their fulfillment in the sacrifice of God's Lamb without blemish, Jesus Christ.

---

[88] Isaiah 40:3-5; Malachi 4:5-6; Matthew 11:9-10
[89] John 1:29
[90] T. Desmond Alexander, *Exodus* (London: Apollos, 2017), 234.

THE SACRIFICES OF LEVITICUS AND THE SACRIFICE OF CHRIST.

Following the Passover event and the great exodus, God gave the Israelites precise directions as to how He was to be worshipped. God told Moses to tell the people of Israel to "make me a sanctuary, that I may dwell in their midst. Exactly as I show you concerning the pattern of the tabernacle, and of all its furniture, so you shall make it."[91] God also selected, and restricted, the priestly work at the tabernacle to only those whom He chose. This we can see from God's choosing of the first priests, "Then bring near to you Aaron your brother, and his sons with him, from among the people of Israel, to serve me as priests."[92]

God not only prescribed the worship place, architecture, furnishings, and the priest, but He also specified the method of worship. One of the most visible reminders of the people's sinfulness was the blood that was required by God for their sins. And this was not a one-time sacrifice, or even just once per year. Their sinfulness before God required sacrifices to be brought to the Lord multiple times per day. As God commanded, "This is the food offering that you shall offer to the Lord: two male lambs a year old without blemish, day by day, as a regular offering. The one lamb you shall offer in the morning, and the other lamb you shall offer at twilight."[93] And it was not only the two lambs that were to be sacrificed daily, but there were also sacrifices required by the people to bring for their own sins as we see in this passage:

> "If his offering is a burnt offering from the herd, he shall offer a male without blemish. He shall bring it to the entrance of the tent of meeting, that he may be accepted before the LORD. He shall lay his hand on the head of the burnt offering, and it shall be accepted for him

---
[91] Exodus 25:8-9
[92] Exodus 28:1
[93] Numbers 28:3-4

to make atonement for him. Then he shall kill the bull before the LORD." (Lev. 1:3-5)

All of this death made for an incredibly bloody scene which served as a constant visual aid of the wages of sin. The innocent animal was a substitute recipient of the wrath of God that the sinful person, or people, deserved. Also, note well the symbolism of the sin being transferred from the guilty person to the innocent animal that was about to die. This bloody substitutionary atonement was an ongoing reminder to the nation of Israel of their sin, the holiness of God, and the punishment that their sin deserved.

Each year thousands of animals were sacrificed; however, one day of sacrifice stood out from all of the others. This was the Day of Atonement. God had ordained this particular day for the sins of the entire nation of Israel's sins to be collectively atoned for each year. In chapter sixteen of Leviticus, God gave detailed instructions for Israel's Day of Atonement. The High Priest was to take two goats. He was to kill one to atone for the sins of the people, but the other was to be released. He was also to symbolically place Israel's sin on the other goat and send him far away into the wilderness.

On this particular day, two animals were used as a sin offering. The animal that was killed was used to teach that propitiation (the appeasement of God for sin), required the death of an innocent substitute to take the place of sinners. The other animal was released, which was used to teach that sin also needed to be removed from the people, expiation.[94] The goat that was kept alive "shall be presented alive before the Lord to make atonement over it, that it may be sent away into the wilderness."[95] The wilderness was far away from the tabernacle. The removal of the sin-bearing goat from the presence of God in the Tabernacle and from the nation of Israel was symbolic of the fact that God removes sins. Such a concept is echoed by the Psalmist who writes, "as far as the east is from the west, so far does he remove our transgressions

---

[94] See Leviticus 16:7-10
[95] Leviticus 16:10

from us."⁹⁶ Now, as for the other goat that was to be killed, God gave exact instructions as well.

> "Then he shall kill the goat of the sin offering that is for the people and bring its blood inside the veil and do with its blood as he did with the blood of the bull, sprinkling it over the mercy seat and in front of the mercy seat. Thus he shall make atonement for the Holy Place, because of the uncleannesses of the people of Israel and because of their transgressions, all their sins." (Lev. 16:15-16)

On this day, and only on this day, the High Priest was allowed to enter into the holiest place in the Tabernacle, the Holy of Holies, where God's presence was manifested. There, the High Priest was to present the blood of an innocent animal before the Lord. This blood represented the death that the people of Israel deserved for their sins against God.

The lessons of propitiation and expiation that were visually taught by the use of the two animals on the Day of Atonement, were entirely fulfilled by the single superior sacrifice of Jesus Christ. Being fully God and fully man, He is the only sacrifice that could actually accomplish both the receiving God's wrath for our sin and full removal of our sin. As the Scottish theologian, John Murray so articulately wrote:

> Jesus, therefore, offered himself a sacrifice and that most particularly under the form or pattern supplied by the sin-offering of the Levitical economy. In thus offering himself he expiated guilt and purged away sin so that we may draw near to God in full assurance of faith and enter into the holiest by the blood of Jesus, having our hearts sprinkled from an evil conscience and our bodies washed with pure water.⁹⁷

---

⁹⁶ Psalm 103:12
⁹⁷ John Murray, *Redemption Accomplished and Applied* (William B. Eerdmans Publishing Company, 2015), 22.

The concept of Jesus' substitutionary, sacrificial death for us is a common theme of the New Testament. The writers understood that Jesus died, but they also regularly brought attention to the purpose of His death. Take, for instance, these verses written by the Apostle Paul:

> For our sake he made him to be sin who knew no sin, so that in him we might become the righteousness of God. (2 Cor. 5:21)

> In him we have redemption through his blood, the forgiveness of our trespasses, according to the riches of his grace. (Eph. 1:7)

> And you, who once were alienated and hostile in mind, doing evil deeds, he has now reconciled in his body of flesh by his death, in order to present you holy and blameless and above reproach before him. (Col. 1:21-22)

> The church of God, which he obtained with his own blood. (Acts 20:28)

As you read over these New Testament Pauline passages, you can't help but hear the wealth of knowledge of the atoning sacrifices of the Old Testament coming forth. In light of looking at the Old Testament first, it becomes difficult to read these Pauline passages without thoughts of the Passover, the sacrificial system of the tabernacle, and the Day of Atonement coming to mind. Even though Paul did not mention such Old Testament events in each of these passages, the truths that they taught certainly come forward as He proclaimed the purpose of Jesus' death.

HEBREWS, BRINGING IT ALL TOGETHER.

While the substitutionary death of Jesus is taught throughout the New Testament, there is nowhere that it is laid out with as much direct comparison to the Old Testament sacrifices as in the book of Hebrews. Take, for example, these passages from the ninth chapter of Hebrews:

> But when Christ appeared as a high priest of the good things that have come, then through the greater and more perfect tent (not made with hands, that is, not of this creation) he entered once for all into the holy places, not by means of the blood of goats and calves but by means of his own blood, thus securing an eternal redemption. For if the blood of goats and bulls, and the sprinkling of defiled persons with the ashes of a heifer, sanctify for the purification of the flesh, how much more will the blood of Christ, who through the eternal Spirit offered himself without blemish to God, purify our conscience from dead works to serve the living God. (Hebrews 9:11-14)

In this passage, the author of Hebrews is teaching that Jesus absolutely and finally fulfills the entirety of the sacrificial system that God had put in place in the Old Testament. The author draws our attention to the fact that Jesus' blood was the supreme sacrifice that secured a once-for-all eternal redemption. His blood was the final blood atonement, of which all other sacrifices symbolically pointed.

Jesus was not only the sacrifice, but He also fulfilled the role of the priest. Jesus Christ dies for our sins, the perfect sinless, righteous one on our behalf and takes the offering of Himself directly to the heavenly temple of God. The passage reveals that the God-ordained tabernacle, priest, and sacrificial system that was put in place by Moses and Aaron was an earthly representation of the ultimate dwelling place of God in Heaven.

Also notice the importance that the author of Hebrews places on blood in the following verse, "Indeed, under the law, almost everything is purified with blood, and without the shedding of blood there is no forgiveness of sins."[98] As theologian Thomas Schreiner writes,

---

[98] Hebrews 9:22

> The pervasiveness of blood is evident in sacrificial practices. Indeed the sacrificial cultus of the OT teaches that there is no forgiveness apart from the shedding of the blood. This is evident from the various sacrifices in Leviticus 1-7 and the Day of Atonement (Leviticus 16). … to be forgiven of sin, as the Day of Atonement indicates, blood had to be spilt. A death had to occur.[99]

The author of Hebrews goes on to compare and contrast between the sacrifice of Jesus and the sacrifices that preceded Him. While the previous sacrifices were instrumental in teaching about sin, sins just punishment before a holy God, the atonement that was needed, etc., those sacrifices were insufficient in and of themselves to deal with sin appropriately. The sacrifices were all pointing forward to the supreme sacrifice that God was going to provide. As the author of Hebrew writes,

> Thus it was necessary for the copies of the heavenly things to be purified with these rites, but the heavenly things themselves with better sacrifices than these. For Christ has entered, not into holy places made with hands, which are copies of the true things, but into heaven itself, now to appear in the presence of God on our behalf. Nor was it to offer himself repeatedly, as the high priest enters the holy places every year with blood not his own, for then he would have had to suffer repeatedly since the foundation of the world. But as it is, he has appeared once for all at the end of the ages to put away sin by the sacrifice of himself. (Hebrews 9:23-26)

While the author of Hebrews brings our attention to the similarities of the previous sacrifices to the sacrifice of Jesus, he certainly drives home the point that the sacrifice of Jesus is different in that it is far superior. Jesus is the "better" sacrifice whose sac-

---

[99] Thomas R. Schreiner, *Commentary on Hebrews*, ed. Köstenberger Andreas J. and T. Desmond Alexander (Nashville, TN: B & H Publishing Group, 2015), 279.

rifice is taken directly into the presence of God Himself to ultimately "put away sin by the sacrifice of himself."

ISAIAH'S PROHPECY OF THE DEATH OF JESUS.

Isaiah was written hundreds of years before Jesus was born; however, this prophecy walks us through the exact scene of the crucifixion of Christ as if Isaiah is an eyewitness. The entire prophecy is packed with prophetic details about the suffering Messiah that would die for the sins of His people. Not only does Isaiah's prophecy detail the death of Jesus, but Isaiah also wrote clearly regarding the purpose of Jesus' death. So, why did Jesus have to die, according to Isaiah? Let's see what reason the prophet gave.

> Surely he has borne our griefs
> and carried our sorrows;
> yet we esteemed him stricken,
> smitten by God, and afflicted.
> But he was pierced for our transgressions;
> he was crushed for our iniquities;
> upon him was the chastisement that brought us peace,
> and with his wounds we are healed.
> All we like sheep have gone astray;
> we have turned—every one—to his own way;
> and the LORD has laid on him
> the iniquity of us all. (Isaiah 53:4-6)

In this passage, it is clearly stated that the coming Messiah was going to suffer and die in place of sinners. Just a quick look over these verses and you can't help but see the purpose in Jesus' death. It is indeed not for Himself or His sin that he is dying, but over and over again, we find that it is because of "our" sins as Isaiah writes: "borne *our* griefs… carried *our* sorrows… *our* transgressions… *our* iniquities."[100]

---

[100] Isaiah 53:4-6

As the sacrificial system of the old testament typified by the sins of the people being transferred to the sacrificial animal, Isaiah prophesied that our sins would be transferred to the Savior. God placed our sins, not symbolically or typologically on Christ, but our sins were truly placed on Jesus Christ, "the Lord has laid on him the iniquity of us all." The Apostle Peter draws from this passage in Isaiah to teach on the atonement of Christ in, "He himself bore our sins in his body on the tree, that we might die to sin and live to righteousness. By his wounds you have been healed."[101] Our righteousness and the healing of our sin-sick souls is only possible due to Jesus bearing our sins upon Himself on the cross. As James Boyce wrote:

> The death of Christ included the penalty in all its fullness. In it he offered up his body and was laid in the grave... His death was not eternal, as would ours have been, arose from the fact that in the execution of the sentence of condemnation, God found in him not such a victim as mere man would have been, unable to atone, or render full satisfaction; but one whose glorious nature gave infinite value to suffering, and who could feel most keenly, yet could bear without destruction, the wrath of God.[102]

As the prophecy of Isaiah continues, pay particular attention to how he brings the lessons taught by the sacrificial system to their typological fulfillment in the prophesied death of the Messiah.

> He was oppressed, and he was afflicted,
> yet he opened not his mouth;
> like a lamb that is led to the slaughter,
> and like a sheep that before its shearers is silent,
> so he opened not his mouth.
> By oppression and judgment he was taken away;

---

[101] 1 Peter 2:24
[102] James Petigru Boyce, *Abstract of Systematic Theology* (Cape Coral, FL: Founders Press, 2006), 328.

> and as for his generation, who considered
> that he was cut off out of the land of the living,
> stricken for the transgression of my people?
> And they made his grave with the wicked
> and with a rich man in his death,
> although he had done no violence,
> and there was no deceit in his mouth. (Isaiah 53:7-9)

Isaiah unambiguously made the connection between the innocent lambs that were required for sacrifice and the innocence, or sinlessness of the supreme Lamb of God, Jesus Christ. The requirement of the blemishless animals of the sacrificial system was meant to show the impeccable quality of sacrifice that God required. Jesus Christ, the Sinless Righteous One, would take on our sins and die as a "lamb that is led to slaughter." As John MacArthur writes,

> For anyone familiar with the New Testament account of Christ's life, death, resurrection and high priestly intercession, there should be no mystery about what Isaiah 53 signifies. It is the complete gospel in prophetic form, a surprisingly explicit foretelling of what the Messiah would do to put away the sins of his people forever.[103]

Lastly, let's look at the substitutionary atonement that the Messiah was to provide. Isaiah writes:

> Yet it was the will of the LORD to crush him;
> he has put him to grief;
> when his soul makes an offering for guilt,
> he shall see his offspring; he shall prolong his days;
> the will of the LORD shall prosper in his hand.
> Out of the anguish of his soul he shall see and be satisfied;
> by his knowledge shall the righteous one, my servant,

---

[103] John MacArthur, *The Gospel According to God: Rediscovering the Most Remarkable Chapter in the Old Testament* (Wheaton, IL: Crossway, 2018), 33.

> make many to be accounted righteous,
> and he shall bear their iniquities.
> Therefore I will divide him a portion with the many,
> and he shall divide the spoil with the strong,
> because he poured out his soul to death
> and was numbered with the transgressors;
> yet he bore the sin of many,
> and makes intercession for the transgressors. (Isaiah 53:10-12)

Isaiah prophesied that the Messiah would be the sacrifice in the place of the "many." Isaiah foretold that the result of the sacrifice would be "righteousness" for those for whom the Messiah died. Isaiah drew from the typological language of the sacrificial system to prophesy what the death of the Messiah would accomplish. The Messiah baring our sins upon Himself would be the punishment (propitiation) and the removal (expiation) of our sins, as was taught on the Day of Atonement. As the great Baptist theologian James Boyce wrote:

> Christ bore the guilt of those for whom he died and thus it became fit that upon him God should inflict the penalty. The result has been the removal of condemnation and the reconciliation effected between God and us. In the removal of these evils, eternal death is taken away.[104]

As you can see, the Old Testament is essential to properly understand why Jesus had to die and what His death accomplished. Unless people understand the lessons of the Old Testament regarding sin and substitutionary sacrifice, the death of Jesus Christ does not make any sense, much less does it sound like good news. However, just by looking over a few places in the Old Testament, we are reminded that 1. Sin deserves the wrath and punishment of God. 2. God provided Israel rescue from sin by way of substitutionary atonement. 3. These sacrifices pointed to the ultimate Lamb of God that would die for sin in our place.

---

[104] Boyce, *Abstract of Systematic Theology*, 328.

BACK TO ROMANS.

As I stated at the beginning of this chapter, the Apostle Paul certainly presented the death of Jesus as a historical fact and as a component of the gospel message. While he did not explicitly address the substitutionary atonement of Jesus Christ in his opening summary of the gospel, it is undoubtedly implied and repeatedly taught further on in his letter to the Romans. As we look at a few examples of such passages from Romans, you might be wondering why I chose not to use these passages alone to explain why Jesus had to die. I sincerely believe that a person can understand the purpose of Jesus' death much better when he or she comes to the subject with a better understanding of the lessons learned from the sacrifices of the Old Testament. So, with all that we have just reviewed: the Passover Lamb, the Levitical sacrifices for people's sins, the Day of Atonement, the commentary of Hebrews, and the atonement prophecy of Isaiah, let's look at few places where Paul proclaims what was accomplished by the death of Jesus.

To begin, let's look at chapter three of Romans.

> ...the righteousness of God through faith in Jesus Christ for all who believe. For there is no distinction: for all have sinned and fall short of the glory of God, and are justified by his grace as a gift, through the redemption that is in Christ Jesus, whom God put forward as a propitiation by his blood, to be received by faith. This was to show God's righteousness, because in his divine forbearance he had passed over former sins. It was to show his righteousness at the present time, so that he might be just and the justifier of the one who has faith in Jesus. (Rom. 3:22-26)

In this passage, Paul is laying out the facts of humanity's sinfulness and God's provision of substitution and salvation through Jesus Christ. All people "have sinned and fall short of the glory of God." We are guilty of sin and incapable of justifying, or making ourselves righteous on our own. What is the solution? As the sacrificial system of the old covenant taught, we need a God-approved innocent substitute to take our place. That substitute is Jesus Christ, who shed His blood, died in our place, received the wrath that we deserve. What do we get in exchange? We receive the righteousness of Jesus Christ.

In and of ourselves, we are unrighteous, ungodly, guilty, sinful lawbreakers who deserve the eternal wrath of God for our sin. However, the substitute that God provided to live and die in our place was blameless before God. In every word, deed, thought, and motive, Jesus was absolutely righteous. As God the Father even announced, "This is my beloved Son, with whom I am well pleased."[105] Jesus lived a perfectly righteous life that was continually pleasing to God. This announcement was not meant to be a momentary approval of Jesus, for Jesus never swayed from perfect righteousness, not even for a moment, as Jesus said, "I always do the things that are pleasing to him."[106]

The innocent, sinless, and righteous life of Jesus is what we must possess for God to be pleased with us as well. But no one can do such a thing. We are all guilty of sin, and cannot pay for it nor remove it. Such guilt is precisely why we need the substitution of Jesus Christ. Our sins are put upon our substitutionary sacrifice, and we receive the record of His righteous life. Paul continues:

> That is why his faith was 'counted to him as righteousness.' But the words 'it was counted to him' were not written for his sake alone, but for ours also. It will be counted to us who believe in him who raised from the dead Jesus our Lord, who was delivered up for our trespasses and raised for our justification. (Romans 4:22-25)

In this passage, Paul taught, once again, that Jesus died, "for our trespasses." Jesus died for our sins. Which is wonderful news, but Paul does not end there, he goes on to teach that we have been justified, made righteous, by God. Our problem of being unrigh-

---

[105] Matthew 3:17
[106] John 8:29

teous sinners before God is solved by God who provided the supreme sacrifice to take our place as a sinner so that we receive the righteousness of Christ Himself. This righteousness is not from us, but given to us by God, through Jesus Christ, as Jonathan Edwards wrote, "When it is said that God justifies the ungodly, it is absurd to suppose that our godliness, taken as some goodness in us, is the ground of our justification…" God receives all the glory for justifying us.

In Romans chapter five, Paul teaches that we have received grace, peace, and access to God through Jesus Christ.

> Therefore, since we have been justified by faith, we have peace with God through our Lord Jesus Christ. Through him we have also obtained access by faith into this grace in which we stand, and we rejoice in hope of the glory of God. (Romans 5:1-2)

Here, Paul is indeed teaching about the accomplishment of Jesus Christ in obtaining grace, peace, and access to God, but hopefully, you can see that Paul is also using lessons learned from the Old Testament to shed light on what the death of Jesus accomplished. For instance, under the sacrificial system of the Old Testament, after the High Priest had made the sacrifice and atoned for the people's sins, he was to return to the people and announce, "The Lord bless you and keep you; the Lord make his face to shine upon you and be gracious to you; the Lord lift up his countenance upon you and give you peace."[107] Notice how even under the old covenant, the grace, peace, and blessing of God was tied to the completion of the sacrifice by the High Priest. But now, those who are in Christ have received a permanent status of grace, peace, and blessing through the One who died for us as the final sacrifice, and the One who is the High Priest who returns from offering Himself to announce, "Peace." As John Murray wrote, "Christ's obedience was vicarious in the full discharge of the demands of righteous-

---

[107] Numbers 6:24-26

ness. His obedience becomes the ground of the remission of sin and of actual justification."[108]

Let's look at one more passage, Romans 5:8-11:

> ... but God shows his love for us in that while we were still sinners, Christ died for us. Since, therefore, we have now been justified by his blood, much more shall we be saved by him from the wrath of God. For if while we were enemies we were reconciled to God by the death of his Son, much more, now that we are reconciled, shall we be saved by his life. More than that, we also rejoice in God through our Lord Jesus Christ, through whom we have now received reconciliation." (Romans 5:8-11)

The subject might be getting a bit repetitive, but you must agree that the Apostle Paul certainly does consider the purpose of Jesus' death as a critical component of the gospel. Here again, we see that it is the blood, or sacrifice, of Jesus that removes us from a position of wrath with God. Jesus atones for our sins, thereby reconciling the relationship, and saving us from God's wrath for our sinfulness. This atonement is so crucial to the gospel that R. C. Sproul wrote, "Therefore, if you take away the substitutionary atonement you empty the cross of its meaning and drain all the significance out of the passion of our Lord Himself. If you do that, you take away Christianity itself."[109]

Summary: So, why did Jesus die? The short answer is, "Jesus died for our sins." Our sins could not be removed without the bloodshed and death of Jesus Christ.[110] The substitutionary atoning death of the Messiah is a common thread that runs through the Bible. The atoning death of the Messiah was typified by the sacrifices of the Old Testament, foretold by the prophets, and predicted

---

[108] Murray, *Redemption Accomplished and Applied*, 17.
[109] R. C. Sproul, *The Truth of the Cross* (Lake Mary, FL: Reformation Trust Pub., 2007), 81.
[110] Hebrews 9:22

in detail by Jesus Christ Himself.[111] Jesus came not just to live the perfect life that we could not live, but He came to pay the price for our sin by His death. Jesus was the ultimate, perfect, and final sacrifice for man's sin. As Martin Lloyd Jones wrote:

> When our Lord died upon the cross he was fulfilling every demand of God's holy law. The righteousness and the justice and the holiness of God were fully satisfied. God poured out his wrath upon sin in the body of his own Son. His soul was made an offering for sin, and all the demands of God in his holiness were satisfied there.[112]

Without the death of Jesus, there is no good news because there is no forgiveness of sins. People need to know that God's love, peace, grace, blessings, reconciliation, redemption, and atonement for sin only come through the substitutionary sacrifice of Jesus Christ. They need to understand that to reject God's provision of sacrifice is to remain in a position of God's wrath. As professor Guy Prentiss Waters has written, "The gospel is a message of salvation, and our sin is one of the things from which we are saved. We may go so far as to say that Paul's gospel is meaningless without a clear understanding of the sin that occasions the need for that gospel."[113] This message is not only wonderful for Christians to dwell on to help enrich our understanding of salvation, but it also needs to be included in our evangelism as well. The gospel is good news, but the benefits of it have come to us by the death of another.

---

[111] Hebrews 9:19-26, Isaiah 53, Psalm 22, John 2:22
[112] Lloyd-Jones and Christopher Catherwood, *The Cross: God's Way of Salvation*, 183.
[113] Guy Prentiss Waters, *The Life and Theology of Paul* (Reformation Trust Publishing, 2018), 31.

Chapter 7

✠

COMPONENT #5: JESUS ROSE FROM THE DEAD.

Paul, a servant of Christ Jesus, called to be an apostle, set apart for the gospel of God, which he promised beforehand through his prophets in the holy Scriptures, concerning his Son, who was descended from David according to the flesh **and was declared to be the Son of God in power according to the Spirit of holiness by his resurrection from the dead,** Jesus Christ our Lord, through whom we have received grace . . . (Rom. 1:1-5)

Jesus not only died, but He also rose from the dead. Can a person deny the resurrection of Jesus and still be saved? According to the Apostle Paul, the resurrection of Jesus from the dead was a vital component of the gospel which he had received and that he preached that others might believe in for salvation. Sinclair Ferguson and Derek Thomas in their book, *Icthus: Jesus Christ, God's Son, Savior,* write:

> Christianity is a religion about facts. It is rooted in the fact of a physical resurrection. Without that Christianity collapses. It is altogether destroyed. 'If Christ has not been raised,' says Paul, 'your faith is futile.' It is useless.[114]

---

[114] Sinclair B. Ferguson and Derek Thomas, *Ichthus: Jesus Christ, God's Son, the Saviour* (Edinburgh: Banner of Truth Trust, 2015), 112.

As Ferguson and Thomas make clear from 1 Corinthians 15:17, Paul put forth his argument for the resurrection of Jesus and even warned, that to deny the resurrection of Christ was to deny historical fact, future promise, and the faith. Let us read what Paul said about the importance of the resurrection of Jesus in the surrounding verses.

> Now if Christ is proclaimed as raised from the dead, how can some of you say that there is no resurrection of the dead? But if there is no resurrection of the dead, then not even Christ has been raised. And if Christ has not been raised, then our preaching is in vain and your faith is in vain. We are even found to be misrepresenting God, because we testified about God that he raised Christ, whom he did not raise if it is true that the dead are not raised. For if the dead are not raised, not even Christ has been raised. And if Christ has not been raised, your faith is futile and you are still in your sins. Then those also who have fallen asleep in Christ have perished. If in Christ we have hope in this life only, we are of all people most to be pitied.
>
> But in fact Christ has been raised from the dead, the first fruits of those who have fallen asleep. For as by a man came death, by a man has come also the resurrection of the dead. (1 Cor. 15:12-21)

Paul made it abundantly clear that the resurrection of Christ was so crucial that without it, the gospel was preached in vain, and any subsequent faith in a gospel which omitted the resurrection of Christ from the dead was also in vain. Paul said that if the resurrection is not preached then, "We are even found to be misrepresenting God."[115] As Ferguson and Thomas point out, Paul further stated, "if Christ has not been raised, your faith is futile, and you are still in your sins."[116] Paul definitely believed the resurrection of Christ to

---
[115] 1 Corinthians 15:14-15
[116] 1 Corinthians 15:17

be of extreme importance to the gospel. Regarding the importance of this element of the gospel, Louis Berkhof, the trusted theologian, in his Sys*tematic Theology,* writes:

> We cannot deny the physical resurrection of Christ without impugning the veracity of the writers of Scripture, since they certainly represent it as a fact. This means that it affects our belief in the trustworthiness of Scripture... What is still more important, the resurrection enters as a constitutive element into the essence of the work of redemption, and therefore the gospel. It is one of the great foundation stones of the Church of God. The atoning work of Christ, if it was to be effective at all, had to terminate, not in death, but in life. Furthermore, it was the Father's seal on the completed work of Christ, the public declaration of its acceptance.[117]

Similarly, the theology of the great Princeton theologian B. B. Warfield emphasizes the extreme importance of the resurrection:

> The original Christianity was preeminently rooted in historical events, and this is particularly so in regard to the resurrection of Jesus. 'If Christianity is entirely indifferent to the reality of this fact, then 'Christianity' is something wholly different from what it was conceived to be by its founders.' That is to say, with the reality of the resurrection, Christianity itself is at stake. If its doctrines are not facts grounded in history, it is not the religion it professes to be. What cannot be denied is that the reality of the resurrection of Christ 'formed the center of the faith of the founders of Christianity.' Jesus himself staked his whole claim upon it, and this was the single and sufficient 'sign' or credential he agreed to give.[118]

---

[117] Louis Berkhof, *Systematic Theology* (Grand Rapids, MI: W.B. Eerdmans Pub., 1996), 349.

[118] Fred G. Zaspel, *The Theology of B. B. Warfield: A Systematic Summary* (Wheaton, IL: Crossway, 2010), 320-321

According to Warfield's theology, if we do not proclaim the resurrection of Christ, then "Christianity itself is at stake." He believed that the very essence, the "center of the faith" is the historical fact and fundamental belief that Jesus died and rose again.

PETER'S RESURRECTION SERMON.

After Jesus had died and rose from the dead, He spent forty more days on earth before ascending into heaven. On the fiftieth day following His resurrection, He sent the Holy Spirit just as He had promised.

> When the day of Pentecost arrived, they were all together in one place. And suddenly there came from heaven a sound like a mighty rushing wind, and it filled the entire house where they were sitting. And divided tongues as of fire appeared to them and rested on each one of them. And they were all filled with the Holy Spirit and began to speak in other tongues as the Spirit gave them utterance.
>
> Now there were dwelling in Jerusalem Jews, devout men from every nation under heaven. And at this sound the multitude came together, and they were bewildered, because each one was hearing them speak in his own language. (Acts 2:1-6)

The supernatural signs from heaven drew a vast crowd that was bewildered and was looking for the reason these things were happening. Peter, as the main representative of the disciples, stood up to preach. What was he going to say to help explain all that was happening? The resurrection, ascension, and exaltation of Jesus Christ:

> Brothers, I may say to you with confidence about the patriarch David that he both died and was buried, and his tomb is with us to this day. Being therefore a prophet, and knowing that God had sworn with an oath

to him that he would set one of his descendants on his throne, he foresaw and spoke about the resurrection of the Christ, that he was not abandoned to Hades, nor did his flesh see corruption. This Jesus God raised up, and of that we all are witnesses. Being therefore exalted at the right hand of God, and having received from the Father the promise of the Holy Spirit, he has poured out this that you yourselves are seeing and hearing. For David did not ascend into the heavens, but he himself says,

'The Lord said to my Lord, "Sit at my right hand, until I make your enemies your footstool."'

Let all the house of Israel therefore know for certain that God has made him both Lord and Christ, this Jesus whom you crucified. (Acts 2:29-36)

Peter let the crowd know that the whole reason they were witnessing this supernatural outpouring of the Holy Spirit was because Jesus was alive. They had killed Jesus, but He rose from the dead, ascended back to heaven, was glorified, and now had sent the Holy Spirit just as He said He would.[119] The resurrection of Christ was not overlooked, skipped over, or treated as tangential in Peter's first sermon. Quite the opposite. The resurrection of Christ was *the* component of his first gospel sermon.

WHAT ABOUT THE ASCENSION?

Although Paul does not mention the bodily ascension of Jesus Christ specifically in his gospel presentation in chapter one of Romans, it does appear that the ascension is assumed as part of what Paul refers to as the "resurrection." This close association of the resurrection and ascension can be seen in the writings of the great theologian Louis Berkhof. He writes, "In a certain sense the ascension may be called the necessary complement and completion of the resurrection. Christ's transition to the higher life of

---

[119] John 7:39; Acts 1:8-9

glory, begun in the resurrection, was perfected in the ascension."[120] The resurrection and ascension are connected in such a way that they are part of the same chain of events, with the ascension and glorification of Christ being at the end.[121] We can even see this in Paul's letter to Timothy, when he writes, "Great indeed, we confess, is the mystery of godliness: He was manifested in the flesh, vindicated by the Spirit, seen by angels, proclaimed among the nations, believed on in the world, taken up in glory."[122]

Christians often incorrectly assume that people know the whole story about Jesus, but do they know His fulfillment of prophecy, His deity, His humanity, His sinless life, His death, His resurrection, and His ascension? Many people know something about the birth and resurrection of Jesus since they both have holidays built around their celebration, but what about His ascension. If the gospel stops with the bodily resurrection of Jesus Christ, then we have an incomplete story. So few people know the real story of Jesus these days, that when evangelizing, it is a good idea to tell the whole gospel, from the Eternal Son of God putting on flesh to the Son of God taking His glorified body back with Him to heaven.[123]

Part of the good news is that in Christ Jesus, we have a Savior who has not only lived and died in our place and then rose from the grave, but one who has also ascended into heaven where He sits at the right hand of the Father.[124] As the writer of Hebrews wrote, "We have this as a sure and steadfast anchor of the soul, a hope that enters into the inner place behind the curtain, where Jesus has gone as a forerunner on our behalf."[125] Jesus has entered heaven and is the forerunner that all believers will eventually follow. The ascension is important and should not be overlooked. As R. C. Sproul has written, "If there is any dimension of the life

---

[120] Berkhof, *Systematic Theology*, 350.
[121] Acts 1:8-9
[122] 1 Timothy 3:16
[123] Daniel 7:13-14; Luke 24:39; Acts 1:9; Phil. 3:21
[124] Matthew 22:41-45
[125] Hebrews 6:19-20

and the work of Jesus that is woefully neglected in the life of the church today, I believe it is His ascension. Yet, in New Testament categories, the ascension is the acme of Jesus' work."[126]

Summary: When you hear the gospel proclaimed, is the resurrection of Jesus Christ from the dead included? The gospel is the story of Jesus, and it is our responsibility to inform people about the whole story. Whether it is intentional or unintentional, leaving out the resurrection of Christ is still a subtraction from the "gospel of God" that was given to Paul by God. The resurrection of Jesus Christ is a crucial component of the good news. This was the ultimate declaration that indeed, He was the Son of God, that He was holy, and that He had successfully paid the price for the sin of all believers. We can trust our Savior because He is not in the ground. Our Savior defeated death, hell, and the grave. This is wonderful news for all who believe in Him. As the Apostle Peter wrote, "Blessed be the God and Father of our Lord Jesus Christ! According to his great mercy, he has caused us to be born again to a living hope through the resurrection of Jesus Christ from the dead."[127]

---

[126] R. C. Sproul, *The Work of Christ: What the Events of Jesus' Life Mean for You* (Colorado Springs, CO: David C Cook, 2012), 181

[127] 1 Peter 1:3

Chapter 8

---※---

COMPONENT #6: JESUS IS CHRIST.

> Paul, a servant of Christ Jesus, called to be an apostle, set apart for the gospel of God, which he promised beforehand through his prophets in the holy Scriptures, concerning his Son, who was descended from David according to the flesh and was declared to be the Son of God in power according to the Spirit of holiness by his resurrection from the dead, **Jesus Christ** our Lord, through whom we have received grace . . . (Rom. 1:1-5)

Is Paul merely stating the first and last name of Jesus, or is there something more? Last names were typically created by adding a word that described a person's place of residence, family association, or occupation along with their other name. We even find this type of thing done with Jesus during His earthly ministry. He was known by the town that He was from as, "Jesus of Nazareth," by His earthly father's name, "Jesus son of Joseph," and by His occupation as, Jesus "the carpenter."[128] These phrases could serve as what we would consider being the last name, or surname, of Jesus. So why do we call Him Jesus Christ?

The word *Christ* comes from the Hebrew word *Mashiach* in which we get the English word *Messiah*. Messiah is the word

---

[128] Mark 10:47; Luke 3:2; Mark 6:3

we find used in the Old Testament to describe the Anointed One that God was going to send. In Greek, the word is *Christos*, in Latin *Christus*, and in English *Christ*. The word "Christ" is the English translation of the word Messiah that means *the anointed*. Therefore, *Christ* is not the last name of Jesus, but it is the title of the role that He is fulfilling. He is Jesus *the* Christ, God's Anointed One. This becomes clear when we see that proving Jesus was the Christ and acknowledging Jesus as Christ was essential in the New Testament. This fact was so important that Paul included it in his summary of the gospel that he had received from God.

THE JEWS WERE EXPECTING THE CHRIST.

While the word "Christ" has somewhat lost its meaning in our modern culture, even to the point that people think it is just the last name of Jesus, this was not so in Judaism. Not only did they know what the word Messiah/Christ meant, but there were also many actively desiring His arrival. God had given many prophecies about the coming Messiah that served as a source of great hope for the people and as a guide to identifying the Christ when He came. These prophecies dealt with His family lineage, His character, His life, His miracles, His death, His resurrection, and even the city in which He was to be born.

Such awareness of the Messianic prophecies among the Jews can be seen even in the birth narrative of Jesus found in the book of Matthew. The arrival of the wise men caused Herod to ask the Jewish religious leaders if there was a prophecy about where their long-awaited king was to be born, and the Jews quickly provided Herod with the precise prophecy that named the city in which the Christ was to be born.

> Now after Jesus was born in Bethlehem of Judea in the days of Herod the king, behold, wise men from the east came to Jerusalem, saying, 'Where is he who has been born king of the Jews? For we saw his star when it rose and have come to worship him.' When Herod the king heard this, he was troubled, and all Jerusalem with him;

and assembling all the chief priests and scribes of the people, he inquired of them where the Christ was to be born. They told him, 'In Bethlehem of Judea, for so it is written by the prophet:

And you, O Bethlehem, in the land of Judah, are by no means least among the rulers of Judah; for from you shall come a ruler who will shepherd my people Israel.' (Matt. 2:1-6)

Here we see the word "Christ" used before they even knew Jesus. "Christ" was not the last name of Jesus, but it did refer to the One that God was to send to lead Israel. Herod did not like the idea of a new king being born, and he wanted to find the Christ so that he could be killed. How would Herod find the Christ? Apparently, all he had to do was to ask Jews who knew the Messianic prophecy about His birthplace.

Many of the Jews were aware of the prophecies and were even looking for the Messiah's arrival. One of the earliest to recognize Jesus as the Christ was Andrew who would soon become one of the Twelve. After Andrew witnesses the interaction between John the Baptist and Jesus, he goes directly to his brother and says to his brother Peter, "'We have found the Messiah' (which means Christ)."[129] Some people, supposedly looking for the Christ, mistakenly, even wondered if John the Baptist was the Christ. "As the people were in expectation, and all were questioning in their hearts concerning John, whether he might be the Christ."[130] The Apostle John even records the story of a person who was not a Jew, but who was still living in expectation of the coming of Christ.

> The woman said to him, 'I know that Messiah is coming (he who is called Christ). When he comes, he will tell us all things.' Jesus said to her, 'I who speak to you am he.' So the woman left her water jar and went away into town and said to the people, 'Come, see a man who told

---

[129] John 1:41
[130] Luke 3:15

me all that I ever did. Can this be the Christ?' They went out of the town and were coming to him. (John 4:25-26)

In this passage, we see that not only is this Samaritan woman aware of prophecies about the coming Messiah/Christ, but that apparently, the other Samaritans in her village were privy to this information as well. As soon as she realized that Jesus may be the Christ, she ran to tell the others the news, and after listening to Jesus themselves, they said, "It is no longer because of what you said that we believe, for we have heard for ourselves, and we know that this is indeed the Savior of the world."[131]

People who witnessed Jesus' teaching and miracles were aware that He was someone special, but many were undecided as to whether Jesus was; Jesus the Christ, Jesus the prophet, or even just Jesus of Nazareth. Here is how John recorded one such dilemma:

> When they heard these words, some of the people said, 'This really is the Prophet.' Others said, 'This is the Christ.' But some said, 'Is the Christ to come from Galilee? Has not the Scripture said that the Christ comes from the offspring of David, and comes from Bethlehem, the village where David was?' So there was a division among the people over him. Some of them wanted to arrest him, but no one laid hands on him. (John 7:40-44)

While some people were confused and divided as to the exact identity of Jesus, one that was not confused was Peter. As we read earlier, when Jesus asked His Disciples, "But who do you say that I am?" Simon Peter replied, 'You are the Christ, the Son of the living God.' And Jesus answered him, 'Blessed are you, Simon Bar-Jonah! For flesh and blood has not revealed this to you, but my Father who is in heaven.'"[132] This statement was not merely the opinion of Peter, but God the Father supernaturally revealed this truth to Peter.

---

[131] John 4:42
[132] Matthew 16:15-16

PAUL CONTINUOUSLY PREACHED THAT JESUS WAS THE CHRIST.

As Paul was on his way to arrest and even pursue the death of Christians, the risen Jesus appeared to him, and overwhelmingly convinced him that indeed He was the Christ. Paul immediately went from trying to rid the world of the people who believe that Jesus is the Christ to trying to convince the world that Jesus is the Christ.

> And immediately he proclaimed Jesus in the synagogues, saying, 'He is the Son of God.' And all who heard him were amazed and said, 'Is not this the man who made havoc in Jerusalem of those who called upon this name? And has he not come here for this purpose, to bring them bound before the chief priests?' But Saul increased all the more in strength, and confounded the Jews who lived in Damascus by proving that Jesus was the Christ. When many days had passed, the Jews plotted to kill him. (Acts 9:20-23)

Virtually every sermon he preached, Paul not only mentioned that Jesus was the Christ, but he also taught on this point repeatedly.

> And Paul went in, as was his custom, and on three Sabbath days he reasoned with them from the Scriptures, explaining and proving that it was necessary for the Christ to suffer and to rise from the dead, and saying, 'This Jesus, whom I proclaim to you, is the Christ.' (Acts 17:2-5)

> When Silas and Timothy arrived from Macedonia, Paul was occupied with the word, testifying to the Jews that the Christ was Jesus. And when they opposed and reviled him, he shook out his garments and said to them, 'Your blood be on your own heads! I am innocent. From now on I will go to the Gentiles.' (Acts 18:5-6)

Even after Paul is imprisoned for preaching that Jesus is the Christ, he does not alter his Christ-centered message in the least.

> 'To this day I have had the help that comes from God, and so I stand here testifying both to small and great, saying nothing but what the prophets and Moses said would come to pass: that the Christ must suffer and that, by being the first to rise from the dead, he would proclaim light both to our people and to the Gentiles.' (Acts 26:22-23)

There is no doubt that Paul viewed Jesus' claim to be Christ a vital component of the gospel. So much so that even when he was threatened with torture, imprisonment, or even death if he did not stop proclaiming that Jesus is the Christ, he still would not remove it from the gospel that he preached.

The Apostle Paul is not alone in his emphasis on Jesus being the Christ. The Apostle John, likewise considered the identity of Jesus as the Christ as of utmost importance. Consider the significance that the Apostle John places on this belief in the following verses:

> Everyone who believes that Jesus is the Christ has been born of God, and everyone who loves the Father loves whoever has been born of him. (1 John 5:1)

> Who is the liar but he who denies that Jesus is the Christ? This is the antichrist, he who denies the Father and the Son. (1 John 2:22)

John does not hold back at all. He says that those who deny that Jesus is the Christ are "liars" and "the antichrist." Clearly, John viewed the rejection of Jesus' fulfillment of the role of Christ as a belief that was contrary to the gospel. He believed Jesus' identity as the Christ to be so important that he even included it in the purpose statement for writing his gospel, "... these are written so that you may believe that Jesus is the Christ, the Son of God, and that by believing you may have life in his name."[133] "Jesus is the Christ," was considered so important to John that he includes it right next to his statement that Jesus is "the Son of God" and lets his readers know that this fact is to be believed to have eternal life.

Summary: Has modern Christianity maintained the same attention to Jesus being the Christ in our communication of the gospel as that of the Bible? Even if the word *Christ* is uttered in a declaration of the gospel today, is just the mention of the word sufficient? As we share the gospel, we must understand that this word has lost virtually all the meaning that it had to the days when Jesus walked the earth. Sadly, many people believe that "Christ" is just a name, and therefore, this component of the gospel will require further explanation. This might take some time, and that is perfectly acceptable. Paul spent significant time persuading people that Jesus was the Christ, the Anointed One that God had promised who would come to save His people, and perhaps we should as well.

---

[133] John 20:31

Chapter 9

COMPONENT #7: JESUS IS LORD.

Paul, a servant of Christ Jesus, called to be an apostle, set apart for the gospel of God, which he promised beforehand through his prophets in the holy Scriptures, concerning his Son, who was descended from David according to the flesh and was declared to be the Son of God in power according to the Spirit of holiness by his resurrection from the dead, **Jesus** Christ our **Lord,** through whom we have received grace . . . (Rom. 1:1-5)

The word *lord* in and of itself means "master," and could be used in that sense to refer to anyone in a position of authority. However, Paul's use of the word in this summary of "the gospel of God" was to declare that Jesus is *the* Lord. There is no master, no authority, no power that is superior to Him. This point is elaborated in Paul's letter to the Philippians when he writes:

Therefore God has highly exalted him and bestowed on him the name that is above every name, so that at the name of Jesus every knee should bow, in heaven and on earth and under the earth, and every tongue confess that Jesus Christ is Lord, to the glory of God the Father. (Phil. 2:9-10)

As you can see, Paul is abundantly clear that there is no one more powerful. Jesus is the supreme authority, and that all people, including all other rulers, and earthly lords, sooner or later bow to Him as Lord.

The Lordship of Christ is no small matter for Paul. He believed in the Lordship of Christ, rested in the Lordship of Christ, and proclaimed the Lordship of Christ as a component of his gospel message. In his letter to the Romans, Paul even taught how Jesus being both *Lord* and *Savior* are so intimately related that you cannot have one without the other. He writes, "if you confess with your mouth that Jesus is Lord and believe in your heart that God raised him from the dead, you will be saved."[134] Those who are saved are those who believe that Jesus rose from the dead, and therefore will openly confess with their mouths that "Jesus is Lord." Paul not only made sure that fellow believers such as the church of Philippi or Rome believed that Jesus is Lord, but he also included this gospel component to those who were opposed to it. Even while on trial before King Agrippa, Paul made sure to include the fact that Jesus is Lord:

> At midday, O king, I saw on the way a light from heaven, brighter than the sun, that shone around me and those who journeyed with me. And when we had all fallen to the ground, I heard a voice saying to me in the Hebrew language, 'Saul, Saul, why are you persecuting me? It is hard for you to kick against the goads.' And I said, 'Who are you, Lord?' And the Lord said, 'I am Jesus.... (Acts 26:13-15)

DO WE MAKE JESUS LORD, OR IS HE LORD?

Subjective truth is a belief that is true because it is right to someone, but the belief may not be deemed valid by others. For instance, some people feel that the color blue is the best color, oth-

---

[134] Romans 10:9.

ers do not; some people believe that chocolate ice cream is superior to all others. However, some people find it disgusting; some people think that eighty-degree days are perfect, while others find that eighty-degree days are too hot. Is the statement, "Jesus is Lord" in the category of subjective truth? No, but professing Christians often place this truth in the realm of subjective truth by their attempts to witness to others. This is often done unintentionally by making a statement like, "Jesus is my Lord, and if you allow Him to, He would be glad to be your Lord as well." Do you see how this statement is presenting "Jesus is Lord," as a subjective truth? While such a statement might come from a professing Christian with good motives, it does not do justice to the unalterable fact that Jesus is Lord. Such a statement makes the Lordship of Jesus contingent upon whether or not the person being witnessed to will acknowledge that Jesus is Lord or not.

The Apostle Paul does not have in mind subjective truth when he places this component in his gospel summary. Instead, he states it as objective truth. Objective truth is not based on emotion, opinion, preference, popularity, or biases. Instead, objective truth is merely true because it is the truth and cannot be changed. This type of truth is ultimately found in God because He is truth, as Jesus said, "I am... the truth."[135] In other words, Jesus being Lord is not based on whether or not you or I, or the person that you are witnessing to, believe Him to be Lord. Jesus just *is* Lord because it is Who He is, and this fact of His being cannot be changed. As R. C. Sproul has written, "That Jesus is objectively the Lord is a common assertion of the New Testament. He is the imperial authority of the entire creation."[136]

Mistaking this truth as subjective, instead of objective, is a complete reversal of the role of Lord Jesus over His creation. Such a mistake puts people in the position of authority to make Jesus Lord, instead of realizing that He is Lord. Such a relativistic view of Jesus distorts Jesus from the all-powerful supreme ruler of all

---

[135] John 14:6
[136] R. C. Sproul, *Renewing Your Mind: Basic Christian Beliefs You Need to Know* (Grand Rapids, MI: Baker Books, 1998),96.

to a God who would like to be the Lord of people, but who must wait on people to give Him such authority. Jesus is in the absolute highest position of power and is Lord of all, and since He is Lord, it is our role *not* to make Him Lord, but to *acknowledge* that He is Lord.

THE APOSTLES AGREED THAT JESUS IS LORD.

Jesus is Lord, is a component of the gospel that was often declared by the Apostle Peter, but it is of particular interest that Peter stated this fact during his first post ascension evangelistic sermon. Peter began his explanation of the events by letting them know that, "for certain that God has made him both Lord and Christ, this Jesus whom you crucified."[137] Think about it, for most of the people listening to Peter, this was the first time they had heard the gospel. The idea that Jesus is Lord must have been a strange and foreign concept. They probably did not think of Jesus as much of a master of anything as they had witnessed Him being arrested, beaten, spat upon, whipped, stripped naked, thorns shoved into his head, nailed to a cross, mocked, ridiculed, and abandoned to die. However, this made it all the more important to teach them that the same Jesus who died in humiliation rose from the dead, conquered death, hell, the grave, and is the sovereign Lord of all.

The Apostle Thomas is known as Doubting Thomas due to his unbelief that Jesus had risen from the dead, even after the other Disciples told him otherwise.

> Now Thomas, one of the twelve, called the Twin, was not with them when Jesus came. So the other disciples told him, "We have seen the Lord." But he said to them, "Unless I see in his hands the mark of the nails, and place my finger into the mark of the nails, and place my hand into his side, I will never believe." (John 20:24-25)

---

[137] Acts 2:36

However, Thomas goes from doubting the full identity of Jesus to fully believing and making a brief but powerful statement about the true identity of Jesus that is on par with Peter's earlier confession when he said, "You are the Christ, the Son of the Living God." Let's see how Thomas goes from Doubting Thomas to Believing Thomas:

> Eight days later, his disciples were inside again, and Thomas was with them. Although the doors were locked, Jesus came and stood among them and said, "Peace be with you." Then he said to Thomas, "Put your finger here, and see my hands; and put out your hand, and place it in my side. Do not disbelieve, but believe." Thomas answered him, "My Lord and my God!" Jesus said to him, "Have you believed because you have seen me? Blessed are those who have not seen and yet have believed." (John 20:28-29)

Thomas goes from doubting to professing that Jesus is Lord and God! For one, we want to notice that Jesus, like the confession of Peter, fully embraces the statement as right and true belief. This is important, for if Thomas had perhaps overstated the identity of Jesus, Jesus, being truth incarnate, would have corrected him. However, instead of correcting Thomas, Jesus fully affirms the statement. And secondly, Jesus says that those not present with them in the room will also be blessed by having the same belief. What belief? That Jesus is Lord and God.

Summary: Jesus is Lord, is not a subjective truth but an objective truth. This means that when we are witnessing and telling them about the person and work of Jesus, we need to make sure that they understand who is sitting on the throne. It is the Lord Jesus, the sovereign creator of the universe, the supreme judge of all humanity. He is Lord and, as Lord He has commanded them to repent and believe in the gospel for salvation.[138]

---

[138] Mark 1:14

Understanding the Lordship of Christ affects how we witness. A person who understands Christ's Lordship might make a statement like this when they are witnessing, "Jesus is the Lord of all, and as Lord, He has commanded you to repent of your sins and to believe in Him for salvation." On the other hand, a person who does not understand the Lordship of Jesus witness more like this, "Jesus sure would like to be Lord of your life. You should give Him a chance." Obviously, one has described the fact that Jesus is Lord, the other has described a Jesus that needs to be made Lord. In a world where people like to think of themselves as lord, in control, powerful, and autonomous, presenting Jesus as Lord and Master can ruffle some feathers, but unless a person is willing to see Jesus for who He truly is, they are still just making up their own version of who they want Him to be.

Chapter 10

COMPONENT #8: SALVATION IS BY GRACE ALONE.

> Paul, a servant of Christ Jesus, called to be an apostle, set apart for the gospel of God, which he promised beforehand through his prophets in the holy Scriptures, concerning his Son, who was descended from David according to the flesh and was declared to be the Son of God in power according to the Spirit of holiness by his resurrection from the dead, Jesus Christ our Lord, **through whom we have received grace** . . . (Rom. 1:1-5)

Though we could continue through the chapter, or even Paul's entire letter to the Romans, to gain a better understanding of the gospel, it seems fitting to end this study of Paul's gospel summary with his use of the word "grace." The word *grace* is so often misunderstood that we miss the grandeur and beauty of this amazing gift of God. However, a correct understanding of grace is essential for a proper understanding of the good news of the gospel.

WHAT GRACE IS, AND WHAT GRACE IS NOT.

Simply defined, grace is unmerited favor received from God. Saving grace is not deserved, earned, or merited by us. Sadly, many people have distorted God's grace by having too high a view of themselves and too low a view of God. Such a skewed view will often lead people to assume that they have worked to achieve God's favor and that He is obligated to give them His saving grace. However, the moment any amount of self-merit enters one's definition of grace, it is no longer the same grace that was taught by the Apostle Paul.

To correctly understand the beauty of saving grace, we need to remind ourselves of what we truly deserve. We are all guilty before God and deserve His wrath. Paul explained to the Romans that sins do not just disappear or go unpunished. Instead, every sin of every sinner will be punished by God. He writes:

> But because of your hard and impenitent heart you are storing up wrath for yourself on the day of wrath when God's righteous judgment will be revealed.
>
> He will render to each one according to his works: to those who by patience in well-doing seek for glory and honor and immortality, he will give eternal life; but for those who are self-seeking and do not obey the truth, but obey unrighteousness, there will be wrath and fury. There will be tribulation and distress for every human being who does evil.... (Romans 2:5-9)

Wrath...judgment...fury...tribulation? Yes, this is the only thing that we truly deserve. However, Paul writes something absolutely amazing at the end of his gospel summary. He writes that he had "received grace." Paul was a sinner who deserved the wrath of God, but now he was no longer a person owed the wrath of God; instead, he had received the free, undeserved, unmerited, saving grace and mercy of God. But, how can a sinner who deserves the wrath of God receive grace?

Many people think of themselves in a much better light than they should. It is human nature to compare ourselves to others, grade on a curve if you will. You might hear people say something like, "Well, I am much better than most people.", or "I do sin a little, but not nearly as much as my friends." Such statements reveal a distorted view of God's holiness and their own sinfulness. As Paul teaches, every sin deserves eternal punishment, and the wrath that each sinner deserves is being stored up for the Day of Wrath when God will fully execute his judgment.

"What about all the good things that I have done? Don't they act as a counterbalance of the bad things?" Although people often assume that they have done enough good to outweigh the bad, that is not the way God operates. God does not place all of a person's good deeds on one side, and all of a person's bad deeds on the other side to determine who will receive grace. Even if this were the case, there would be nothing for God to place on the "good" side of the scale, for the Bible says, "We have all become like one who is unclean, and all our righteous deeds are like a polluted garment.", or as Paul writes, "None is righteous, no, not one."[139] While we might think ourselves to be "pretty good," the Bible paints a much different picture of who we are by nature. As Paul writes in Ephesians:

> As for you, you were dead in your transgressions and sins, in which you used to live when you followed the ways of this world and of the ruler of the kingdom of the air, the spirit who is now at work in those who are disobedient. All of us also lived among them at one time, gratifying the cravings of our flesh and following its desires and thoughts. Like the rest, we were by nature deserving of wrath.[140]

"By nature deserving of wrath," that is who we are. Wrath is what we deserve, and wrath is what God owes us.

Salvation is not given to those who are doing better in life than others. God does not look to see who is working the hardest at being good to determine who deserves salvation. Those who think they are deserving of salvation because of their own merit are the furthest away from salvation. Just look at the parable Jesus

---

[139] Isaiah 64:6, Romans 3:10
[140] Ephesians 2:1-3

told of the Pharisee and the tax collector. The Pharisees depended heavily on their good works and believed that they had earned righteousness; however, tax collectors were the lowest of the low in Jewish society and were known to be horrible sinners. Let's see what Jesus says of these two men who came to the temple to pray:

> Two men went up into the temple to pray, one a Pharisee and the other a tax collector. The Pharisee, standing by himself, prayed thus: 'God, I thank you that I am not like other men, extortioners, unjust, adulterers, or even like this tax collector. I fast twice a week; I give tithes of all that I get.' But the tax collector, standing far off, would not even lift up his eyes to heaven, but beat his breast, saying, 'God, be merciful to me, a sinner!' I tell you, this man went down to his house justified, rather than the other. For everyone who exalts himself will be humbled, but the one who humbles himself will be exalted. (Luke 18:10-14)

The Pharisee pridefully trusted in himself and bragged about his goodness to God. However, it was not the "good" Pharisee's prayer that Jesus approved of, but the "sinful" tax collector's prayer, who acknowledged his sinfulness and his need for mercy. The tax collector understood his position before God. He knew that he was a sinner in need of mercy and that he was in dire need of salvation from God. However, the Pharisee did not admit his sinfulness, or need of any mercy, and instead boasted of his own righteousness to God.

At one-time Paul, himself was one such Pharisee and not just any Pharisee.[141] He had climbed the ranks and was sort of *the Pharisee of Pharisees*, yet by the grace of God, he finally saw himself for the sinner that he was and realized that everything *good* he was doing was useless to earn his salvation.

> But whatever gain I had, I counted as loss for the sake of Christ. Indeed, I count everything as loss because of the

---

[141] Acts 22:3-5

> surpassing worth of knowing Christ Jesus my Lord. For his sake I have suffered the loss of all things and count them as rubbish, in order that I may gain Christ and be found in him, not having a righteousness of my own that comes from the law, but that which comes through faith in Christ, the righteousness from God that depends on faith . . . (Phil. 3:7-9)

Paul realized that all of his self-righteousness had the total combined worth of a pile of trash. For many years, he had worked very hard to earn righteousness as a strict adherent of the law, yet once he encountered true salvation by grace, he understood that all he had done to try to earn salvation was useless. He now saw the error of his ways, understood his inability to earn righteousness, and looked to the only truly righteous One, God incarnate; Jesus Christ. By the grace of God, through faith in Christ Jesus, Paul had gained everything. What is more valuable than being saved from sin and the wrath and curse of God that we deserve as sinners? Nothing. Additionally, what is more wonderful than knowing that this salvation does not rest on us and our own record, but on the perfect record of Jesus Christ, the Son of God?

It is impossible, to wrap our minds around the nature of God's grace completely, but in Ephesians, the Apostle Paul attempts to enlighten us once again as to the magnificent beauty of God's grace to undeserving recipients:

> But God, being rich in mercy, because of the great love with which he loved us, even when we were dead in our trespasses, made us alive together with Christ—by grace you have been saved—and raised us up with him and seated us with him in the heavenly places in Christ Jesus, so that in the coming ages he might show the immeasurable riches of his grace in kindness toward us in Christ Jesus. For by grace you have been saved through faith. And this is not your own doing; it is the gift of God, not a result of works, so that no one may boast. (Eph. 2:4-9)

According to this passage, who should receive the credit for salvation? The answer is, obviously, "God." However, so many professing Christians still think that they have done something to deserve God's grace in salvation. Yet, Paul says that salvation, "is not your own doing; it is the gift of God." Some will at least agree that they need grace to be saved, but they still believe that salvation is a mixture of grace and their own good works. However, any amount of self-worth or self-merit changes the unmerited nature of God's grace to a grace that is merited. We must remember that grace is not a reward, it is an undeserved gift from God. As Martin Lloyd Jones wrote:

> Grace is a great word in the Bible, the grace of God. It is most simply defined in these words—it is favour shown to people who do not deserve any favour at all. And the message of the gospel is that any one of us is saved and put right for eternity, solely and entirely by the grace of God, not by ourselves… Do what you like, you will never save yourself… We deserve nothing but hell. If you think you deserve heaven, take it from me you are not a Christian.
>
> Any man who thinks that he deserves heaven is not a Christian. But for any man who knows that he deserves hell, there is hope. Out goes all your self-righteousness. It is all by grace, and entirely the mercy and compassion and the grace of God. It is God, who, in spite of us, and in spite of the world being what it is, sent his own Son into this world and then sent him to the cross.[142]

Martyn Lloyd Jones, like Paul, preached salvation by faith, in Christ that was received purely by the grace of God. Such saving grace is unmixed with human works. Even our faith, as Paul writes, "is not our own doing; it is the gift of God, not a result of

---

[142] Martyn. Lloyd-Jones and Christopher Catherwood, *The Cross: God's Way of Salvation*, 74-75

works, so that no one may boast."[143] God does not believe for us, we believe, but we only do so because He has chosen to give us saving grace. What do we do with such wonderful news of salvation by grace alone? The only thing we can do: praise God.

UNDESERVED GRACE.

Who better to understand grace, and teach on grace, than the man who considered himself the least deserving of God's grace? We know much about Paul's hatred of Christ and hatred of all Christians, but also of his radical change that was accomplished by the grace of God. As Paul writes of himself, He says,

> …though formerly I was a blasphemer, persecutor, and insolent opponent. But I received mercy because I had acted ignorantly in unbelief, and the grace of our Lord overflowed for me with the faith and love that are in Christ Jesus. The saying is trustworthy and deserving of full acceptance, that Christ Jesus came into the world to save sinners, of whom I am the foremost.[144]

Paul was calling himself the foremost, or the chief sinner. As he looked back on his life, he fully realized that he had done nothing to deserve God's grace. In fact, Paul had done everything to deserve the wrath of God. Yet, in spite of his sin, God saved him and gave him mercy and grace.

Paul understood that it was not only him, in his persecution of Christians that made him an enemy of God. He realized that all of humanity was by nature, an enemy of God, deserving of wrath. Yet as all of his talk on sin, judgment, and wrath painted the dark canvass background that allowed the beauty of the gospel of grace to shine forth. As we see here in chapter five of Romans:

> ... but God shows his love for us in that while we were still sinners, Christ died for us. Since, therefore, we have

---

[143] Ephesians 2:9
[144] 1 Timothy 1:13-15

now been justified by his blood, much more shall we be saved by him from the wrath of God. For if while we were enemies we were reconciled to God by the death of his Son, much more, now that we are reconciled, shall we be saved by his life. More than that, we also rejoice in God through our Lord Jesus Christ, through whom we have now received reconciliation.[145]

It is clear that Paul, over and over again teaches that no one can merit, earn, work for, or deserve salvation. Paul was saved by the pure sovereign grace of God being given to him. As he told the Corinthians, "But by the grace of God I am what I am."[146] Paul always attributed his salvation fully to the work of God, and none of it to himself. As Charles Spurgeon, the "Prince of Preachers," preached:

> Paul ascribed his own salvation to the free favor of God. He believed himself to be a regenerate man, a forgiven man, a saved man—and he believed that condition of his was the result of the unmerited favor of God. He did not imagine that he was saved because he deserved salvation, or that he had been forgiven because his repentance had made an atonement for his sin! He did not reckon that his prayers had merited salvation, or that his abundant labors and many sufferings had earned that gift for him at God's hands. No, he does not for a moment speak of merit—it is a word which Paul's mouth could not pronounce in such a connection as that. His declaration is, 'It is by God's free favor that I, Saul of Tarsus, have been converted, and made into Paul the Apostle, the servant of Jesus Christ. I attribute this great change entirely to the goodwill, the Sovereign benignity, the undeserved favor of the ever-blessed God.'[147]

---

[145] Romans 5:8-11
[146] 1 Corinthians 15:10
[147] Charles Spurgeon, "Sermon No. 3084 Paul's Parenthesis," March 1908, 2, accessed October 11, 2016.

Spurgeon, like Paul, understood that salvation was purely by the grace of God. Humanity cannot do one single thing to help or contribute to its own salvation.

ADDING TO THE GOSPEL.

Adding your own works to the gospel of grace is bad math. As mentioned, many times, the gospel is a message that consists of components, and the gospel message should not be added to or subtracted from. Salvation by grace alone, through faith alone, in Christ alone often sounds just *too alone* for people, so they add something to it; their works. However, any mixture of works and grace is no longer salvation by grace. Such a works/grace salvation vastly underappreciates the perfect work that Jesus Christ did to accomplish our salvation. He and He alone lived the perfect life in our place and died on the cross for our sins, rising from the dead as proof of his redeeming work and a pledge to all who believe in Him. To add our works of rubbish to His perfect and holy work is to say, "God, you did your part pretty well, but it just was not quite enough, but with the addition of my good works, we can save me." Such a view of saving grace is a horrible distortion of the truth.

SAVED BY WORKS OR TO WORKS?

A lot of people get salvation by works and salvation for works mixed up. Even though they sound similar, they are theological opposites. In the first case of salvation by works, a person believes that they have done something to deserve salvation by their good life, lack of sin, and etc. However, salvation by grace is the understanding that salvation has come by the pure unmerited favor of God, and that God has saved you so that you may begin to work for Him. As believers, we are not saved because of our good works, but we are saved by grace to do good works as Paul wrote, "For we are his workmanship, created in Christ Jesus for good works, which God prepared beforehand, that we should walk in them."[148] Similarly, Jesus in acknowledging the right order of salvation and works said, "You did not choose me, but I chose you and appointed you that you should go and bear fruit and that your fruit should abide."[149]

Summary: Everything we do in life seems to be based upon our personal merit. If you want to make a good grade at school, then you must actively study, do homework, take tests, and turn in completed assignments. If enough time, effort, and energy are poured out, then the reward will hopefully be a good grade, and that grade will be based upon the work that you have done to deserve it. If you want to get a raise at your place of employment, then you must not only meet but also often exceed what is expected of you. If you're going to have good friends, then you must put in time with them for those relationships to stay strong. The closest thing we have to a relationship based on grace is a healthy marriage, but even that example falls far short when compared to the grace of God given in salvation.

In the end, no other example of love compares to the kind of undeserved love that God displays in the salvation of sinners. His love is not caused by anything in us. There is nothing a person can do to earn even the smallest portion of their salvation. It is truly unmerited. As Spurgeon once preached, "Salvation is not of works, but of Grace alone! And they who do not obtain salvation in this way will as surely perish as the blasphemer and the drunk! There is but one way of salvation—the way of free favor. That was the way in which Paul went, and that is the way in which we must go if we would enter into eternal life!"[150]

---

[148] Ephesians 2:10
[149] John 15:16
[150] Charles Spurgeon, "Sermon No. 3084 Paul's Parenthesis," March 1908, 2, accessed October 11, 2016.

CONCLUSION TO PART I:

Although salvation is not just a list of facts about Jesus, it is certainly not less than these facts. As Christians, we know that "All Scripture is breathed out by God and profitable for teaching, for reproof, for correction, and for training in righteousness, that the man of God may be complete, equipped for every good work."[151] We are not allowed to make up our own private beliefs about God, and we are certainly not allowed to create our own versions of the gospel. Instead, we are to seek to understand the truth by allowing God's Word to teach, reproof, correct, train, and equip us.

God's Word reveals that the gospel has specific information in it that is both true and factual. This information must remain the same or else the gospel of God becomes a different message. Since God provides a specific message and works through it to bring salvation, we are limited in our proclamation of the gospel. The Apostle Paul received "the gospel of God," and he made sure to deliver all of the gospel, with no subtractions or additions. Paul had no right to change the message, and neither do we. As the theologian, Graeme Goldsworthy has written:

> The Bible itself gives us the needed information that the gospel is a message with a definable content, and that it is to be believed if we are to be saved. There is enough biblical evidence to justify our understanding of the gospel as the event, or the proclaimed message of that event, which is set forth by God as the object of our faith and trust if we are to be saved.[152]

Much of Christianity has drifted away from seeing the gospel as a set message and has taken creative license; in which each person just creates, believes, and proclaims whatever he or she desires, as the gospel. However, this is not what the Bible teaches.

---

[151] 2 Timothy 3:16-17
[152] Graeme Goldsworthy, *Preaching the Whole Bible as Christian Scripture: The Application of Biblical Theology to Expository Preaching* (Grand Rapids, MI: W.B. Eerdmans, 2000), 82.

As we have seen from the Apostle Paul's letter to the Romans, the gospel has specific content. Paul made it abundantly clear that the gospel is all about the identity of Jesus and what He did to bring about salvation. As Martin Lloyd Jones wrote of Paul and the Apostles preaching of the gospel:

> . . . the glory of the gospel is that it is primarily an announcement of what God does, and has done, in the Person of Jesus Christ. That was the essence of Paul's gospel, as he proceeds to show in the remainder of the Epistle. That was the gospel which was preached by all the apostles. They preached Jesus as the Christ. They made a proclamation, an announcement. Primarily, 'the good news'… They began by stating facts and explaining what they meant. They preached, not a programme, but a person . . . That was the message. Its entire emphasis was upon what God had done. Its content was God's way of salvation and of making men righteous. Here indeed was something to be proud of as a message.[153]

In a society that is increasingly relativistic, biblically illiterate, and therefore gospel ignorant, it is the duty of Christians to proclaim this gospel clearly and completely. Cultural relevance at the cost of changing the gospel is not a valid option. If we omit critical components of the gospel or add extra components to the gospel, we are treading where mankind has no authority to tread.

Many people call themselves Christians but believe and proclaim differing gospels. How can this be? Do all of the various gospels possess the power to save? Speaking on the unity of faith that is empowered by the gospel, Paul writes, "Since we have the same spirit of faith according to what has been written, 'I believed, and so I spoke," we also believe, and so we speak."[154] Both Paul and the church of Corinth were of the same faith because they had both received and believed in the same gospel. Could that be said

---

[153] Martyn Lloyd-Jones, *The Plight of Man and the Power of God* (Ross-shire: Christian Focus Publications, 2009), 103-104.
[154] 2 Corinthians 4:13

of professing Christians today? Do we believe in the same gospel as Paul? If not, then we are not even of the same faith!

Some people think that they are Christians because they have walked an aisle, said a prayer, joined a church, were baptized, or felt emotionally stirred one Sunday morning. While these things could possibly accompany real salvation, they should not be relied on for salvation. Salvation must include belief in the true gospel, or salvation did not occur.

The truths of the gospel are vital to salvation. Believe them, proclaim them, but don't change them. Jesus is the fulfillment of the good news foretold by the prophets, Jesus is the Son of God, Jesus is human, and the Seed of David and Jesus is the Messiah/Christ, who lived, died, rose from the dead, and is the Lord of all. Let us strive to follow in Paul's example in our own communication of the gospel. And it is this message about this person that is "the power of God for salvation for all who believes."[155] Let us fight the tendency to subtract from or add to God's gospel, and instead "contend for the faith that was once for all delivered to the saints."[156]

---

[155] Romans 1:16
[156] Jude 1:3

PART II:

CONSEQUENCES OF CHANGING GOD'S GOSPEL.

Chapter 11

ARE PROFESSING CHRISTIANS PROCLAIMING THE GOSPEL CORRECTLY?

Let us imagine that John, a professing Christian, has been concerned about the salvation of his co-worker, Andy, who has never been to church and who lives an extremely sinful lifestyle. During lunch one day, John shares his testimony with Andy about how he used to feel empty inside, but how he now feels complete after becoming a Christian. As the conversation develops, John decides to go for it and make the big push to turn Andy into a Christian. John tells Andy, "You know, God loves you and has a great plan for your life. If you just invite Jesus into your heart, you could be on your way to heaven like I am." Andy, seemingly interested, says, "This sounds exactly like what I have been looking for. What do I have to do?" John quickly replies, "You just need to say the sinner's prayer." Andy says, "Well, sure, why not. I'll give it a try. What's the prayer I'm supposed to say again?" An ecstatic John says, "Well, bow your head, close your eyes, just repeat this after me, and really mean it, 'Dear Jesus, ….'"

At the end of the prayer, John informs Andy that he is now saved and on his way to heaven. John then informs Andy, "Now that you are saved you should come to church with me Sunday and walk the aisle at the end of service to make this official." Andy does precisely what he is told to do by John. The very next Sunday

Andy goes to church with John, walks the aisle, and tells the pastor that he said the prayer with John. Upon hearing this statement, the pastor congratulates Andy on his salvation and says, "Well, next, you need to get baptized, and we can take care of that right now." Once again, Andy agrees. Right before the pastor submerges Andy into the water, the pastor asks him once again, "Andy have you asked Jesus to come into your heart." Andy replies, "Oh yes, I said the prayer." The pastor smiles and follows through with the baptism. At which time, the pastor announces to the congregation that Andy has been saved, baptized, and is now a Christian and a full member of their church.

What a tremendous evangelistic success story! Or was it? A lot was happening in Andy's conversion story, but was true salvation a part of that story? Andy followed the instructions and checked off all the to-be-saved activities that John and the Pastor instructed him to do. But, is it possible that even though Andy followed all the instructions given to him (to say the prayer, to ask Jesus into his heart, to walk the aisle, to get baptized and to join the church) that he is still just as unsaved as before his Christian friend, John, witnessed to him?

Perhaps, to understand Andy's, so-called, "salvation" better, we must ask, "Did John share the gospel with Andy?" John did share many popular words used in evangelism with Andy; however, John failed to communicate the only message that is the "power of God for salvation to everyone who believes."[157] If Andy had never heard the gospel, and if John never actually presented the gospel to Andy, then this conversion was no success story at all. In fact, all that has been done to, supposedly, make Andy a "Christian" could have put him in a far *worse* place than before John even "witnessed" to him. Andy has now been led to believe that he is a Christian, even though he is not. Sadly, Andy still remains just as unsaved as he was before.

Andy trusted in the various prescribed steps and methods to turn him into a Christian, but all those techniques were powerless to save. Even though John, the pastor, and the members of the

---

[157] Romans 1:16

church all genuinely desired for Andy to be saved and wanted to rejoice—genuinely—in his salvation, there was one thing missing from the story: the gospel. How could Andy be saved if he was not even told of the person and work of Jesus Christ? As the Scottish Professor, John Murray wrote:

> We must know who Christ is, what he has done, and what he is able to do. Otherwise, faith would be blind conjecture at the best and foolish mockery at the worst. There must be apprehension of the truth respecting Christ. Sometimes, indeed, the measure of truth apprehended by the believing person is small, and we have to appreciate the fact that the faith of some in its initial stages is elementary. But faith cannot begin in a vacuum of knowledge.[158]

Information with no content and with no biblical basis can never bring about salvation. There must be something to believe in, but not just anything will do. The object of our faith must be Jesus Christ, the Son of God. This is why Murray rightly wrote, "Faith cannot begin in a vacuum of knowledge." Yet it is precisely this "vacuum" in which modern Christianity is finding itself. Faith has become a term that can be defined however one chooses. One might have faith, but if it is not faith in the gospel, then it is certainly not saving faith, and he or she is not a Christian. Such, "faith" is nothing but make-believe, and up to each person to create a feeling or belief of his or her own choosing. However, the gospel, opposite of an empty faith, contains all the necessary information needed for salvation.

John was right in his desire to witness to Andy, but how he went about doing so was incorrect. Sadly, the passion of a Christian to evangelize does not automatically mean that true evangelism occurs. Evangelism takes more than desire; it requires the gospel. Paul wrote, "How then will they call on him in whom they have

---

[158] John Murray and Carl R. Trueman, *Redemption Accomplished and Applied* (Wm. B. Eerdmans Publishing, 2015), 116.

not believed? And how are they to believe in him of whom they have never heard?"[159] How could Andy call on the one of whom he had never heard unless John told him? How could Andy have been saved if the gospel was not even presented? So, if Andy was not saved, what did John accomplish, what did the pastor's affirmation provide, what does the church membership mean? A *false convert* has been made who is now a *false member* of the church with a *false hope* of salvation because of a *false witness* by a professing Christian.

Though the story with John and Andy is fiction, unfortunately, this type of scenario plays out in real life on a regular basis. False conversions are the ever-present danger when professing Christians rely on modern evangelistic techniques and language that talk around the gospel but never actually proclaim it. If there is no gospel presented, then there is no evangelism taking place. As J. I. Packer writes in *Evangelism And The Sovereignty of God*:

> According to the New Testament, evangelism is just preaching the gospel, the evangel. It is a work of communication in which Christians make themselves mouthpieces for God's message of mercy to sinners. Anyone who faithfully delivers that message, under whatever circumstances, in a large meeting, in a small meeting, from a pulpit, or in a private conversation, is evangelizing. Since the divine message finds its climax in a plea from the Creator to a rebel world to turn and put faith in Christ, the delivering of it involves the summoning of one's hearers to conversion. If you are not, in this sense, seeking to bring about conversions, you are not evangelizing; this we have seen already. But the way to tell whether in fact you are evangelizing is not to ask whether conversions are known to have resulted from your witness. It is to ask whether you are faithfully making known the gospel.[160]

---

[159] Romans 10:14
[160] Packer, *Evangelism and the Sovereignty of God*, 45.

Many Christians, like John in the opening story, know people who need to be saved and have a real desire to see them become Christians. This desire is good. As Paul expressed his evangelistic desire to the Corinthians, "To the weak I became weak, that I might win the weak. I have become all things to all people that I might save some. I do it all for the sake of the gospel."[161] Sadly, many Christians who desire to see people saved, as Paul did, do not have Paul's desire to be proficient in the one thing that can lead to salvation: the gospel.

We, as Christians, must constantly remind ourselves that God uses the knowledge of the gospel to accomplish salvation. Therefore, we must present the gospel of God to others that they might believe. Otherwise, like John in our story, we are being false witnesses of the gospel, creating false Christians, and populating our churches with people who claim to be Christians but who have not even heard, much less, believed in the gospel. R. C. Sproul, rightly observed:

> I think the biggest danger is that churches are filled with people who have made a profession of faith but are not in a state of grace. Justification is by the possession of faith, and anyone who possesses it is certainly called to profess it. But you don't get into the kingdom of God by raising your hand, by walking an aisle, by praying a prayer, or by signing a card. All of these acts are good but they're externals. Unfortunately, we tend to focus on these things.[162]

---

[161] 1 Corinthians 9:22-23
[162] Sproul, *The Truth of the Cross,* 162.

Chapter 12

ARE ALL GOSPELS *THE* GOSPEL?

> I am astonished that you are so quickly deserting him who called you in the grace of Christ and are turning to a different gospel—not that there is another one, but there are some who trouble you and want to distort the gospel of Christ. But even if we or an angel from heaven should preach to you a gospel contrary to the one we preached to you, let him be accursed. As we have said before, so now I say again: If anyone is preaching to you a gospel contrary to the one you received, let him be accursed.
>
> For am I now seeking the approval of man, or of God? Or am I trying to please man? If I were still trying to please man, I would not be a servant of Christ. (Gal. 1:6-10)

Paul had witnessed to the Galatians by proclaiming "the gospel of God" that "is the power of God for salvation to everyone who believes."[163] However, something horrible was happening in Galatia, and Paul needed to take corrective action. False witnesses were presenting a false gospel. They were distorting the original message from God into something more to their liking. Paul was filled with righteous indignation because a false gospel was supplanting the real gospel. Paul was rightfully upset that false teach-

---

[163] Romans 1:1,16

ers had come to the Galatians with a distorted gospel, but he was "astonished" that the believers in Galatia were putting up with a "different" gospel as if it were an insignificant matter.

IS THE GOSPEL STILL BEING DISTORTED?

It appears that there is just as much of, if not more of, a state of emergency in our day than there was even in Galatia. It has become so common for professing Christians to distort the gospel that there is little astonishment about this travesty and far more general acceptance of this egregious practice. As we have seen, distortions to the gospel can happen much easier than we sometimes imagine. Gospel distortion can be done by communicating an inadequate gospel and by the wrong communication of the gospel. The commonality of distorting the gospel has turned much of modern "Christianity" into a perpetual false gospel factory. Instead of viewing the situation as the Apostle Paul did in Galatia when he sounded the alarm of heresy and commanded people to return to the original gospel, we have become so accustomed to hearing the distortions that they have numbed us into apathy. The acceptance of multiple gospels within Christianity has become Christianity's greatest danger. As Paul Tripp has preached, "The greatest threat to Christianity is not activist Atheism. The greatest threat to Christianity is false Christianity. The greatest threat to the gospel is a false gospel."[164]

The gospel is not made of wax or clay, and we cannot manipulate it in any way that we see fit. Any creative license taken to reshape the gospel, even in the name of Christianity, is still wrong. It is an unalterable message that has been "once for all delivered."[165] Regarding the ever-changing gospel of modern Christianity, Michael Horton, in his book *Christless Christianity*, has written:

---

[164] Paul D. Tripp, "One Thing - Mark 10:17-34," SermonAudio, 2011, Introduction, accessed December 03, 2016, http://www.sermonaudio.com/.
[165] Jude 1:3

Efforts to translate the gospel into contemporary language actually aim at making the gospel not only more understandable but more believable. The problem is that the gospel is so counterintuitive to our fallen pride that it cannot be believed apart from a miracle of divine grace. And because it is through the gospel itself the Spirit accomplishes this feat, we remove the one possibility for genuine conversion that we have in our arsenal. Lost in translation is the gospel itself—and therefore the only hope of genuine transformation as well as forgiveness.[166]

How should we respond when we hear of distorted gospels being proclaimed? The Apostle Paul serves as a perfect example. For Paul, changing the gospel was no small matter, and neither should it be to us. He dealt with this issue head-on, and his response was one of righteous anger and sadness. Paul was emotionally stirred, but he was also convinced that he must call out the false gospel and compel the people to hold on to the one true gospel. He knew that his silence would only allow the false gospel to continue to spread. Paul had to speak out if he wanted to stop the spread of the false gospel.

In his commentary on Galatians, Martin Luther, the great reformer of the 16th century, summarized the situation in Galatia with utmost clarity when he wrote:

> Here we learn to see the devil's tricks. No heretic comes to us claiming errors and the title of the devil; nor does the devil himself come as a devil in his own likeness... In spiritual matters when Satan appears white, like an angel or God Himself, he disguises himself in a most deadly way and offers for sale his most deadly poison instead of the doctrine of grace, the Word of God, the Gospel of Christ. That is why Paul calls the doctrine of the false apostles, Satan's ministers, a different gospel—

---

[166] Michael Scott. Horton, *Christless Christianity: The Alternative Gospel of the American Church* (Grand Rapids, MI: Baker Books, 2008), 240.

but derisively. This is like saying, 'You Galatians now have other evangelists and another gospel. My Gospel is despised by you now; you no longer value it.'[167]

Martin Luther, like Paul, did not take changing the gospel lightly. Luther was bold and clear when he wrote that the "different" gospels are made of "deadly poison" spread by "false apostles, Satan's ministers." Therefore, Paul warned, "If anyone is preaching to you a gospel contrary to the one you received, let him be accursed."[168] Paul's warning is a message that modern Christianity seems to have taken far too lightly. It is no little thing to change the gospel of God. As John Macarthur writes,

> ... corruptions of vital biblical truths are not to be trifled with, and the purveyors of different gospels are not to be treated benignly by God's people. On the contrary, we must take the same approach to false doctrine that Jesus did, by refuting the error, opposing those who spread the error, and contending earnestly for the faith.[169]

Paul even warned that those presenting a different gospel were in danger of receiving the curse of God because they had proclaimed a gospel which is different from the gospel of God. It was a gospel which was *not* "the power of God for salvation to everyone who believes."[170] False teachers had created a distorted gospel that was powerless to save. Regarding the exclusivity of the gospel and God's abhorrence of those who change it, Martin Luther wrote:

> Paul therefore concludes that there is no gospel besides what he himself had preached. But he had not preached a gospel of his own devising, but the one God had

---

[167] Martin Luther, *Galatians*, ed. Alister McGrath and J. I. Packer (Wheaton, IL: Crossway Books, 1998), 49-50.
[168] Galatians 1:8-9
[169] John MacArthur, *The Jesus You Can't Ignore: What You Must Learn from the Bold Confrontations of Christ* (Nashville, TN: Thomas Nelson, 2008), xvi.
[170] Romans 1:16

promised through his prophets in the Holy Scriptures (Rom.1:2). Therefore, he pronounces himself and others, even an angel from heaven, to be certainly condemned if they teach anything contrary to this Gospel.[171]

Would you say that the gospel which Paul preached is still the gospel that is most often proclaimed today, or are the gospel distortions more common? Alternatively, have the different gospels become so normative that we no longer feel astonished by them or a desire to call out those who are bearing such false witness? Are Christians today equally defending the same gospel that Paul so adamantly defended? What would Paul's reaction be if he sat through Sunday Worship Service at the church you attend? Would Paul be pleased with the gospel that was being preached? What would Paul's reaction be if he heard the most popular evangelists of today proclaiming the gospel? What would Paul's response be if he heard *you* sharing the gospel? Would he be pleased that you are still sharing the same gospel that he shared, the gospel that he received from God?

DON'T PROCLAIM A GOSPEL OF GRACE PLUS WORKS.

> For am I now seeking the approval of man, or of God? Or am I trying to please man? If I were trying to please man, I would not be a servant of Christ. (Gal. 1:10)

Seeking the approval of people, and not that of God is still the electricity that keeps the false gospel factory alive and well today. Professing Christians who desire to be accepted by the world, often change the gospel, in hopes that more people will find it less offensive. However, if we change God's message to please people what does that say about our innermost desires? Whom do we want to please with our communication of the gospel: God or man? Certainly, we know the right answer to such a question. No

---

[171] Luther, *Galatians*, 53.

Christian *should* desire to create a different gospel that is displeasing to God simply to please people. However, creating a different gospel can be far subtler than one might think.

In Galatia, it appears that the "different gospel" still had much of the original gospel content, which may be why the Galatians were not as "astonished" by the different gospel as much as Paul. Bible teacher, John Stott, believed these false witnesses' addition to the gospel was a bold affront to the gospel of grace alone, Stott writes:

> They did not deny that you must believe in Jesus for salvation, but they stressed that you must be circumcised and keep the law as well. In other words, you must let Moses finish what Christ has begun. Or rather, you yourself must finish, by your obedience to the law, what Christ has begun. You must add your works to the work of Christ. You must finish Christ's unfinished work.[172]

The original gospel of God's grace had been mixed with human works resulting in a distortion of the gospel. And now the "Christian" culture of Galatia seemed to be putting Paul under pressure to make the same additions to his communication of the gospel. However, Paul knew well the message that he had received from God, and he knew that no one could contribute anything to his or her salvation. Salvation was by the pure grace of God. Paul knew that if he gave in to the pressure to alter the gospel that he would compromise in such a way that he too would deserve the wrath of God.

Instead of surrendering, or compromising in the least, Paul "did not yield in submission even for a moment, so that the truth of the gospel might be preserved for you."[173] Paul chose to remain a true witness of the gospel by "preserving" the gospel of grace. God's grace in salvation and mankind's working for salvation *cannot* both be components in the gospel communication. As Luther wrote:

---

[172] John R. W. Stott, *The Message of Galatians: Only One Way* (Leicester, England: Inter-Varsity Press, 1986), 22.
[173] Galatians 2:5

> It seems such a little thing to mix the law and the Gospel, faith and works; but this does more mischief than human reason can conceive, for it not only blemishes and obscures the knowledge of grace, but it also takes away Christ, with all his benefits, and utterly overshadows the Gospel.[174]

Grace is offensive to the natural man, who believes that he does not need grace. People do not mind *grace* if it merely means a little help from above while they still get to contribute. However, this is a deadly mixture because it creates another false gospel. There can be no mixing of works and grace in the gospel message that saves. On this point, James Montgomery Boice wrote:

> Is there anything that we can contribute to our salvation? Only the sin from which we need to be saved, for we are the objects of divine grace. Yet the constant temptation is to slip the human element back into the equations. Theologians call this 'synergism,' a term that comes from the Greek word *syn*, meaning "with," and *ergos*, meaning 'work.' In theology, synergism is the belief that we work together with God to accomplish and apply our salvation. But this is fatal to any sound doctrine of salvation, for it has the inevitable result of increasing the place of man and thus diminishing the glory of God in salvation.[175]

In a similar vein, gospel proclaimer and grace defender, Paul Washer wrote,

> The instant that even the most minute work is added to or mingled with the doctrine of salvation, Christianity becomes a works religion, justification becomes a thing to be earned, God becomes the debtor of the people, and people are able to boast before Him. This is why the

---

[174] Luther, *Galatians*, 49-52.
[175] Boice and Philip Graham Ryken, *The Doctrines of Grace*, 36.

apostle Paul labors with all his might in his writings to accentuate the depravity of humanity and prove their utter inability to please God in the flesh.[176]

Boice and Washer both point out that even the smallest amount of works added to the doctrine of salvation renders it powerless to save. Unfortunately, many professing Christians like to think that they have contributed in some *small* way to their salvation. For instance, I once heard a friend attempt to describe his salvation by saying, "I believe that God definitely did most of the saving. Jesus did his ninety-nine percent, and I only had to do my one percent." At first, his words may sound quite humble since, after all, he did give God most of the credit for saving him. Nevertheless, contained in his *humble* statement is the addition of works to God's grace. The point is that the false gospel which Paul vehemently preached against can slip in easily if we are not on guard. John Stott warned, "To make men's works necessary to salvation, even as a supplement to the work of Christ is derogatory to His finished work. It is to imply that Christ's work was in some way unsatisfactory and that men need to add to it and improve on it."[177] Adding anything to the perfectly sufficient work of Christ is to deem His work lacking and in need of our work to fill in His insufficiencies.

EVEN THE APOSTLE PETER STRUGGLED.

Peter was driven to please God and to remain faithful to the gospel of grace message that he had received, even in the face of persecution. As Luke recorded:

> But Peter and the apostles answered, 'We must obey God rather than men. The God of our fathers raised Jesus, whom you killed by hanging him on a tree. God exalted him at his right hand as Leader and Savior, to give repentance to Israel and forgiveness of sins. And

---

[176] Paul Washer, *The Gospel Call and True Conversion* (Grand Rapids, MI: Reformation Heritage Books, 2013), 30.
[177] Stott, *The Message of Galatians*, 25.

we are witnesses to these things, and so is the Holy Spirit, whom God has given to those who obey him.'

When they heard this, they were enraged and wanted to kill them... And when they had called in the apostles, they beat them and charged them not to speak in the name of Jesus, and let them go. Then they left the presence of the council, rejoicing that they were counted worthy to suffer dishonor for the name. And every day, in the temple and from house to house, they did not cease teaching and preaching Jesus as the Christ. (Acts 5:29-33; 40-42)

Peter would not change his message to please these men and even considered himself, "worthy to suffer dishonor for the name." Peter was honored to be beaten for proclaiming the gospel so clearly.

Yet even the Apostle Peter, the one who, at one time, was ready to be beaten to proclaim the gospel, was later pressured by supposed Christians, to make a "slight" adjustment to the message of the gospel. What was the addition to the gospel message that Peter added, that made Paul so angry that he called Peter out? Peter was allowing another ingredient—works—to become a necessary component of the message of the gospel. The Apostle Paul refused to accept this change to the gospel, and had to call Peter out for this mixture of grace and works that Peter's actions were teaching. Paul writes:

> But when Cephas came to Antioch, I opposed him to his face, because he stood condemned. For before certain men came from James, he was eating with the Gentiles; but when they came he drew back and separated himself, fearing the circumcision party. And the rest of the Jews acted hypocritically along with him, so that even Barnabas was led astray by their hypocrisy. But when I saw that their conduct was not in step with the truth of the gospel, I said to Cephas before them all, 'If you, though a Jew, live like a Gentile and not like a Jew, how can you force the Gentiles to live like Jews?'

> We ourselves are Jews by birth and not Gentile sinners; yet we know that a person is not justified by works of the law but through faith in Jesus Christ, so we also have believed in Christ Jesus, in order to be justified by faith in Christ and not by works of the law, because by works of the law no one will be justified. (Gal. 2:11-16)

A seasoned Christian and Apostle had to be reprimanded for letting works get mixed with grace. Peter knew this was wrong, but he was momentarily more concerned about the opinions of certain men more than the decree of God. If even the Apostle Peter could succumb to such pressure then we, who are not Apostles, must be especially on guard to ensure that we do not make the same mistake in our communication of the gospel. John MacArthur, in his book *Ashamed of the Gospel*, writes:

> Preaching the Word is not always easy. The message we are required to proclaim is often offensive. Christ Himself is a stone of stumbling and a rock of offense. 'The message of the cross is a stumbling block to some, mere foolishness to others. The natural person does not accept the things of the Spirit of God, for they are folly to him, and he is not able to understand them because they are spiritually discerned' (1 Cor. 2:14). Why do you suppose Paul wrote, 'I am not ashamed of the gospel' (Rom. 1:16)? Surely it is because so many Christians are ashamed of the message we are commanded to proclaim.[178]

EVEN JESUS' GOSPEL COMMUNICATION WAS OFFENSIVE.

What about Jesus Himself, God in the flesh? Did He alter His message to please more people? No, in fact, He did quite the oppo-

---

[178] John MacArthur, *Ashamed of the Gospel: When the Church Becomes like the World* (Wheaton, IL: Crossway Books, 1993), 44.

site. Take the feeding of the five thousand in the book of John, for example. Jesus performed the miracle of feeding thousands of hungry people. The people loved getting the free food, and Jesus was instantly the most popular man around, so much so that they wanted to make Him king. As the Apostle John wrote:

> When the people saw the sign that he had done, they said, 'This is indeed the Prophet who is to come into the world!' Perceiving then that they were about to come and take him by force to make him king, Jesus withdrew again to the mountain by himself. (John 6:14-15)

Moments later, however, His following drastically decreases and His approval ratings drop like a rock because His message, though true, was difficult for them to understand. As Jesus said:

> 'Truly, truly, I say to you, unless you eat the flesh of the Son of Man and drink his blood, you have no life in you. Whoever feeds on my flesh and drinks my blood has eternal life, and I will raise him up on the last day. For my flesh is true food, and my blood is true drink. Whoever feeds on my flesh and drinks my blood abides in me, and I in him.' (John 6:54-56)

This teaching of Jesus irritated the people. They wanted the good news of more free food, but instead, Jesus taught the good news about salvation through Him, "the bread of life."[179] As a result, "After this many of his disciples turned back and no longer walked with him."[180]

Thousands of people had gathered to hear Him. Jesus had achieved success, right? However, no sooner than He had succeeded in gathering a huge crowd, He offended them by His teaching, and virtually everyone left. Had He failed? Though that could be the opinion of some church growth strategists, Jesus had not failed. Jesus knew that the gospel was going to be offensive to

---

[179] John 6:35
[180] John 6:66

many of the people who heard Him, but He did not soften the message to appease the masses. Christ was not looking for large crowds of half-hearted, superficial followers. His concern was for the truth and the clarity of the message that would bring men to repentance and true salvation.

After most of the people had left, Jesus asked Peter and the other Disciples, "Do you want to go away as well?" Simon Peter answered him, "Lord, to whom shall we go? You have the words of eternal life."[181] Peter realized that the most important thing about Christ was not the physical and temporal needs that He could fulfill, but it was His words that were of immense importance and eternal value. Peter gave the perfect answer to Jesus' soul-searching question, "You have the words of eternal life."[182] Peter's greatest need, when it came to Jesus, was not found in supernatural food to feed his body but was found in the supernatural words of Christ that fed his soul. The message Jesus preached appeared to have offended almost everyone, but to those who were being saved the same offensive words were also the words of life.

OUR GOSPEL WILL BE OFFENSIVE AS WELL.

We should never measure successful gospel communication by the number of people who are left unoffended upon hearing it. The measure of success is found in truth conveyed, regardless of whether it offends or not. Jesus Christ, the Son of God, made no attempt to remove the offense of the message, and neither should we. May we not distort, twist, soften, or hold back any portion of the gospel just because the message may be offensive to some. I am sure we would all agree that it is better to be offended for a moment by hearing the true gospel than not to be offended by hearing a false gospel, and yet go on to receive the wrath of God for all of eternity.

Paul let the Corinthians know that they should not expect everyone to receive the gospel joyfully. He said, the gospel that

---

[181] John 6:67-68
[182] John 6:68

he preached was "a stumbling block to the Jews and folly to Gentiles," but he also affirmed that it is the only message that saves those who believe.[183] Jesus likewise warned:

> Do you think that I have come to give peace on earth? No, I tell you, but rather division. For from now on in one house there will be five divided, three against two and two against three. They will be divided, father against son and son against father, mother against daughter and daughter against mother, mother-in-law against her daughter-in-law and daughter-in-law against mother-in-law. (Luke 12:51-53)

We are warned in Scripture by Christ and the Apostles that the true gospel is going to offend some people. However, the offense of the gospel is never a reason to create a different gospel. This means that we, as Christians, are to stay the course and to continue proclaiming the same God-given gospel even if some people take offense. Anthony Hoekema, a well-known professor of systematic theology, in his book *Saved by Grace*, wrote:

> The work Christ has done for our salvation must be clearly and carefully set forth. This should be done in language which is understandable to people today, and in a way that is relevant to present-day needs and problems. Important as it is to be relevant, however, the preacher must first of all be faithful to the Scriptures. There is a sense in which the message of the crucified Christ will always seem irrelevant and offensive. It is not pleasant to be told that we are sinners, by nature objects of God's wrath, unable in our own strength to work our way out of this predicament.[184]

---

[183] 1 Corinthians 1:23-25
[184] Anthony A. Hoekema, *Saved by Grace* (Grand Rapids, MI: W.B. Eerdmans Pub., 1989), 68.

Our role as Christians is to guard the true gospel against change or distortion. We are not in the business of public appeasement, and we must not allow public opinion to sway our mission. As Greg Gilbert, in his book *What is the Gospel?*, has written:

> The gospel is a stark message, and it intrudes into the world's thinking and priorities with sharp, bracing truths. Sadly, there has always been a tendency among Christians—even among evangelicals—to soften some of those edges so that the gospel will be more readily acceptable to the world.[185]

While we must be discerning and acknowledge the sad fact that there is great pressure to modify the gospel message to conform to the world's desires, our acknowledgment should not lead to gospel compromise. We must not forget how quickly and easily that even professing Christians can become false witnesses, especially when their goal is to please people more than God. In writing about the pressure Christians face to alter the gospel to satisfy the culture, Paul Washer warns:

> When our culture no longer desires what we have, then we give them what they want…We are only catering to a godless culture in order to keep it within our walls. In the end, the gospel is gone, God is not honored, and the culture goes to hell.[186]

Let us make every effort to know and understand the true gospel and to preserve and guard the true gospel as we communicate it to others. We must not allow the culture to change our message, but we must rest in the fact that the message will change the culture.

---

[185] Greg Gilbert, *What Is the Gospel?* (Wheaton, IL: Crossway, 2010), 21.
[186] Washer, *The Gospel's Power and Message*, 58-59.

Chapter 13

IS THE WRONG GOSPEL CREATING FALSE CHRISTIANS?

A false convert is a person who has *not* been truly transformed and regenerated by the Holy Spirit, although that person may claim that such an event has taken place. False converts have not placed their trust in the true gospel, and their faith is misplaced. Many Christians *witness* with a genuine desire for others to be saved, but if they do not communicate the gospel, then they have presented a false method of salvation: a different gospel that is based on something besides the gospel of God. Regardless of their motives, *false witnesses* produce *false converts* by proclaiming *false gospels*.

Do you remember our friends, John and Andy, from our story earlier? Let us see how Andy was led to become a false convert. Andy did everything that his Christian friend and the pastor of the church told him to do to become a Christian. However, they never gave Andy the gospel of Jesus Christ to believe in for his salvation. Which means that Andy is still dead in his sins and will still face the judgment and punishment from God resulting in an eternity in hell, yet well-meaning Christians told Andy that everything was just fine because he had followed their formula of salvation.

False converts are often led to believe that they are at peace with God, even though they are truly not. God called out the false prophets in Jeremiah's day for doing virtually the same things which many professing Christians are doing today. Of the false prophets, God said, "They have healed the wound of my people lightly, saying, 'Peace, peace,' when there is no peace."[187] Jeremiah was given the difficult task of preaching that the people were in sin, needed to repent, and needed to turn to God. Meanwhile, the false prophets, who also claimed to speak for God, would tell the people that everything was perfectly fine between them and God. This "Peace when there was no peace" message caused them to think wrongly of their relationship with God. They saw no need to repent of their sin and turn to God because the prophets told them that they were in good standing with God. If professing Christians, pronounce "peace" to people while they are still enemies of God, then they are doing the same thing the false prophets did in the days of Jeremiah by giving people false hope while denying the real condition of their soul.

The horrible state of the false convert is one in which they live under the false assurance of salvation that they have neither received nor understood. Sadly, false converts are being made every day by professing Christians who distort the gospel message, convince others to believe it, and then assure them of their salvation. However, it takes more than calling a person a "Christian" for them to be a Christian. It takes more than saying "peace" for a person to be truly at peace with God.

YOU WILL KNOW THEM BY THEIR FRUIT.

Even if we trust that a Christocentric gospel of grace was preached, caution should still be taken before any official declaration as to the person's salvation. Speaking to those who are so quick to announce someone converted, George Whitfield, pastor during The Great Awakening, said:

> I am glad you know when persons are justified. It is a lesson I have not yet learnt... That makes me so cautious now, which I was not thirty years ago, of dubbing converts so soon. I love now to wait a little, and see if

---

[187] Jeremiah 6:14

people bring forth fruit; for there are so many blossoms which March winds you know blow away, that I cannot believe they are converts till I see fruit brought forth. It will do converts no harm to keep them a little back; it will never do a sincere soul any harm.[188]

Whitfield's point is clear: there is much danger in proclaiming a person saved when they may not truly be saved. The danger of false conversion is especially true when the proclamation is made in the heat of the moment without any time to check on the fundamental beliefs and the life of the new convert. Jesus never said, "You will know them because they went forward in an altar call," or, "You will know them because they claim to be Christians." Jesus said:

> You will recognize them by their fruits. Are grapes gathered from thornbushes, or figs from thistles? So, every healthy tree bears good fruit, but the diseased tree bears bad fruit. A healthy tree cannot bear bad fruit, nor can a diseased tree bear good fruit. Every tree that does not bear good fruit is cut down and thrown into the fire. Thus you will recognize them by their fruits. (Matt. 7:16-20)

Salvation is, of course, by grace alone, through faith alone, and in Christ alone. We are not attempting to mix works into salvation when we say that there must be a change in a person who is truly saved. Salvation does not come from good works, but good works do come from salvation. "For we are his workmanship, created in Christ Jesus for good works, which God prepared beforehand, that we should walk in them."[189] If a person has been saved, he has been justified, which then leads to the process of sanctification. A new believer will not completely stop sinning, but they will grow to hate the sin they once loved and will increasingly grow in love for the God whom they once despised. Evidence of true conversion is that change will occur. As the Apostle Paul says,

---

[188] Murray, *The Invitation System*, 32-33.
[189] Ephesians 2:10

"Therefore, if anyone is in Christ, he is a new creation. The old has passed away; behold, the new has come."[190] The Apostle John also speaks of the difference that should be in a true convert's life when he writes, "If we say we have fellowship with him while we walk in darkness, we lie and do not practice the truth."[191] In the same epistle, John also writes:

> And by this we know that we have come to know him, if we keep his commandments. Whoever says "I know him" but does not keep his commandments is a liar, and the truth is not in him, but whoever keeps his word, in him truly the love of God is perfected. By this we may know that we are in him: whoever says he abides in him ought to walk in the same way in which he walked. (1 John 2:3-6)

Countless numbers of false converts sadly live under the mistaken belief that they are right with God even though their lives provide evidence to the contrary. Perhaps they may have walked an aisle, said a sinner's prayer, asked Jesus into their heart, or made a decision for Jesus without ever hearing the gospel. Such false converts may call themselves "Christians," and they may be called "Christians" by others. They may even be further assured of their Christian identity by a pastor and the members of a local church, but one thing is clear: Christ knows those who are truly His. As Jesus said, "I am the good shepherd. I know my own and my own know me."[192] One of the scariest and most foreboding passages in all of Scripture is a warning from the lips of Jesus Christ, Himself, about the day that false converts will be exposed. He said:

> Not everyone who says to me, 'Lord, Lord,' will enter the kingdom of heaven, but the one who does the will of my Father who is in heaven. On that day many will say

---

[190] 1 Corinthians 5:17
[191] 1 John 1:6
[192] John 10:14

to me, 'Lord, Lord, did we not prophesy in your name, and cast out demons in your name, and do many mighty works in your name?' And then will I declare to them, 'I never knew you; depart from me, you workers of lawlessness.' (Matt. 7:21-23)

As Christians, we must keep this warning in mind even when we evangelize. The last thing we want to do is to make a person think that they are saved even though they are not. We may get a person to do, or pray, something, but if there is no repentance from sin, then there is no salvation. On the subject of true and false converts, A. W. Pink wrote:

> Multitudes desire to be saved from hell (the natural instinct of self-preservation) who are quite unwilling to be saved from sin. Yes, there are tens of thousands who have been deluded into thinking that they have "accepted Christ as their Savior," whose lives show plainly that they reject Him as their Lord.[193]

Pink's speculation, that "tens of thousands" of professing Christians were living a delusion in his day should be even more alarming to us today. For if anything, the number of those living in that delusion has only increased as the true gospel of God has become so commonly supplanted with different gospels.

ONCE SAVED, ALWAYS SAVED?

The Bible makes it abundantly clear that true believers will not lose their salvation. We should take much comfort in this wonderful truth. Passages, such as these bring tremendous peace to one's life:

> In him you also, when you heard the word of truth, the gospel of your salvation, and believed in him, were sealed with the promised Holy Spirit, who is the guar-

---

[193] Pink, *Studies on Saving* Faith, 36.

antee of our inheritance until we acquire possession of it, to the praise of his glory. (Eph. 1:13-14)

Blessed be the God and Father of our Lord Jesus Christ! According to his great mercy, he has caused us to be born again to a living hope through the resurrection of Jesus Christ from the dead, to an inheritance that is imperishable, undefiled, and unfading, kept in heaven for you, who by God's power are being guarded through faith for a salvation ready to be revealed in the last time. (1 Peter 1:3-5)

I give them eternal life, and they will never perish, and no one will snatch them out of my hand. My Father, who has given them to me, is greater than all, and no one is able to snatch them out of the Father's hand. (John 10:28-29)

The true believer has been sealed and guaranteed salvation by God. However, such assurance is given only to those who have "heard the word of truth, the gospel of your salvation, and believe in him." Not all men share this assurance of eternal glory, no matter how much they would like to believe they do. If they have not heard and believed the true gospel of God, any perceived assurance of the security of their salvation, is nothing but deception.

These are false converts who have not believed in Christ for salvation; yet, they firmly believe that they are, and forever will be, saved. It is not that they have lost their salvation somewhere along the way, but that from the beginning, they never had salvation. You cannot lose what you never possessed. "Once saved, always saved" is biblically true, but the belief could be better summarized by saying, "If saved always saved."

You might be asking, "What does this have to do with false converts?" Many Christians attempt to comfort their friends, who doubt their salvation, by having them recall the time and place when they think that they were saved. For instance, one comforting Christian might ask his troubled friend, "Well, didn't you ask

Jesus into your heart at church camp when you were in the Sixth Grade?" "Yes," replies the troubled Christian. "Well, there you have it," assures the comforting Christian. "Don't worry about your salvation anymore. If you asked Him into your heart back then, you can trust that He is still there now."

The best way to keep a false convert unsaved is by continuing to reinforce the wrong message by which they were "converted": a false gospel void of saving power. Remember, many people who call themselves Christians may be false converts who desperately need to be evangelized. Well-meaning Christians may try to comfort false converts by reminding them of past commitments; however, what the false convert needs most is to hear the truth of the gospel.

HOW DO YOU WITNESS TO A FALSE CONVERT?

The only hope for the false convert is the gospel, and that is what we must proclaim to them. As Paul asks in Romans, "How then will they call on him in whom they have not believed? Moreover, how are they to believe in him of whom they have never heard? And how are they to hear without someone preaching?"[194] Instead of checking on someone's salvation by asking them if they have walked an aisle or asked Jesus into their heart, we must ask them more probing questions. Paul told the Corinthians to, "Examine yourselves, to see whether you are in the faith. Test yourselves. On the other hand, do you not realize this about yourselves that Jesus Christ is in you? —unless indeed you fail to meet the test!"[195]

To be in the faith, you do need to know something of the faith that you are in. An excellent way to go about witnessing to, or discerning if a person is a false convert is to ask them questions about their faith. Not questions like, "Have you decided to follow Christ?", or "Have you said the sinner's prayer?" Such questions do not delve into the deeper issue of true saving faith. Questions about faith must be specific and must deal with the fundamen-

---

[194] Romans 10:14
[195] 2 Corinthians 13:5

tal issues of salvation. Instead, use questions that might prove to be more revealing of whether the person even knows the gospel. Such as: "What is sin?", "Who is Jesus?", "What did Jesus do to provide salvation?", "What is the gospel?", "What is belief?", or, "What is repentance?" As you recall, the gospel that saves is a gospel that contains information, and although saving faith is not merely about reciting facts, we never want to downplay that the facts are essential to saving faith.

FALSE CONVERTS CREATE MORE FALSE CONVERTS.

Let's check back in with our friend Andy as he returns to work Monday following his "conversion." After the whirlwind experience of spending a weekend becoming a "Christian," Andy is excited to tell a few of his co-workers about his conversion to Christianity. He tells them about the prayer that John led him in and about going forward to be baptized to become a member of the church. "That is interesting," says one of Andy's co-workers. "I have been looking for more meaning in my life, as well. Maybe I should try that too. Now, exactly what do I need to do to become a Christian?" Andy, who has learned from example, says, "Well, just repeat this prayer after me . . ."

A chain of false conversion has begun. It all started with a Christian named John, who desired to see that his friend Andy became saved, but he failed to give him the gospel. Now John has passed this *mis*communication to Andy who then passes it along to another. Like a contagion that spreads from human contact, the false gospel has been proclaimed and believed, and now it will be further proclaimed leading others to believe falsely that they too have become Christians.

Summary: Without clear gospel communication, there is no evangelization, and there is no true salvation. For there to be real conversions, the real gospel must be proclaimed. We must heed the command of Paul to Timothy when he wrote, "Keep a close watch on yourself and on the teaching. Persist in this, for by so doing you will save both yourself and your hearers."[196] One prominent professor made the following observation regarding the state of theology and evangelism in our time:

> Evangelism and theology have not proved to be compatible partners, at least in the modern period of the Christian tradition. The relationship perhaps has more the character of a stormy courtship ending in separation rather than a well-established marriage.[197]

Unguarded teaching about the gospel that is divorced from biblical authority and theology has enormous ramifications in evangelism. These ramifications are severe and eternal as they result in false converts being made by well-meaning Christians. The problem is further compounded when false converts repeat the process and draw others into a net of false security. The error is spread because someone down the line did not "keep a close watch on … the teaching." Paul's admonition is as much needed in our time as it was in Paul's time. There is a great divide between the teaching of men and the teaching of Christ and the Apostles found in Scripture regarding salvation. We must guard this true teaching and hold fast to it.

---

[196] 1 Timothy 4:16
[197] Stephen K. Pickard, "Evangelism and the Character of Christian Theology," in *The Study of Evangelism: Exploring a Missional Practice of the Church*, ed. Paul Wesley Chilcote and Laceye C. Warner, 138.

Chapter 14

---※---

ARE YOUR FELLOW CHURCH MEMBERS SAVED?

A false church member is an unsaved person who has been accepted as a member by a local church. The prerequisite for becoming a member of a local church is that the person must first be a member of *the* Church: the invisible Church, the Church Universal, namely the body of Christ. These terms do not speak of a specific congregation or denomination, but they do describe all people who are true believers who make up the body of Christ regardless of their local church affiliation.

We see this type of language being used often by Paul when he wrote to believers who were members of different churches, yet all members of the same Body of Christ. To the Romans, he wrote, "For as in one body we have many members, and the members do not all have the same function, so we, though many, are one body in Christ, and individually members one of another."[198] Similarly, in First Corinthians, Paul wrote, "Now you are the body of Christ and individually members of it."[199] Likewise, to the Ephesians, he wrote, "And he put all things under his feet and gave him as head over all things to the church, which is his body..."[200] It is clear from Scripture that the body of Christ is all people everywhere who

---

[198] Romans 12:4-5
[199] 1 Corinthians 12:27
[200] Ephesians 1:22-23

have been saved by Christ, and that the unsaved are not a part of His body.

Part of the local church's role is to confirm, to the best of its ability, that a person seeking membership is genuinely saved before being granted membership by a local church.[201] Not that there is an absolute test, but adherence to foundational beliefs of Christianity, such as the person and work of Jesus Christ, should be explored to see if the object of their faith is truly in the right place. Salvation by Jesus Christ puts them into the Body of Christ. Once they have become members of the Body of Christ, they should also become members of the *local* church. This membership to the local church should be an external affirmation of a person's inner conversion.

The gospel acts as the guardian of the entrance to membership in the local church. If it is assumed of everyone who desires to join the local church that they believe in the gospel with no process of verification, then the guardian of the church is bypassed and ignored. Churches should not assume that those seeking membership know much about the Bible, church membership, or even the gospel. As Al Mohler, President of the Southern Baptist Theological Seminary has observed:

> Secularized Americans should not be expected to be knowledgeable about the Bible. As the nation's civic conversation is stripped of all biblical references and content, Americans increasingly live in a Scripture-free public space. Confusion and ignorance of the Bible's content should be assumed in post-Christian America.[202]

Such confusion means that the church must be careful to make sure that those seeking membership know, and have believed, the gospel that their membership implies. Churches open their doors to receiving and giving assurance of salvation to false converts when they do not adequately check on the status of the person's

---

[201] Romans 1:7; 1 Cor. 1:2; Acts 2:41,42; Acts 5:12-14

[202] Al Mohler, "The Scandal of Biblical Illiteracy: It's Our Problem.," Christianity - Faith in God, Jesus Christ - Christian Living, Trivia, Paragraph 6, accessed December 03, 2016, http://www.christianity.com/.

soul. It is a disservice to the gospel, the holiness of the church, and to a church's witness in its community when local churches bestow membership of non-believers into a body that is to be made only of believers. Regarding this matter, theologian Millard Erickson writes:

> Traditionally, the church was thought of as distinct from the world, as standing over against and intended to transform it. …the church possesses the gospel, the good news of salvation and the world, which is lost and separated from Christ, can be saved or reunited with him only by hearing that gospel, believing, and being justified and regenerated.[203]

There is to be a distinct difference of belief from those who are of the world, and those who are of Christ. The local church should not falsely affirm those who are not believers by granting them membership. It is not enough for a person just to express a desire to be a church member; there must, in the least, be the presence of the same core beliefs. John MacArthur teaches that such fundamental theological agreement should be mandatory before local church membership is granted. He writes:

> Scripture makes clear, for example, that we must take a zero-tolerance stance toward anyone who would tamper with or alter the gospel message (Gal. 1:8-9). And anyone who denies the deity of Christ or substantially departs from His teaching is not to be welcomed into our fellowship or given any kind of blessing (2 John 1:7-11).[204]

What happens if someone's beliefs are not honestly checked and belief in the gospel is not verified, and membership is granted to anyone who shows interest? The result is that the church becomes populated with counterfeit Christians. If this becomes

---

[203] Erickson, *Christian Theology*, 1038.
[204] MacArthur, *The Jesus You Can't Ignore*, xiii.

the common practice of the local church, it is entirely possible that false converts could begin to outnumber the real converts. It would not be long before unconverted people are running the church, teaching in the church, and continuing to create more false converts all in the name of Christianity. They may call themselves a church, yet what holds them together is not the gospel. As Mark Dever writes, "Any unity they experience is a unity based on a false message."[205]

Solution: In our story about John and Andy, John tried to witness to Andy, yet he presented a distorted gospel. Andy believed it and was told that he was a Christian by both John and the pastor. Andy was baptized and became a member of the church without ever even hearing the gospel much less believing the gospel. As a result, a false convert was granted membership into the local church without being an actual member of the Body of Christ.

What could have been done to prevent such a thing from happening? It is highly possible that it all could have been avoided if John would have communicated the real gospel to Andy. However, even though John had presented a false gospel to Andy, the local church should have done more to make sure that Andy understood the gospel and had placed his faith in the true gospel. This takes time, effort, and open discussion between the one seeking membership and the local church's leadership.

In their book *The Deliberate Church: Building Your Ministry on the Gospel*, authors Mark Dever and Paul Alexander, writing on the importance of the gospel in church membership interviews, write:

> The most important question for the protection of the purity of the church is to ask them to explain the Gospel... This may be intimidating for some, but that's okay—it is better for them to stutter in front of you now than to stand speechless before the Lord on the last day. Look for the basics—God, man, Christ, response—even

---

[205] Dever, *The Church: The Gospel Made Visible*, 26.

if they don't use the exact vocabulary. If they leave anything out, graciously ask leading questions. If they are still unable to articulate it, say it for them, and ask them if they have repented of their sins and believed in the Gospel. If they still seem shaky on their understanding (not just articulation) of the Gospel after this conversation, encourage them to go through an evangelistic Bible study with a mature member before recommending them for membership.[206]

The membership process may take some time and may require multiple meetings between a pastor or elder and the one seeking membership. There is much more to lose than there is to gain by rushing a possible false convert through membership. While the front doors of a church should be open to all, the door of membership is through the gospel. There is no doubt that every true Christian, pastor, and evangelist wants more people to be saved and wants more people to join their local church, but in our desire to see the salvation of souls and growth in our churches we must not speed past the gospel to gain a member.

---

[206] Mark Dever and Paul Alexander, *The Deliberate Church: Building Your Ministry on the Gospel* (Wheaton, IL: Crossway Books, 2005), 64.

CONCLUSION TO PART II:

So, how could John have done a better job of witnessing to Andy? How could you strive to prevent a similar scenario from playing out in your own life? The answer to these questions is not overly complicated. It is simply found in the right communication of the gospel. As Paul Washer writes:

> Do we recognize that the power to save is found uniquely in the gospel? The gospel of Jesus Christ is the power of God for salvation. It is not just the core, or part of what is needed, but the whole. For it to have a great effect upon men, it only needs to be proclaimed. It does not require a revision to make it relevant, an adaption to make it understood, or a defense to validate it. If we stand up and proclaim it, it will do the work itself.[207]

As Christians, we should strive to grow in our understanding of the gospel so that we can present a factual, life-giving message to a lost and dying world. The gospel is no small matter; it is the epicenter of the Word of God, and it is the "power of God for salvation to all who believe."[208] Understanding the power and importance of the gospel should cause every Christian to be stirred to prepare our minds for action and to be sober-minded so that we may dwell on the glories of the gospel, and therefore strive to be better communicants of the gospel.[209] As A. W. Pink wrote, "The 'evangelism' of the day is superficial to the last degree, but it is also radically defective. It utterly lacks a foundation on which to base an appeal for sinners to come to Christ."[210] May we not find Pink's words true of us today. In our desire to see people converted to Christianity and to see our churches grow, we must not allow our gospel proclamation to become "radically defective" by changing the message.

---

[207] Washer, *The Gospel's Power and Message*, 58.
[208] Romans 1:16
[209] 1 Peter 1:13
[210] Pink, *Studies on Saving Faith*, 6.

It is our responsibility as messengers of the gospel to deliver it just as it was sent. As the Apostle Paul challenged Timothy, "Do your best to present yourself to God as one approved, a worker who has no need to be ashamed, rightly handling the word of truth."[211] Obviously, it is a possibility that Christian's do not handle the word of truth correctly, or else Paul would not have warned Timothy about the dangers of such a mistake. However, many modern Christians appear to heed no such warning and fondly embrace the wrong handling of the word of truth. Such distortion of the gospel should not be applauded, but rejected, as Paul did in his letter to the Galatians. We, like Timothy, should strive to present ourselves to God as one who God approves of and handles His gospel rightly. As Will Metzger has written, "We all need to reexamine our evangelism to make sure that we do not simply talk around the gospel or that we are so interested in applying the gospel (getting results) that we slight the theological content."[212] Our desire should be to handle the gospel accurately and honestly, and we do so by communicating it as God has given it without addition or subtraction.

---

[211] 2 Timothy 2:15
[212] Will Metzger, *Tell the Truth: The Whole Gospel to the Whole Person by Whole People: A Training Manual on the Message and Method of God-centered Witnessing to a Grace-centered Gospel* (Downers Grove, IL: InterVarsity Press, 2002), 180.

PART III:

POPULAR, YET UNBIBLICAL, WORDS USED TO SPEAK OF SALVATION.

Chapter 15

---❀---

AN EVALUATION OF CURRENT EVANGELISTIC TECHNIQUES AND QUESTIONS.

Do popular methods of evangelism clearly communicate the gospel? Many professing Christians use words and phrases to share the gospel which are confusing, misleading, lacking, and in some cases, entirely wrong. As we have covered, the gospel is a message that contains vital information that is necessary for belief and salvation. The last thing any Christian wants is for the saving message from God to be altered in such a way that it is no longer the correct message and has no power to save. However, we must admit that some well-meaning professing Christians are altering the gospel into something that is not remotely close to a biblical definition of the gospel.

The modern tendency to change the gospel message reminds me of the old game of "Gossip." The game begins by writing a sentence down on paper to keep as the original, and then the writer whispers the message into the next person's ear. That person, in turn, whispers the message into another person's ear and so the message continues through a room of people. The last one to hear the message writes it down and then compares it to the original. Most of the time, the message has been so altered along the way that it no longer resembles the original message. Now, I know there are sometimes jokesters in the bunch who might try to change it intentionally, but even when there is persistent effort to convey the exact message, it usually comes out different. Can this happen to the gospel even among professing Christians? Yes, if we do not stay true to the original message and allow ourselves to depend just on what we have heard others say, then we could easily pass a message to others which is not in keeping with the original.

In this section, we are going to take popular methods of gospel communication and see how well they hold up to a comparison with the biblical definition of the gospel. If you have grown up in the church, then the odds are you have heard some of these "evangelistic" phrases used by your friends, family, and even ministers. Perhaps, you too have even uttered some of these phrases. However, we do not want the test of whether these statements speak accurately about the gospel to be based on widespread usage or even our own usage of them.

Looking back at my own life, I can easily recall, that even though I was saved, and desired others to be saved, I did not know exactly how to share the gospel. Later in life, my desire to evangelize grew stronger, and eventually, I even became a vocational evangelist traveling throughout the U.S. and internationally. Being an evangelist, I felt an immense amount of pressure to make sure that I was proclaiming the true "gospel of God." But, I was astonished to find that many of the other evangelists that I was around seemed to take evangelism lightly, and were not that concerned about getting the gospel right. Sadly, there were many times that I witnessed "evangelistic" messages spoken, invitations given, people supposedly saved, yet the gospel had not been proclaimed.

However, the accuracy of which I proclaimed the gospel and called people to respond to it weighed heavily on my conscience. In fact, the longer I was an evangelist, the more I critiqued my own evangelistic practices. I had a growing appreciation of the gospel, and less appreciation for the other things that so often mark an evangelist: high-energy, emotional manipulation, and of course the sad reality of merely seeking high numbers of decisions for Christ. I say this to let you know that, over the years, I have seen many methods of evangelism; some good and some bad. I can also say that I too know what it is like to struggle to find the words to articulate the gospel clearly.

Looking back, I'm sure there were times when I did not present the gospel as clearly as I should have. I would read books on the gospel and evangelism, but I struggled to see the connection between the methods that were taught and what I read in the Bible. Over the years, I began to realize that much of what I thought was evangelism was not evangelism. I realized that there had been a shift in modern evangelism from biblical evangelism. The emphasis was no longer on the message of the gospel and the call to believe. Instead, what was now commonly referred to as "evangelism" was someone proclaiming a message that was *not* the gospel but *called* the gospel, followed by a command to respond publicly.

As we begin this study, let me say that just because someone uses some of these methods to proclaim the gospel does not mean that he or she is not a Christian. It also does not mean that he or she is set on trying to deliver an intentionally false gospel to lead people to hell. For the most part, it seems that those who use this type of language when speaking of salvation do so innocently, and they genuinely believe that they are accurately speaking about the gospel and salvation. Their motive may be pure; however, it is possible that their message may not be.

With that said, do your best to look at each of these evangelistic questions and methods analytically to determine if they are good descriptions of the "gospel of God" that we just studied. As you consider each evangelistic technique, ask yourself questions like:

1. How does this statement compare to the list of components in the gospel summary of Paul in chapter one of Romans?

2. Have components been added into the gospel that should not be there?

3. Have components been taken out of the gospel, which makes the message an incomplete and inadequate gospel?

4. Is Jesus presented as God and man, or just one or the other?
5. Is Jesus, His identity, and what He accomplished, the primary subject matter of the gospel being shared?
6. What are people called upon to do? Are they to repent, believe, make a decision, invite, say a prayer, or do something else?
7. Does God receive all the glory for the salvation, or does man get some of the glory as well?
8. Did Jesus or the Apostles use such words to speak of salvation?

As we dig into the comparison of modern evangelism to that of biblical evangelism, let me once again reiterate the importance of personally knowing and believing in the right gospel. For it is not only other people that need to hear and believe in the right gospel, but it is you as well. What is the gospel that you have believed in for your salvation? Is it the right gospel? Burk Parsons, the editor of *Tabletalk* Magazine, warns:

> The gospel is absolutely fundamental to everything we believe. It is at the core of who we are as Christians. However, many professing Christians struggle to answer the question: What is the gospel? When I teach, I am astounded by how many of my students are unable to provide a biblically accurate explanation of what the gospel is, and what's more, what the gospel is not. If we don't know what the gospel is, we are of all people the most to be pitied—for we not only can't proclaim the gospel in evangelism so that sinners might be saved, but we in fact may not be saved ourselves.[213]

We must admit, as Burk Parsons did, that there are many professing Christians who are not actual Christians because they do

---

[213] Burk Parsons, "What Is the Gospel?" *Tabletalk* 39, no. 1 (January 2015): 2.

not know the gospel. Understandably, some professing Christians do know the gospel but have a difficult time stating it. Either way, we must admit that it is entirely possible that many professing Christians could have relied on some of the evangelistic techniques and practices of our day that have little or nothing to do with the gospel of God.

Chapter 16

DO YOU HAVE A RELATIONSHIP WITH GOD?

I have chosen to start with this question because it is considered to be the most popular, yet unclear method of evangelism used today. And, as we will see, there is also an underlying theological error that is at the core of this evangelistic method that needs to be examined. First of all, think about what truths are being conveyed to a person by this kind of statement: "Do you have a relationship with God?" What does this question mean? Is there even such a thing as a human who does not have a relationship with God? Now, I know what the Christian asking the question may be implying, but based upon the Bible everyone is in *some kind* of relationship with God, and it is for this reason that this question can be misleading.

The Apostle Paul makes our natural relationship with God quite clear:

> And you were dead in the trespasses and sins in which you once walked, following the course of this world, following the prince of the power of the air, the spirit that is now at work in the sons of disobedience—among whom we all once lived in the passions of our flesh, carrying out the desires of the body and the mind, and were by nature children of wrath, like the rest of mankind. (Eph. 2:1-3)

Just by nature, our relationship with God is terrible. We are naturally (automatically) spiritually dead, followers of Satan, followers of the world and other sinners, disobedient to God, living for ourselves, and as far as a relationship goes, enemies of God. Regarding this natural relationship, Martyn Lloyd Jones wrote:

> We are in the wrong relationship to Him. His wrath is upon us. We have made it impossible for Him to bless us. His Holy nature demands that He must punish us and our transgressions. What can we do about it? Nothing! ... Can nothing be done? God be thanked, the gospel of Christ provides the answer, as we have already seen. God has dealt with our sins in Christ.[214]

"Wrong relationship," "wrath," "punishment?" This is not good news. It is horrible news, and that is the point that Jones was trying to make. However, it is the bad news that people must understand before they will see any need for their relationship with God to be reconciled. Instead of asking people if they have a relationship with God, we should be warning them of the automatic relationship that all of humanity has with God without Christ. We should be willing to take the time to explain the wrath that humanity deserves and what God has done to provide salvation.

To understand the broken relationship that humanity has with God, one must first understand the problem of sin which all of humanity faces, and what that means to our relationship with God. Adam, the first man, represented not only himself but also all who would ever be born from him. In other words, he represented all humanity. God had given Adam and Eve His law to follow:

> And the LORD God commanded the man, saying, "You may surely eat of every tree of the garden, but of the tree of the knowledge of good and evil you shall not eat, for in the day that you eat of it you shall surely die. (Gen. 2:16-17)

---

[214] Lloyd-Jones, *The Plight of Man and the Power of God*, 108.

However, they rejected God's rule, disobeyed His clear command, and they sinned against God.

> So when the woman saw that the tree was good for food, and that it was a delight to the eyes, and that the tree was to be desired to make one wise, she took of its fruit and ate, and she also gave some to her husband who was with her, and he ate. (Gen. 3:6)

Adam and Eve were both created by God and were originally sinless. Their innocence allowed them to enjoy an intimate relationship with God and to be in His presence, unlike anything humanity will ever experience again on this side of heaven. However, mankind's relationship with God changed when Adam disobeyed God's command. Adam and Eve were forbidden from entering back into the Garden of Eden because of their sin.

All humanity has been corrupted by the Fall of Adam, so much so that we cannot fix ourselves or right our position before God. As Paul says in Romans, "Therefore, just as sin came into the world through one man, and death through sin, and so death spread to all men because all sinned."[215] David also acknowledged that he had been a sinner since birth when he wrote, "Behold, I was brought forth in iniquity, and in sin did my mother conceive me."[216] By exposing the true relationship that people have with God, people hear the truth, which opens the door for presenting how they can have "peace with God."[217]

WE ACTIVELY SIN AGAINST GOD.

Sin occurs not only by our outward actions, but it also happens within the motivations of our desires and thoughts. Sin can be a matter of actively going against God's rules, or even not doing what we know we should be doing. As James writes, "So whoever

---

[215] Romans 5:12
[216] Psalm 51:5
[217] Romans 5:1

knows the right thing to do and fails to do it, for him it is sin."[218] While Christians should see this concept of sin as basic, for others, sin and its biblical definition may be foreign to their thinking. In a society that no longer views God as God and sin as sin, even basic biblical terms may need to be clarified when communicating the gospel message. We want to make sure our terminology means the same thing to our hearers as it does for us. A quick study on sin helps add to the understanding of the relationship we naturally have with God in our sinful condition.

The Ten Commandments were given to Moses by God for His people to obey. These Ten Commandments, which used to hang in every public school and courthouse, have all but been removed from public view. Not only have the Ten Commandments been evicted from the public square, but sadly they have been removed from the walls, and more importantly, the teaching of churches. Not that long ago, it was common for Christian parents to teach their children the Ten Commandments and to encourage the memorization of the Ten Commandments. However, such practices have been all but lost in our increasingly secular society, and even amongst many professing Christians. So, before we go any further, let's review the Ten Commandments.

1. You shall have no other gods before me.
2. You shall not make for yourself a carved image, or any likeness of anything that is in heaven above, or that is in the earth beneath, or that is in the water under the earth.
3. You shall not take the name of the LORD your God in vain…
4. Remember the Sabbath day, to keep it holy.
5. Honor your father and your mother.
6. You shall not murder.
7. You shall not commit adultery.
8. You shall not steal.

---

[218] James 4:17

9. You shall not bear false witness against your neighbor.
10. You shall not covet...[219]

Of what use are these commandments to us? First, they reveal God's holy standard and teach us our duty to Him and our duty to others. Secondly, the Ten Commandments expose humanity's inability to be perfectly obedient to His Law. When we violate His Law and reject His authority, we commit the act called *sin*. As Martin Luther preached in the sixteenth century, "The Law revealeth the disease: the Gospel ministereth the medicine."[220] Luther also advised that the Law of God should be preached before the gospel because it,

> ... reveals and teaches how to recognize sin. Secondly, when now sin is recognized and the law is so preached that the conscience is alarmed and humbled before God's wrath, we are then to preach the comforting word of the Gospel and the forgiveness of sins, so that the conscience again may be comforted and established in the grace of God...[221]

DOES GOD GRADE ON A CURVE?

Now it is interesting how some people will grade themselves as they read over the Ten Commandments. For instance, if they admit that they have used God's name in an irreverent manner, and they admit that they once took something that was not theirs, they might grade themselves at an 80 percent, which does not seem too bad, as that is still considered a "B" in most schools. However, that is an "F" in God's school. As James writes:

> For whoever keeps the whole law but fails in one point has become accountable for all of it. For he who said,

---

[219] For a full reading of the Ten Commandments see Exodus 20:1-17
[220] Luther, *Sermons: By Martin Luther*, 219.
[221] Martin Luther, *Luther's Works*, ed. Jaroslav Pelikan and Helmut T. Lehman, Vol. 40 (Philadelphia: Fortress, 1965), 82-83.

> 'Do not commit adultery,' also said, 'Do not murder.' If you do not commit adultery but do murder, you have become a transgressor of the law. (James 2:10-11)

By God's standard, we would have to be 100 percent perfect at fulfilling all of His righteous requirements. Such perfection is where we run into a big obstacle because we are not perfect. We all know that we have broken God's Laws, and because of that, we are guilty of sin. All of humanity, like Adam and Eve, has chosen to follow our desires rather than the commands of our Maker.

Some people may admit that they have broken a couple of Laws, but Jesus raises the bar even higher when He teaches on this issue. He lets His audience know that violating God's Laws is not just about the sins committed on the outside, but it also concerns those committed on the inside. Jesus said:

> You have heard that it was said to those of old, 'You shall not murder; and whoever murders will be liable to judgment.' But I say to you that everyone who is angry with his brother will be liable to judgment; whoever insults his brother will be liable to the council; and whoever says, 'You fool!' will be liable to the hell of fire. (Matt. 5:21-22)

Therefore, to break the Law, "Do not murder," you do not have to kill someone literally, but even just being wrongfully angry at a person or by insulting someone is a violation of God's Law. In this example, Jesus says that even calling someone a fool is enough to cause the individual to spend eternity in hell. As you can see, God's rules are much easier to break than we often think, and the consequence far more severe.

Jesus then teaches on adultery in this same passage and once again reveals to His hearers that this law is much more easily broken than many of them may have realized. "You have heard that it was said, 'You shall not commit adultery.' But I say to you that everyone who looks at a woman with lustful intent has already committed adultery with her in his heart."[222] In other words, to break this command does not even require a physical, sexual act, but just a lustful thought.

Often, we think that God sees what we do in the same way that people around us see what we do. However, God knows everything about us, including our thoughts and motives as we have seen from Jesus' teaching on murder and adultery. Think about that for a moment. We view our thoughts as safe and private, obscured from the view of others. The most secret place on earth is in your mind. Who can truly see your thoughts? God can, and He knows exactly what you are thinking. As Jesus said, "Nothing is covered up that will not be revealed, or hidden that will not be known. Therefore, whatever you have said in the dark shall be heard in the light, and what you have whispered in private rooms shall be proclaimed on the housetops."[223] We have no privacy as we stand before God. He truly knows everything about us. He knows all that we have done and He knows every thought that we have. His knowledge is perfect. As David wrote:

> O LORD, You have searched me and known me! You know when I sit down and when I rise up; you discern my thoughts from afar. You search out my path and my lying down and are acquainted with all my ways. Even before a word is on my tongue, behold, O LORD, You know it altogether. (Psalm. 139:1-4)

When we understand that God knows everything about us, including our thoughts and motives, it should cause us to see more clearly the reality of our sin.

THE GREATEST COMMANDMENTS.

As good of an expression of God's laws for humanity as the Ten Commandments are, Jesus added even more clarity to

---

[222] Matthew 5:27-28
[223] Luke 12:2-3

the issue when He taught that the greatest commandments of all are to "love the Lord your God with all your heart and with all your soul and with all your mind and with all your strength" and to "love your neighbor as yourself.' There is no other commandment greater than these."[224] In these two commands, we find the center from which all of God's law for humanity flows. First and foremost, each of us is to love God with all of our heart, soul, mind, and strength. This is a total and complete love of God that goes far beyond merely striving not to break the Ten Commandments. Is there anyone that has succeeded in fulfilling this command of God? No, all humanity is guilty of insufficiently loving God.

The next command Jesus gave was to "love your neighbor as yourself." A practical outworking and a test of one's love of God is his or her love of others. It is one thing to love a perfectly holy, good God, but it is quite another to sacrificially love the flawed, sinful people that we are around every day. The Apostle John elaborates on Jesus' teaching by writing that, "If anyone says, 'I love God,' and hates his brother, he is a liar; for he who does not love his brother whom he has seen cannot love God whom he has not seen. And this commandment we have from him: whoever loves God must also love his brother."[225]

The teachers of the law in Jesus' day prided themselves at "keeping" the Ten Commandments, but Jesus wanted them to understand that obedience to God goes much deeper than checking the box on each of the Ten Commandments. Jesus was using these two commands, which He called "the greatest commandments," to help reveal all of humanity's guiltiness before God. No one loves God completely, and no one sacrificially loves their neighbors as themselves 100% of the time. As the Apostle Paul says, "All have sinned and come short of the glory of God."[226]

---

[224] Mark 12:28-31
[225] 1 John 4:20-21
[226] Romans 3:23

LAW BREAKERS WILL BE JUDGED.

Now that it has been established that our natural relationship with God is one of guilt and separation because of sin, it logically follows that we must consider what this means for us. Regarding this issue, theologian Millard Erickson states:

> . . . sin is a broken relationship with God. The human has failed to fulfill divine expectations, whether by transgressing limitations that God's law has set or by failing to do what is positively commanded there. Deviation from the law results in a state of guilty or liability to punishment.[227]

Mankind is guilty, and there will be an ultimate judgment before God. The author of Hebrews wrote, "And just as it is appointed for man to die once, and after that comes judgment."[228] A judgment by God should be more than just a little bit concerning because we are by nature in a relationship of wrath because of our sin.

The Book of Revelation describes, to some degree, what this judgment and punishment will be like:

> Then I saw a great white throne and him who was seated on it. From his presence earth and sky fled away, and no place was found for them. And I saw the dead, great and small, standing before the throne, and books were opened. Then another book was opened, which is the book of life. And the dead were judged by what was written in the books, according to what they had done. And the sea gave up the dead who were in it, Death and Hades gave up the dead who were in them, and they were judged, each one of them, according to what they had done. Then Death and Hades were thrown into the lake of fire. This is the second death, the lake of fire. And

---

[227] Millard J. Erickson, *Christian Theology* (Grand Rapids, MI: Baker Book House, 1998), 918.
[228] Hebrews 9:27

if anyone's name was not found written in the book of life, he was thrown into the lake of fire. (Rev. 20:11-15)

Passages like this help us to see the reality and future outcome of the relationship that unsaved humanity has with God. Not only are we guilty before God, but He also keeps a record of all we have done. One day that book will be opened, and we will be judged, sentenced, and punished by the God who is Judge over all creation.

THE ANGER OF GOD.

Jonathan Edwards, the great pastor, and evangelist of the Great Awakening made sure to represent the natural relationship unredeemed man has with God accurately, as you can see from this excerpt of his sermon *Sinners in the hands of an angry God*:

> So that, thus it is that natural men are held in the hand of God, over the pit of hell; they have deserved the fiery pit, and are already sentenced to it; and God is dreadfully provoked, his anger is as great towards them as to those that are actually suffering the executions of the fierceness of his wrath in hell, and they have done nothing in the least to appease or abate that anger, neither is God in the least bound by any promise to hold them up one moment; the devil is waiting for them, hell is gaping for them, the flames gather and flash about them, and would fain lay hold on them, and swallow them up; the fire pent up in their own hearts is struggling to break out: and they have no interest in any Mediator, there are no means within reach that can be any security to them. In short, they have no refuge, nothing to take hold of; all that preserves them every moment is the mere arbitrary will, and uncovenanted unobliged forbearance of an incensed God.[229]

---

[229] Jonathan Edwards, "Select Sermons," - Christian Classics Ethereal Library, Sinners in the Hands of an Angry God, accessed October 19, 2016, http://www.ccel.org/ccel/edwards/sermons.sinners.html.

Jonathan Edwards was not known for asking people, "Do you have a relationship with God?", but he was known for telling people exactly what their relationship was without Christ as their Savior, and describing the consequences of that relationship in detail.

God's punishment for those that are in a relationship of wrath is described in many places in the Bible. To get a better understanding of what we need to be saved from, it is good to look at how the Bible describes the punishment people will receive for their sins. For example:

> His winnowing fork is in his hand, to clear his threshing floor and to gather the wheat into his barn, but the chaff he will burn with unquenchable fire. (Luke 2:17)

> They will suffer the punishment of eternal destruction, away from the presence of the Lord and from the glory of his might. (2 Thess. 1:9)

> And they shall go out and look on the dead bodies of the men who have rebelled against me. For their worm shall not die, their fire shall not be quenched, and they shall be an abhorrence to all flesh. (Is. 66:24)

> And many of those who sleep in the dust of the earth shall awake, some to everlasting life, and some to shame and everlasting contempt. (Dan. 12:2)

> And the smoke of their torment goes up forever and ever, and they have no rest, day or night. (Rev. 14:10-11)

> The poor man died and was carried by the angels to Abraham's side. The rich man also died and was buried, and in Hades, being in torment, he lifted up his eyes and saw Abraham far off and Lazarus at his side. And he called out, 'Father Abraham, have mercy on me, and send Lazarus to dip the end of his finger in water and cool my tongue, for I am in anguish in this flame.' (Luke 16:22-24)

Who deserves such judgment and punishment? We have all sinned against God, broken His commands, and deserve punishment. Such is the natural relationship all mankind has with God, the good news of Jesus Christ can only mend the relationship. Teaching on the importance of God's Law and God's Gospel, Bible teacher and pastor John Stott wrote:

> We cannot come to Christ to be justified until we've first been to Moses to be condemned. Once we have gone to Moses and acknowledged our sin, guilt and condemnation, we must not stay there, we must leave Moses and go to Christ.[230]

The Law exposes us to the harsh reality of our sinful condition and the inability to save ourselves by meeting the Law's standards. We have sinned many times, and we cannot erase them. We continue to break God's rules, and we can't completely stop. We need to be saved from the relationship that we are in because of our sinfulness. It is an understanding of the Law and our inability to meet its demands that cast our hope of salvation away from ourselves to the gospel of grace that is found in Jesus Christ. The God-man is the only One that can mend the broken relationship between God and man.

Summary: So, does the question, "Do you have a relationship with God?" work to describe the relationship status between God and man appropriately? Does it speak truthfully of the bad news of sin, judgment, punishment, and the relationship of wrath in which we are naturally born and need to be saved? We, as Christians, must be cautious if we choose to use this evangelistic question, because it may not convey what we think it conveys to the non-Christian. While the Christian may truly be trying to check on the individual's salvation, the non-Christian may not have any knowledge of the gospel that is needed to believe in for salvation. Likewise, the

---

[230] John R. W. Stott, *The Message of Galatians: Only One Way* (Leicester, England: Inter-Varsity Press, 1986).

non-Christian does not fully understand the relationship of wrath that they are currently in with God. If this question is used, the Christian should never just accept a "Yes" answer as meaning that the person is saved. It is possible that the person answering may have no idea about the question that he or she has been asked.

We must paint an accurate picture of people's natural state before God and the good news of the gospel. The good news is about the Savior that came to fix our relationship with God by dying on the cross, taking our sins on Himself, paying the price that sin demands, removing the wrath we deserved, and who made perfect peace between God and us. As Isaiah said of the Messiah, "But he was pierced for our transgressions; he was crushed for our iniquities; upon him was the chastisement that brought us peace, and with his wounds we are healed."[231]

---

[231] Isaiah 53:5

Chapter 17

HAVE YOU MADE A DECISION FOR CHRIST?

Over the years, many non-believers have been instructed to make a decision for Christ. These non-believers often receive assurances from the Christian that if they will just make a decision for Christ, then they will be forever right with God. Is this biblical evangelism? Again, what we find is a vague question that is supposedly speaking about salvation. However, does this question communicate the gospel? Is this question meant to ask if the individual has heard the gospel, confessed their sin, repented of their sin, and believed in Jesus for salvation? If this is what is meant by "Make a decision for Christ," then more explanation is needed.

As a pastor, I have counseled many people who have "made a decision for Christ." When I hear these words come from someone's mouth, I always have them explain what they mean by that statement. I will admit that some will accurately explain the gospel and their belief in the gospel for their salvation. In this case, even though their statement of, "I made a decision for Christ" is a vague statement, they have allowed it to become a type of shorthand for meaning something different than the words that are being spoken.

While some who use the phrase, "I made a decision for Christ," do know the gospel and have believed in it for salvation, some have gone on to reveal that they know nothing about the gospel, but can only explain a moment where they agreed to someone's plea to decide for Jesus. Is this salvation? Does deciding for Christ equate to believing in the gospel?

Unfortunately, the high-pressure invitations, in which many pastors and evangelist exhort their hearers to make a decision for Christ have caused many people to do exactly as they are instructed, but is that salvation? Truly, neither high-pressure tactics nor good decision-making skills are what we need for true salvation. As John MacArthur writes:

> Unfortunately, many people go through life caring nothing for Christ but believing they are Christians only because they responded with a childhood 'decision.' Their hope of heaven hangs solely on the memory of that event. I'm afraid that in many cases it is a vain and damning hope.[232]

Believing in Christ for salvation is far more than just making a good choice. As MacArthur points out, "Believing isn't easy. It is not hard. It is impossible in human terms."[233] As the Apostle Paul writes, "The natural person does not accept the things of the Spirit of God, for they are folly to him, and he is not able to understand them because they are spiritually discerned."[234] This passage makes it clear that the only decision we can make in our sinful condition, regarding Christ, is not a good one. Paul says that, in and of ourselves, we cannot "accept the things of the Spirit of God... they are folly", and that we are "not able to understand them." Humanity is called upon to believe in the gospel, but even our belief is a gift from God, as is our desire to repent.[235] Often Christians attempt to force people to make a decision as if it is just as simple as deciding which shoes to buy, which soda to drink, or where to eat dinner.

---

[232] John MacArthur, *The Gospel According to the Apostles: The Role of Works in the Life of Faith* (Nashville, TN: Word Pub., 2000), 197.
[233] Ibid., 199.
[234] 1 Corinthians 1:14
[235] Ephesians 2:8-9; Acts 11:8

Even if we get them to make a decision, what have we done? Is their faith in Jesus Christ, the Son of God, and His atoning work, or is their faith in their decision? As you can see, using the, "make a decision for Christ" type of language instead of proclaiming the gospel, and trusting God to work in and through the gospel to bring about salvation can be confusing, misleading, and possibly lead to a false sense of salvation. Regarding the use of these empty evangelistic words, Mark Dever, in his book, *The Gospel & Personal Evangelism*, writes:

> Who can deny that much modern evangelism has become emotionally manipulative, seeking simply to cause a momentary decision of the sinner's will, yet neglecting the biblical idea that conversion is the result of the supernatural, gracious act of God toward the sinner?"[236]

The Apostle Paul was certainly not manipulative when he preached the gospel. He understood that his role was to proclaim the gospel for his audience to hear and believe, yet at the same time, he acknowledged that salvation was still of the Lord. We can see this in Luke's record of Paul's witness to the Gentiles; "And when the Gentiles heard this, they began rejoicing and glorifying the word of the Lord, and as many as were appointed to eternal life believed."[237] Likewise, we are called to proclaim the gospel, but we must still acknowledge the fact that we are fallen, sinful, spiritually dead, lovers of sin, and that without the grace of God we cannot be saved. Salvation is more than weighing out the decision to be for Christ or to not be for Christ. Truly, no one even can decide for Christ without God supernaturally moving in their lives first. As the Apostle John wrote, "No one can come to me unless the Father who sent me draws him."[238]

A person's faith for salvation must not be in a decision. If it is, then that is "decisionism," which is the belief that a decision

---

[236] Mark Dever, *The Gospel & Personal Evangelism* (Wheaton, IL: Crossway Books, 2007), 80.
[237] Acts 13:48
[238] John 6:44

is what saves a person. True Christians *do* decide to love Christ; however, it is not the decision to love Christ that saves them, but their love towards Christ is a response to the grace Christ has shown them by saving them. As Paul wrote in Ephesians, "But God, being rich in mercy, because of the great love with which he loved us, even when we were dead in our trespasses, made us alive together with Christ—by grace you have been saved."[239] As the pure grace of God regenerates a person, God gives them a new heart with new desires to trust in Christ for salvation.

Summary: In your mind, what does "making a decision for Christ" mean? It is possible that some Christians have put meaning into these words that is just not self-evident by an examination of the words themselves? However, we must admit that these words, in and of themselves, are confusing in the least, and in reality, have nothing to do with the gospel. Not only is it confusing and void of gospel content, but it also shifts the one who is saving from God, to man. Remember, no one is saved simply by making a good decision; instead, it is the one who "believes" that will not "perish but have eternal life."[240]

Our job as Christians is not to make people decide for Christ; rather, it is our role to proclaim the gospel and allow the Holy Spirit to work through the gospel to bring about repentance and belief. As Graeme Goldsworthy, writing on the difference between the gospel and gospel response, wrote, "The distinction between the message and the demand to believe it is vital. It means that preaching the gospel must involve more than simply calling on people to make a decision."[241]

---

[239] Ephesians 2:4-5
[240] John 3:16
[241] Goldsworthy, *Preaching the Whole Bible as Christian Scripture*, 82.

Chapter 18

WOULD YOU LIKE TO ASK JESUS INTO YOUR HEART?

This is another question that is thought to be evangelistic by many well-meaning Christians, but it is also one of the most confusing questions ever used to speak of salvation. Honestly, stop and think about the meaning of, "Would you like to ask Jesus into your heart?" The question has nothing to do with sin, confession of sin, repentance from sin, who Jesus is, what Jesus did, or any of the components of the gospel covered by the Apostle Paul in Part I of this study. Instead, the entire focus is merely to ask Jesus to come into one's heart. How exactly does a person invite Christ into his or her heart? Should we, as Christians, invite unsaved people to tell God to come into their hearts? Do we really think that such an invitation for God to enter one's heart is equivalent to salvation? Writing on this issue, R. C. Sproul stated:

> People think that the gospel is having a warm relationship with Jesus or asking Christ into your heart. Those things are important, but they are not the gospel. The gospel focuses on the person of Christ, what Christ accomplished, and how the benefits of Christ are appropriated to the Christian's life by faith.[242]

---

[242] R. Mohler Albert et al., *Feed My Sheep: A Passionate Plea for Preaching* (Orlando, FL: Reformation Trust Pub., 2008), 85.

Telling people to ask Jesus to come into their heart is not the same as sharing the gospel. Simply put, this evangelistic question is no gospel declaration at all. It is an incomplete and inadequate gospel. Some might argue that the "asking Jesus into your heart" style of evangelism is not meant to be the gospel, but instead a description of how a person should respond to the gospel. However, neither this method of sharing the gospel or this response to the gospel can be found in the Bible. In the end, it has absolutely no Scriptural support.

WHAT ABOUT ROMANS 10:9-10?

Some proponents of the "Ask Jesus into your heart" style of evangelism often cite Romans 10:9-10 as a proof text for their methodology. So, let us examine this passage to see if such a substantiation can be made. The verse in question is, "that if you confess with your mouth, 'Jesus is Lord,' and believe in your heart that God raised Him from the dead, you will be saved. For with your heart you believe and are justified, and with your mouth you confess and are saved." This passage does contain the word "heart," but it is certainly missing any imperative to "ask Jesus into one's heart." Instead, once again, we find a response to the gospel that should sound quite familiar by now: "believe."

Paul did not create a different method of salvation different from the one he taught earlier in Romans when he wrote that the gospel "is the power of God for salvation to everyone who believes."[243] Nor did Paul alter the gospel from his earlier statements. This passage is taken from the same letter where he had clearly articulated the gospel from the beginning. Paul is still referring to the same gospel, and he is still commanding the same response to the gospel in chapter ten of Romans as he was in chapter one of Romans. His use of the word "heart" is to teach that belief in Jesus is more than a verbal statement. Genuine salvation involves deep faith that upon regeneration, flows out of a per-

---

[243] Romans 1:16

son's innermost being, and overflows to a verbal confession that correlates.

We can see a similar use of the word *heart* throughout scripture, for instance, Jesus' words, "You shall love the Lord your God with all your heart and with all your soul and with all your strength."[244] Here the word "heart" is again used to show a deep, all-inclusive love that we are to have for God. This is how Paul used the word as well. In short, Romans 10:9-10 does not validate the "Ask Jesus into your heart" method of evangelism. But, reiterates the same response to the same gospel that the Apostle Paul has been teaching all along.

The fact of the matter is that Paul never used this style of evangelism. What about Jesus? Does Jesus ever command someone to ask Him into his or her heart? No. What about the Apostles? Do the Apostles ever command their audience to *ask* or *invite* Jesus into their heart? No. Instead, Jesus and the disciples proclaim the gospel and command people to believe.

"BUT THIS METHOD IS EASIER FOR CHILDREN TO UNDERSTAND?"

John MacArthur, in addressing the superficiality and oversimplification of popular evangelistic strategies, writes:

> Too many people whose hearts are utterly cold to the things of the Lord believe they are going to heaven simply because they responded positively as children to an evangelistic invitation. Having 'asked Jesus to come into their hearts,' they were then taught never to examine themselves and never to entertain any doubt about their salvation.[245]

Sadly, as MacArthur mentioned, many people seem to think that this is an excellent way to communicate the gospel to children at

---

[244] Mark 12:30
[245] MacArthur, *The Gospel According to the Apostles*, 197.

a level that they can understand. I would argue that the opposite is the case. Telling a child, or anyone, to "Ask Jesus into your heart" is not a way to present the gospel that is easier for them to understand; instead, it complicates, confuses, and can easily lead them into some wrong beliefs regarding salvation.

Try to explain this method of being "saved" to a child who only knows of the heart as an organ in his chest and get ready for some serious confusion. One such boy, when asked if he knew the reason that he bowed his head to pray, explained, "That puts my brain closer to my heart where Jesus lives." While such a statement sounded bizarre to the mature believers around the child, the boy's odd theology is the logical outworking of their teaching the child to ask Jesus into his heart.

It is far more logical (and biblical) to present children with the information of who Jesus is and what He has done. Give the proper object of belief so that they may believe and be saved. Changing the gospel or the call to believe it, into something different does not make the gospel more understandable. Such oversimplification is not helpful to anyone. It is dangerous to the one giving it and the one receiving it because it is a distortion of the gospel.

THE BIBLE DOES SPEAK ABOUT RECEIVING A NEW HEART.

What about the Bible? Doesn't the Bible speak about the heart? We do find passages that reference the heart and salvation, but we see none that instructs us to "Ask Jesus into our heart." The Bible tells us that God gives us a new heart, which is descriptive of God's work in salvation. As God said through Ezekiel the prophet:

> And I will give you a new heart, and a new spirit I will put within you. And I will remove the heart of stone from your flesh and give you a heart of flesh. And I will put my Spirit within you, and cause you to walk in my statutes and be careful to obey my rules. (Ez. 36:26-27)

Notice that God is the one who takes the initiative and is the change-agent in this passage. This passage has nothing to do with a person asking Jesus to come into their heart; instead, it has everything to do with God supernaturally saving people, giving them a new heart, a new desire to love Him, hate sin, and being born again by the action of God. God's Word does tell us to do many things with our heart: "trust in the Lord with all your heart," "love the Lord your God with all your heart," etc. . . . but it never tells us to ask Him into our hearts.[246]

The Holy Spirit indeed indwells believers, but even this is not something that people are to ask for; instead, the indwelling of the Holy Spirit is given at salvation. As Paul wrote, "In him you also, when you heard the word of truth, the gospel of your salvation, and believed in him, were sealed with the promised Holy Spirit, who is the guarantee of our inheritance until we acquire possession of it, to the praise of his glory.[247] The Ephesians heard the gospel, "the word of truth," believed, and were saved. However, there is no mention of anyone inviting Jesus or the Holy Spirit to come into their heart. Once again, the emphasis is on the proclamation of the gospel and the proper response to the gospel: believing. As Graeme Goldsworthy has written,

> When the question 'How do you know God will accept you?' is answered by 'I have Jesus in my heart,' 'I asked Jesus into my life,' 'The Holy Spirit is in me,' and so on, the real gospel basis for assurance needs to be reviewed. We rejoice when the answer comes in the third person: 'God gave his only Son to die on the cross for me,' 'Jesus died, rose, and is in heaven for me.' When the focus is on the finished and perfect work of Christ, rather than on the yet unfinished work of the Spirit in me, the grounds for assurance are in place.[248]

---

[246] Proverbs 3:5, Deuteronomy 6:5
[247] Ephesians 1:13-14
[248] Goldsworthy, *Preaching the Whole Bible as Christian Scripture*, 95.

Summary: "Have you asked Jesus into your heart?" is a favorite evangelistic question for many Christians, yet we do not find anything like this commanded in scripture. This is another example of a statement that might mean one thing to a Christian, but there would be no way for a non-Christian to decipher the correct meaning from these words. We, as Christians, should never seek to create our own *easier* version of the gospel, nor should we make up our own *easier*, but a fallacious response to the gospel. By doing so, we have created a wrong response to the gospel than what is commanded of us by God.

What if someone you are witnessing to says, "I asked Jesus into my heart when I was eight." Should you trust that the person has believed in the gospel of God for salvation? No, because he or she has not described anything having to do with salvation. Instead, explore what the person means by this statement. It is possible that the individual is saved, but that he or she has just picked an inadequate expression of salvation. However, it is also possible that the individual may have never even heard the real gospel and that he or she has an entirely incorrect view of the gospel and of salvation. This is why it is crucial to ask even professing Christians about the gospel.

Likewise, it is possible that some well-meaning Christians may mean something more than what is actually stated when they say, "Have you ever invited Jesus into your heart?" It is possible that they mean, "Have you ever heard the gospel, and believed in it for your salvation?" However, the Christian's words used to express such a thought are falling far short of clear gospel proclamation. It should never be our purpose to witness to someone in a way that convolutes the gospel. If our goal is to share the gospel and to call upon people to believe the gospel for salvation, then that is precisely what we should do.

Chapter 19

JESUS IS KNOCKING. WILL YOU LET HIM IN?

I can still recall the artwork from my childhood of Jesus standing at a wooden door knocking and wanting to come in, but sadly, there was no doorknob on His side of the door. The picture was to serve as an evangelistic visual aid for those who believed that Jesus could not open the door to one's heart unless the person opened the door to his or her heart and let Jesus enter. However, is this image of Christ knocking on the door of our hearts an accurate depiction of salvation? Should we ask people to open their hearts' door to let Jesus in?

This image of Christ knocking and the question of, "Will you let Him in?" is pulled from a verse from the book of Revelation that says, "Behold, I stand at the door and knock. If anyone hears my voice and opens the door, I will come in to him and eat with him, and he with me."[249] Does this passage mean that Jesus is at the door of our hearts wanting and waiting to come in, but He cannot unless we open the door to let Him in? It appears to, but to get this understanding of the verse, one would have to read it out of context.

Even just a reading of the verse that precedes it helps us to see that evangelism is not the emphasis of the metaphor. The passage states, "Those whom I love, I reprove and discipline, so be

---

[249] Revelation 3:20

zealous and repent."[250] In context, we see that the passage in question was written to the members of The Church at Laodicea, who were living in unrepentant sin. They were His Church already, and He desired to commune with them, but they needed to confess their sins in keeping with true repentance. Jesus loved them, and He was correcting them by calling out their sinful behavior.

The command for Christians to continue to turn from their sins was a common command of Jesus and the Apostles. For instance, Peter commanded the elect: "As obedient children, do not be conformed to the passions of your former ignorance, but as he who called you is holy, you also be holy in all your conduct, since it is written, 'You shall be holy, for I am holy.'"[251] Paul commanded the believers in Rome, "Do not be conformed to this world, but be transformed by the renewal of your mind, that by testing you may discern what is the will of God, what is good and acceptable and perfect."[252] However, the point of Peter, Paul, and Jesus with these particular statements was not the conversion of the lost, but the sanctification of the saved. Jesus was not using the door-heart metaphor to teach Christians how to evangelize. Regarding this point, Dr. Sproul writes:

> Usually the evangelist applies this text to the unconverted, saying: 'Jesus is knocking at the door of your heart. If you open the door, then He will come in.' In the original saying, however, Jesus directed His remarks to the church. It was not an evangelistic appeal.
>
> So what? The point is that seeking is something that unbelievers do not do on their own. The unbeliever will not seek. . . Seeking is the business of believers. . . Seeking is the result of faith, not the cause of it.[253]

---

[250] Revelation 3:19
[251] 1 Peter 1: 14-16
[252] Romans 12:2
[253] R. C. Sproul, "Is Jesus Knocking at the Heart of the Unbeliever?" Ligonier Ministries, February 10, 2017, accessed April 19, 2017, http://www.ligonier.org/blog/jesus-knocking-heart-unbeliever/.

In the manner that Revelation 3:20 is often interpreted, the omnipotent creator of the world, Jesus, the Son of God who has all authority in heaven and earth is portrayed as powerless to save. He is left outside, hoping, and praying that someone will let Him in. If Jesus wanted into a door, even the fictitious door of one's heart, there is no power anywhere that could keep Him out, even if a doorknob was missing.

Perhaps, the only scripture that can be referenced as to a door being opened to someone's heart would be found in the sixteenth chapter of Acts:

> One who heard us was a woman named Lydia, from the city of Thyatira, a seller of purple goods, who was a worshiper of God. The Lord opened her heart to pay attention to what was said by Paul. And after she was baptized, and her household as well, she urged us, saying, 'If you have judged me to be faithful to the Lord, come to my house and stay.' And she prevailed upon us. (Acts 16:14-15)

Lydia, did have the door of her heart opened, was saved, and even baptized; but, was this due to her opening her heart to let Jesus come in? No. As Luke records, "The Lord opened her heart." In the example of Lydia's conversion, we find that Paul proclaimed the gospel to Lydia, and the Lord opened her heart so that she would believe the gospel. One thing that is definitely not found in Lydia's conversion, is any mention of her opening the door to let Jesus come into her heart. In fact, it is the exact opposite. As we see throughout scripture, God sovereignly calls people to Himself for salvation. He does this through the gospel and the inner working of the Holy Spirit. The doors that people have put up to keep Him out are no obstacle to Him, for as Jesus said, "All that the Father gives me will come to me."[254]

---

[254] John 6:37

Summary: "Jesus is knocking on the door to your heart. Will you let Him in?", does appear to be evangelistic when the passage is removed from its original context, but in context, with the proper audience in mind, we can see that it was written to people who already had salvation. There is no gospel presented in this statement or the question. The gospel focus is also shifted from the person and work of Christ, to a door and a person who is opening that door to Jesus. What is this door, and how does the opening of it save one's soul from the wrath of God?

Not only is this question confusing, but it can also lead someone to agree to do something that does not equate to salvation, yet they now believe themselves to be saved. What if we get the non-believers to agree to open their hearts' doors to Jesus? Does this mean that they have heard the gospel, repented of their sins, and have believed in the person and work of Jesus Christ for their salvation? As you can see, using this passage for evangelism could be quite confusing to the hearer.

In the end, we do not have a single biblical example of Jesus or the Apostles telling people to do such a thing to be saved. This is another example of words that supposedly speak of salvation, but upon closer examination, do not.

Chapter 20

INSTRUCTING A PERSON TO TELL JESUS TO COME INTO HIS LIFE.

As with the other statements, we are forced to ask if this one contains anything pertaining to the gospel. This type of extreme shorthand evangelism, has become quite popular but, truthfully, it does not convey any information that could be considered the gospel. It is an empty statement. There is no foundation laid regarding personal sin, the need for repentance and forgiveness, or even the need for salvation. Simply put, this is not the gospel, and even if the gospel was presented to a person, such a statement as, "Now all you must do is tell Jesus to come into your life, and you'll be saved," would not be an appropriate response to the gospel. Nowhere in the Bible are we commanded to tell anyone to ask Jesus to come into his or her life.

Summary: This statement is theological vacuous. In and of itself, it lacks any gospel components, and it could mean just about anything one could imagine. We must remember that the gospel is a real message, and our job is to tell that message. As Michael Horton writes in his book, *Christless Christianity*:

> What distinguishes Christianity at its heart is not its moral code but its story—a story of a Creator who, although rejected by those he created in his image, stooped to reconcile them to himself through his Son.

This is not a story about the individual's heavenward progress but the recital of historical events of God's incarnation, atonement, resurrection, ascension, and return and the exploration of their rich significance. At its heart, this story is a gospel: the Good News that God has reconciled us to himself in Christ.[255]

Instead of instructing someone to tell Jesus to come into his or her life, we should take our time to share the details of the gospel and the clear command to believe in that gospel.

---

[255] Michael Scott Horton, *Christless Christianity: The Alternative Gospel of the American Church* (Grand Rapids, MI: Baker Books, 2008), 103.

Chapter 21

---✣---

DO YOU WANT TO BECOME A CHRISTIAN?

At first glance, this seems to be a great way to speak of salvation, since the word "Christian" is right there in the question? However, this type of question would require much explanation since the word *Christian* is so loosely defined these days. We should never assume that others define the word *Christian* as we do. For example, as a Christian, you may attempt to witness to others by telling them that you became a Christian as a teenager, and now you love telling others about how they can become Christians themselves. However, what you as a Christian might think that you are communicating with them may not be getting communicated at all. You might think that he or she already has heard the gospel of God and knows that when you say the word "Christian," that you mean a person who has been saved from their sins by Jesus Christ. However, the term, without being explained, may not convey as much as you think. The hearer of such a question about becoming a Christian might believe that you are asking them to try to be a better person, stop some bad habit or that you want them to start attending church.

Of course, there is nothing wrong with using the word *Christian*. One of the titles given to those who believed in Jesus early in church history was "Christian."[256] However, it is a term

---

[256] Acts 11:26; Acts 26:2; 1 Peter 3:16

used to describe those who have believed in the gospel, but it is not used, in and of itself, to evangelize. We do not find any examples of Jesus or the Apostles asking people to become Christians. Instead, we see them proclaiming the gospel and commanding people to repent and believe in it, and once they do, they are referred to as Christians.

Summary: Do not put the cart before the horse. Proclaim the gospel and allow it to transform lost sinners into Christians, but don't expect anyone to agree to want to be a Christian before the gospel is even shared. Keep in mind that the word *Christian* has a multitude of meanings these days. Never assume that people have the same definitions to the words that you are using when witnessing. The word *Christian* might be the equivalent of a *believer* to you, but to others, it might just mean a person who is kind, goes to church or walks the elderly across the street.

Chapter 22

HAVE YOU INVITED (OR ACCEPTED) JESUS TO BE YOUR PERSONAL SAVIOR?

This evangelistic question seems to have a lot of potential. After all, it does have the word "Jesus" in it, and the word "personal" and, to top it off, it even uses the word "Savior." What more could you possibly want in an evangelistic question? However, upon closer inspection, as in the other examples, this statement puts the lost sinner in a position that, according to the Bible, does not exist. It has a way of putting the creature in charge of telling the Creator what to do. As A. W. Tozer observed:

> The whole 'Accept Christ' attitude is likely to be wrong. It shows Christ [appealing] to us rather than us to Him. Instead, the way it is worded puts Jesus in a position of weakness and man in a position of strength. It makes Him stand hat-in-hand awaiting our verdict on Him, instead of our kneeling with troubled hearts awaiting His verdict on us.'[257]

The emphasis of this style of evangelism is on what the person does to accomplish salvation rather than on Jesus and what He does to bring about our salvation. We are recipients of salvation,

---

[257] A. W. Tozer, *That Incredible Christian* (Harrisburg, PA: Christian Publications, 1964), 18.

but we do not save ourselves, nor do we contribute. As J. Gresham Machen wrote, "Such a wonderful change is not the work of man; faith itself is given us by the Spirit of God. Christians never make themselves Christians, but they are made Christians by God."[258]

Salvation is not based on human effort, but on the unmerited favor of God. The concept of grace is difficult to wrap our minds around because we are used to working for what we get; however, we must guard against a work and reward mentality from slipping into our communication of the gospel. The word *invite* is one such word that attributes some of the *work* of salvation to the individual rather than the whole of salvation to Christ alone. The "invite" or "accept" terminology puts the person in the driver's seat of their salvation in a way that is contrary to what we find in Scripture.

Instead of depicting humanity as utterly helpless in rescuing itself, the words "invite" or "accept" have a way reversing the roles in salvation by portraying God in a position of weakness, and man in the position of power. John MacArthur writes:

> The Western church has subtly changed the thrust of the gospel. Instead of exhorting sinners to repent, evangelicalism in our society asks the unsaved to 'accept Christ.' That makes sinners sovereign and puts Christ at their disposal. In effect it puts Christ on trial and hands the judge's robes and gavel to the inquirer—precisely opposite of what should be. Ironically, people who ought to be concerned about whether Christ will accept them are being told by Christians that it is the sinner's prerogative to 'accept Christ.' This modified gospel depicts change of heart as 'decision for Christ' rather than a life-transforming change of heart involving genuine faith, repentance, surrender, and rebirth unto newness of life.[259]

We must remember that God is God: the eternal, holy, omnipotent, sovereign, creator, and final judge. God needs nothing and,

---

[258] J. Gresham Machen, *What Is Faith?* (Edinburgh: Banner of Truth Trust, 1991), 203-204.

[259] MacArthur, *The Gospel According to the Apostles*, 197.

as He is sufficient unto Himself, He is not helplessly waiting and wishing that His creation will accept or invite Him into their lives. In all actuality, we are the ones who need to be accepted by, and invited to, Him. We are the ones who need His forgiveness so that we can be accepted. We are the ones who, like Adam and Eve, have sinned against Him, and need to be brought back into His blessed presence.

Is this style of evangelism used by Jesus or the Apostles? After examining the New Testament, author David Platt writes,

> . . . you will not find an emphasis on accepting Jesus. We have taken the infinitely glorious Son of God, who endured the infinitely terrible wrath of God and who now reigns as the infinitely worthy Lord of all, and we have reduced him to a poor, puny Savior who is just begging for us to accept him. Accept him? Do we really think Jesus needs our acceptance? Don't we need him?[260]

As we look at the Scriptures, we do not see such an invitation. Instead, we see commands to believe in the gospel. Mark records one such example in his Gospel, ". . . Jesus came into Galilee, proclaiming the gospel of God, and saying, 'The time is fulfilled, and the kingdom of God is at hand; repent and believe in the gospel.'"[261] Jesus commanded the people to repent and believe, but he never begged them to invite Him in. We also see this in the sermons of the Apostles—in Acts, for example—when the Philippian jailer asked Paul and Silas, "'Sirs, what must I do to be saved?' And they said, 'Believe in the Lord Jesus, and you will be saved, you and your household.'"[262] We see this type of language in the teaching of Christ and by the Apostles. The call to salvation is not for the hearers to "invite," but the command for salvation is to "believe."

---

[260] David Platt, *Radical: Taking Back Your Faith from the American Dream* (Colorado Springs, CO: Multnomah Books, 2010), 37.
[261] Mark 1:14-15
[262] Acts 16:30-31

PERSONAL SAVIOR?

Beyond just looking at how the words *invite* or *accept* are used, it is also interesting how the phrase "personal Savior" is used today with such endearment by many Christians, but how others can easily misunderstand it. While, "personal Savior," may imply to a Christian that he has been reconciled to God by Christ, we must be careful that "personal Savior" does not come across as relativism. In other words, it is possible for our non-believers to interpret, "personal Savior" as the Christian saying, "I have found a good Savior for me, but whatever you choose is fine as well." Jesus is indeed each believer's personal Savior, but we must emphasize that He is also the only Savior of anyone who is to be saved. Walter Chantry, editor of *Banner of Truth* magazine, in his book *Today's Gospel: Authentic or Synthetic*, writes:

> Our ears have grown accustomed to hearing men told to 'Accept Jesus as your personal Saviour,' a form of words which is not found in Scripture. It has become an empty phrase. These may be precious words to the Christian—'personal Saviour.' But they are wholly inadequate to instruct a sinner in the way of eternal life.[263]

To some, "Jesus is my personal Savior," could be taken as, "Well that is nice for you, but I am going to look for a different religious leader that fits my personal needs." It is important to communicate that Jesus is the one and only possible way of salvation. As the Apostle Peter said, "… there is salvation in no one else, for there is no other name under heaven given among men by which we must be saved."[264] While our salvation by Jesus is indeed personal, we need to be careful that we avoid accidentally teaching that Jesus is just our own personal preference. We want to make sure that all who hear about our Savior understand that there

---

[263] Walter Chantry J., *Today's Gospel: Authentic or Synthetic?* (London: Banner of Truth Trust, 1970), 48-49.
[264] Acts 4:12

"…is one God, and there is one mediator between God and men, the man Christ Jesus."[265]

Summary: While this phrase is popular and seems to sound Christian, it does need some help and correction. If we want to stay faithful to salvation that is by grace alone, we must be clear that Jesus is the one and only Savior of the world and the work of salvation is His to do. What if instead of saying, "Have you invited/accepted Jesus as your personal Savior," we said something like, "Do you know who Jesus is? Do you know what He has accomplished so that you may be accepted by God?" Such a change keeps God in the position of authority and reveals our helplessness. This change still uses "acceptance" terminology, but it shows that we are the ones in need of God's acceptance through the atoning work of Christ rather than by anything we have done to earn it.

As Christians, we need to put more thought into the wording of our evangelistic questions. It is not wrong to use questions to witness; however, the questions do need to be biblically correct and speak truthfully of the gospel. While it is impossible to get the full gospel into one or two questions, we do want such questions to at least contain truths of the gospel which can lead to a broader proclamation and discussion of the gospel.

---

[265] 1 Timothy 2:5

Chapter 23

HAVE YOU SAID THE SINNER'S PRAYER?

Many evangelists, preachers, professing Christians, and evangelistic tracts often imply that by repeating a specific prayer, a person can be saved. This technique has become so popular that to utter a word against "The Sinner's Prayer" would be deemed heresy by many professing Christians. However, we must realize that there is absolutely no record of "The Sinner's Prayer" in the Bible. Neither Jesus nor the Apostles even hint that such a prayer exists. Jesus nor the Apostles ever say anything remotely similar to, "Please bow your head, close their eyes, repeat this prayer after me, and you'll be saved."

"The Sinner's Prayer" sounds formal and necessary, but where do we find this specific prayer taught or modeled in the Word of God? Well, we don't find it anywhere in Scripture, nor do we find it in early church history. This type of evangelistic response was not created until relatively recent times. Also, of interest, is the fact that there is not one set version of "The Sinner's Prayer," but there are many versions of such prayers in circulation. Listen to or read any of the versions of the so-called "Sinner's Prayer," and you will understand that they differ significantly. As David Platt has observed,

> Our attempt to reduce this gospel to a shrink-wrapped presentation that persuades someone to say or pray the

right things back to us no longer seems appropriate. That is why none of these man-made catchphrases are in the Bible. You will not find a verse in Scripture where people are told to 'bow your heads, close your eyes, and repeat after me.' You will not find a place where a superstitious sinner's prayer is even mentioned.[266]

Even though we do not have a single biblical example of such a practice being used, today it seems to be unheard of to suggest that a sinner could be saved without uttering some version of the sinner's prayer. Many probably wonder if salvation can even occur if the sinner's prayer has not been prayed. After all, isn't it during the prayer that a person is saved?

In the unlikely event that you are unfamiliar with a sinner's prayer, let me explain how it is often used. Towards the close of an evangelistic meeting or church service, or at the end of a gospel tract, it is common for instructions to be given to the listener or reader to repeat a specific prayer for salvation. This is commonly referred to as "The Sinner's Prayer." Once a person finishes repeating the prayer, he or she is assured that salvation has occurred.

Let us look at an example of one such prayer. This example comes from the back page of a copy of the New Testament that is used by a major denomination for evangelistic projects.

ARE YOU READY TO RECEIVE GOD'S INVITATION TO ETERNAL LIFE AND HOPE?

If so, please pray the following prayer, Remember, it is not the words you use, but the attitude of your heart. If you pray this prayer sincerely Jesus will come into your life and in Him, you will have eternal life and hope.

"Dear God, I know that Jesus is Your Son and that He died on the cross and was raised from the dead. Because I have sinned and need forgiveness, I ask Jesus to come

---

[266] David Platt, *Radical: Taking Back Your Faith from the American Dream* (Colorado Springs, CO: Multnomah Books, 2010), 37.

into my heart. I am willing to change the direction of my life by acknowledging Jesus as my Lord and Savior, and by turning away from my sins. Thank You for giving me forgiveness, eternal life, and hope. In Jesus' name. Amen." [267]

Well, what do you think? Do you approve of the gospel content and the response to the gospel that is given in this sinner's prayer? Here are some questions to think about regarding this sinner's prayer and others that you come across.

1. Was the true gospel presented before initiating the prayer, or is the prayer being used as the gospel presentation?
2. Is the emphasis on confession, repentance, and belief in the gospel?
3. Is there a response to the gospel that is not commanded in the Bible, such as asking Jesus to come into your heart, or even having to recite a specific prayer to be saved?
4. Is belief in the gospel emphasized for salvation or is saying the words of the prayer emphasized for salvation?
5. Is salvation presented by grace alone in Christ alone, or could the prayer be viewed as a contributing work that earns salvation?
6. Where does the assurance of salvation rest? Is it on Jesus Christ and His completed work, or is the assurance on prayer?
7. Is the prayer being turned into a mandatory, and extra-biblical step for salvation?

---

[267] *The Invitation: New Testament* (Nashville, TN: Holman Bible Publishers, 2006), 243

Such sinner's prayers commonly include an assuring statement that affirms a person's salvation upon proper repetition of the prayer. This assertion can be seen in the last sentence of instruction that precedes the example sinner's prayer just given, "If you pray this prayer sincerely Jesus will come into your life." Such assurance can be dangerous because the words of the prayer have been given power that they do not possess. Once again, humanity is wrongly given the reigns over salvation, and God is merely at his bidding. Instead of a sinner relying on the person and work of Jesus Christ, the sinner is told to rely on his or her own words to command the Creator of the universe to come into his life. Such prayers suggest that if the individual will "Just repeat this prayer," then like a magical incantation, God will save them, or even worse they have now saved themselves. There is more to conversion than just getting someone to recite certain words in a particular order.

The other day, I spoke to a woman who oversaw her denomination's countywide evangelistic outreach. I had known this woman for quite some time, so I felt comfortable talking to her about their evangelistic plan. She informed me that they were going to attempt to knock on every single door in their county in an attempt to reach the entire county for Jesus. Apparently, lots of energy and volunteers would go into such a monumental task. I then asked her what the outreach group planned to do on their door-to-door evangelistic campaign, once someone opened the door. Sadly, she told me that it was their goal "To get as many people as possible to repeat 'The Sinner's Prayer.'" Notice that she did not say that it was their goal to "share the gospel," or to "tell them about Jesus," but to get them to say, "The Sinner's Prayer." It became apparent, after listening to her talk, that she genuinely believed that the repetition of this prayer would result in salvation.

After listening to her plan to evangelize the entire county, I applauded her zeal, boldness, and organizational skills. However, I also politely asked her a few questions that I hoped would cause her more introspection of their evangelistic strategy. For example, "Okay, so if your group succeeds in getting people to say the words of this prayer, will they then be saved?", and "What exactly are the words that save the person?" and, "What if a person does not know who Jesus is or what He has done to accomplish salvation when he or she says the prayer? Is he or she still saved?" After asking her such questions, and conversing for a while she began to realize that there was something quite significant missing from their evangelistic strategy, and the forgotten something was no small matter: it was the gospel. Instead of relying on God to draw people to Himself through the proclamation of the gospel, she, and her team were relying on their ability to get people to recite a prayer.

As another example, recently I was visiting a church where I, once again, witnessed a sinner's prayer being used in a dangerous manner. I watched a young man walk down the aisle during a time of Invitation and then watched as that same young man was taken back to be prepared for baptism. Within a matter of four minutes, the young man went from walking forward to being baptized. My concern over this young man's rapid baptism (knowing that the gospel had not been presented during the sermon that specific day), led me to ask the pastor to explain what steps he took to ensure, as best as one can, that the people he baptized were truly saved. He smiled, and said, "Well, that's easy. I just have them say 'The Sinner's Prayer' right before I baptize them." I was completely shocked that this pastor who had been in ministry for decades had empowered "The Sinner's Prayer" as if it was the "power of God unto salvation" rather than the gospel.

SO, SHOULD YOU LEAD SOMEONE IN "THE SINNER' PRAYER?"

If a person has heard the true gospel, and if by the grace of God, he or she is willing to confess, repent, and believe in the gospel for his or her salvation, then what is there left to do? Is a formal sinner's prayer required to seal the deal? Of course not, and to make it such a prayer necessary for salvation is to add an extra component to the gospel that God did not include. No specific sinner's prayer is needed to receive salvation. If a person has believed in the gospel and repented of their sin, then salvation has already come.

So, what do you do with someone who has just heard the gospel, believed in it and repented of his or her sins? It does seem to be an appropriate time to pray with them, but not "The Sinner's Prayer." Instead, use this as an opportunity to lead them in a prayer of thanking God for salvation, or maybe a prayer for strength to overcome sin and to pursue Godly living now that they are saved. This type of evangelism helps the new believer to resist the temptation to attribute his or her salvation to a prayer and to see that salvation has supernaturally come to them by the unmerited grace of God. We have nothing in and of ourselves to contribute to our salvation, and that includes, "The Sinner's Prayer."

Summary: Though many Christians often view an official sinner's prayer as a *requirement* for salvation, there is just *no* biblical requirement of such a prayer ever given by neither Jesus nor His Apostles. Since a specific sinner's prayer is never used, commanded, or even recommended in the Bible, we must question its necessity in today's evangelism. Moreover, if this scripted prayer has been added to the gospel, as an extra step that must be completed by the individual to secure salvation, then we are drifting perilously away from the biblical salvation that is by grace through faith. When sinful man attempts to add anything to the gospel, we can be sure that the addition will put mankind in the position of deserving merit rather than desperately needing grace.

God did not provide a specific prayer for us to pray for salvation or a prayer for us to make others say for them to be saved. Instead, He gave us something to be believed: the gospel. We must be cautious to present the gospel correctly and to also correctly instruct people as to what they are to do with the gospel.

Did you say "The Sinner's Prayer?" If so, this does not mean that you *are not* saved, but it also does not mean that you *are* saved. People have been saved who have said a sinner's prayer, and people have remained unsaved after repeating a sinner's prayer. Is your faith in Christ, or is your faith in "The Sinner's Prayer?" This is important, because faith in prayer does not save, but faith in Christ most certainly does. Now, if you have said a sinner's prayer and did have faith in Jesus Christ and His work as the object of your salvation, then you have been saved, not because of the prayer, but in spite of the prayer. Your salvation was a supernatural gift from God. It is God who regenerated you, made you aware of your sins, the need of a Savior, and gave you faith to believe the gospel of Jesus Christ for salvation: to God be the glory.

Chapter 24

DO YOU KNOW THAT GOD LOVES YOU?

This statement can easily be taken by the non-Christian to mean that God already loves them with a saving love without them ever repenting of sin and believing in God's Savior. This can be confusing to a non-Christian and even doctrinally misleading. While the Christian may be attempting to tell the person of the need for Christ, by applying the love of God to the sinner pre-emptively, they have removed the persons need of the gospel. A non-believer could hear such a statement of God's love and easily assume, "Well if God already loves me, then why do I need to change from my sinful ways? Why do I even need Jesus or need to be saved if God already loves me?" Writing on this matter, James Montgomery Boice wrote:

> Apart from Christ everyone is at war with God, regardless of what some may believe or say. We are God's enemies. We resist him in every way we possibly can; we would kill him if we could. And that is what we did, when God became man in the person of Christ! Jesus' death has brought God and those whom God has given him together. Paul told the Romans that while 'we were God's enemies, we were reconciled to him through the death of his son.' (Rom. 5:10)[268]

---

[268] Boice and Philip Graham Ryken, *The Doctrines of Grace*, 121.

Can telling an unrepentant person that, "God loves you," be considered a valid evangelistic method when the Bible tells us that the unrepentant person is under God's wrath? Paul said that we are "by nature children of wrath."[269] Paul also wrote that, "All have sinned and fallen short of the glory of God," and that "the wrath of God is revealed from heaven against all ungodliness and unrighteousness of men, who by their unrighteousness suppress the truth."[270] Similarly, John writes, "Whoever believes in the Son has eternal life; whoever does not obey the Son shall not see life, but the wrath of God remains on him."[271]

The whole point of salvation is that we have sinned against the Holy God who created us, and we will suffer wrath for all of eternity because we rightly deserve it. We deserve His wrath because we have rebelled against the Sovereign Ruler of all Creation. As Paul writes, "For although they knew God, they did not honor him as God, or give thanks to him, but they became futile in their thinking, and their foolish hearts were darkened."[272] He goes on to say, "There will be tribulation and distress for every human being who does evil…For there is no partiality with God."[273] The whole purpose of the gospel is to announce to sinners under the wrath of God how they can be rescued. They are in extreme danger, and they will face an almighty, holy, righteous, all-powerful, judge one day. As the Psalmist wrote, "God is a righteous judge, and a God who feels indignation every day. If a man does not repent, God will whet his sword; he has bent and readied his bow; he has prepared for him his deadly weapons, making his arrows fiery shafts."[274]

When Christians begin their evangelism efforts with, "God loves you," they are skipping the wrath of God against sinners, and the work of Jesus Christ to remove that wrath, and are presumptu-

---

[269] Ephesians 2:3
[270] Romans 1:18;3.23
[271] John 3:36
[272] Romans 1:21
[273] Romans 2:9-11
[274] Psalm 7:11-13

ously announcing God's love upon people before the good news of salvation through Jesus Christ is given. Paul Washer writes:

> As stewards of the gospel of Jesus Christ, we do no service to men by making light of sin, skirting around the issue, or avoiding it altogether. Men have only one problem: they are under the wrath of God because of their sin. To deny this is to deny one of the most foundational doctrines of Christianity. It is not unloving to tell men that they are sinners, but it is the grossest form of immorality not to tell them.[275]

Instead of beginning evangelism with the love of God, it would be far more biblical, as John the Baptist, Jesus, the Apostles, and many prophets demonstrated to call people to confess their sinfulness and need of forgiveness by God. We need to let the lost know that God does not love them in their unrepentant condition. He is not happy with them, and that they are, in fact, an object of His wrath.

Let the bad news be *bad*, and let the good news be *good*, and let the Holy Spirit, through the gospel of God, supernaturally work to transform people from unrepentant sinners who deserve His wrath to repentant sinners saved by grace, through faith in Jesus Christ. The importance of the gospel in salvation cannot be underestimated. As R. C. Sproul has written:

> People are not excited about the gospel because they tacitly assume that there is no great need for it. We are told that God loves everybody unconditionally; that He accepts us just as we are. If that were true, we would have no need to flee from our guilt and sin to embrace the gospel.[276]

---

[275] Washer, *The Gospel's Power and Message*, 76.
[276] R. Mohler Albert et al., *Feed My Sheep: A Passionate Plea for Preaching* (Orlando, FL: Reformation Trust Pub., 2008), 80.

Proclaiming, "God loves you" to people that are under God's wrath is much like what the false prophets did during the days of Jeremiah. The false prophets told the people that they were at peace with God, even though God was angry with them. Instead of telling people the truth about their sin and its offense to God, they comforted them with a kind sounding but an untrue message. In speaking about the false prophets, God said, "They have healed the wound of my people lightly, saying, 'Peace, peace,' when there is no peace."[277] The false prophets fooled the people by telling them that they were at peace with God, but they were not at peace with God. In fact, His wrath was about to be poured out upon them. Let us not be the voice of false prophets in our day, by saying "peace, peace" or "love, love" when God says the opposite. The Word of God is clear that those who hate God and who have rejected His Son will die in their sins and face eternal judgment and punishment unless they repent.

As Christians, we are particularists and not universalists. In other words, we know that the Bible says that all people are not, and will not be saved. There will be some in heaven and some in hell, which means that we believe that only a particular people will be saved. The opposite view is universalism, which is the view that all people will be saved no matter what they believe, even if they reject salvation by Christ. Many Christians attempt to witness in a way that comes dangerously close to presenting universal salvation of all humankind. J. I. Packer, warning of such evangelism writes, "But if we start by affirming that God has a saving love for all, and Christ died a saving death for all, and yet balk at becoming universalists, there is nothing else that we can say."[278] God's saving love is not automatically given to all humans, but it is automatically given to the God-man: Jesus Christ, the Son of God. God loves His Son and all of those who have been saved by the Son. The beauty of the gospel is that we do not have to remain children of wrath, but

---

[277] Jeremiah 6:14
[278] J. I. Packer, introduction, in *The Death of Death in the Death of Christ*, by John Owen (Edinburgh: Banner of Truth Trust, 1983), http://www.the-highway.com/Death.html.

through Christ, we can become children of God and objects of his mercy, compassion, love, and grace.

We must not take one attribute of God, such as His love, and turn that into His only attribute as if God is just a big heart in the sky. This would be a severe distortion of God as He has revealed Himself in His Word. Yet, this is often the false image of God we present when we evangelize. Well-meaning Christians will often present only the love of God to witness because love is much less offensive than wrath. Even the unregenerate will proclaim God's love as the hope they have for their eternal destiny. It is common to hear an unsaved person say, "I believe that God is love and a loving God would never send anyone to hell." A wrong gospel presentation can cause people to have a completely different god in mind than the God revealed in Scripture. Mark Dever writes:

> If a right theology of God provides the framework, or grid, for right teaching, then a focus on the gospel provides the center, or point, of right teaching. As we have seen, false teaching about God separates God's people from him and builds a community around a being who does not exist. Furthermore, if the God preached is not offended by sin and does not judge sinners, then the gospel itself is short-circuited. People are lied to in a manner which imperils their salvation. The right teaching of the true church, therefore, centers itself upon a right understanding of the gospel.[279]

Summary: We must not announce God's love at the exclusion of the person and work of Jesus Christ. God's love is for Christ and all of those who are found in Christ. If we tell people that God loves them before they are found in Christ, we have deceived them, created a false image of God, and have removed the bad news that makes the good news: good. We must communicate the biblical truth of both the seriousness of sin and the solution that is found only in Jesus Christ.

---

[279] Mark Dever, *The Church: The Gospel Made Visible* (Nashville, TN: B & H Academic, 2012), 26.

Chapter 25

GOD LOVES YOU AND HAS A GREAT PLAN FOR YOUR LIFE.

If God loves you, then it just makes sense that God has a great plan for your life, right? Here, once again, we must ask if we are giving the benefits of salvation out before someone is even a child of God. If an individual is rejecting God, rejecting the Savior, and living in sin, does God still have a plan for her or his life? Of course He does, but it is not the "great plan," of blessing that the individual may have in mind. The Apostle Paul wrote of such a person:

> Do you suppose, O man—you who judge those who practice such things and yet do them yourself—that you will escape the judgment of God? Or do you presume on the riches of his kindness and forbearance and patience, not knowing that God's kindness is meant to lead you to repentance? But because of your hard and impenitent heart you are storing up wrath for yourself on the day of wrath when God's righteous judgment will be revealed.
>
> He will render to each one according to his works: to those who by patience in well-doing seek for glory and honor and immortality, he will give eternal life; but for those who are self-seeking and do not obey the truth, but obey unrighteousness, there will be wrath and fury. (Rom. 2:3-8)

When we tell people the gospel, we have no guarantee that the person we are witnessing to will believe the gospel or reject it. Since this is true, we should not guarantee them what God has not yet given them. Pastor John Cheeseman saw the dangers of such evangelistic techniques and even warned against the use of them:

> The benefits enjoyed by the Christian — joy, peace, fulfillment, meaning in life — are often made the ground of an appeal to the unsaved. This is, of course, a motive well-designed to lead the natural man to 'make a decision' for Christ, but it is misleading when divorced from the preaching of the wrath of God against sin, the need for a complete change of nature and the demand for true repentance, all of which are found in the New Testament gospel.[280]

Scripture is clear that God does love those for whom Christ died and does have a marvelous plan for all who are saved. As Paul says, "And we know that for those who love God all things work together for good, for those who are called according to his purpose" (Rom. 8:28). However, it is wrong to bestow upon an unsaved person the blessings and gifts of God that are only given to those who are found in Christ.[281] As Shane Rosenthal, executive producer of the White Horse Inn national radio program, writes:

> Effective, Christ-centered, evangelism must therefore be based on the 'facts' of Christianity, not the 'effects.' When you think about this, it makes perfect sense. Just about any religion or ideology can make a difference in a person's life, and yet, all of these different belief systems cannot be simultaneously true.[282]

---

[280] John Cheeseman, *The Grace of God in the Gospel* (London: Banner of Truth Trust, 1972)

[281] See Ephesians. 1:3-10

[282] Shane Rosenthal, "When the Message Obscures the Message," Reformation Ink, 1995, Theological Training, accessed February 20, 2012, http://homepage.mac.com/rosenthal/reformationink/classic.htm.

God's love and blessings are not guaranteed for those who have not repented and believed in God's one and only Savior. Besides, we must not mislead people into professing Christ as their Savior just to try to get what they feel will be a "great plan for their life."

Summary: Is the gospel of God being shared in the statement, "God loves you and has a great plan for your life?" Not at all. Instead, people are told prematurely that a better life waits because God loves them. What gospel components are included in this type of witnessing? Seemingly none. What does such a change of plans even mean? Is there a call to admit sinfulness, to repent, and to believe in Jesus Christ? Even if someone does decide they want to give God's plan a chance, whatever that means, is he or she doing so just for personal gain or because he or she loves God and desires to live in obedience to Him for His glory? In his book, *God Has a Wonderful Plan For Your Life: The Myth of the Modern Message*, evangelist and author Ray Comfort, writes:

> Those who look to the cross as a token of God's love will never doubt His steadfast devotion to them, regardless of their circumstances. But those who come to Christ seeking a wonderful life will think that their happiness is evidence of God's love, and therefore when trials come and their happiness leaves they may think that God has forsaken them—or worse, that He doesn't exist.[283]

This phrase, "God loves you and has a great plan for your life" should *not* be used for evangelism. Instead, it should be reserved for those who are already saved as a reminder of God's love and His plan to complete the salvation that He has begun.[284] Simply put, no one gets the love of God or the blessings of God without first believing the gospel. It is only after one has repented and believed in the gospel that they can have the assurance of God's great redemptive plan for their lives.

---

[283] Ray Comfort, *God Has a Wonderful Plan for Your Life: The Myth of the Modern Message* (Bellflower, CA: Living Waters Publications, 2010), 43.
[284] Hebrews 12:2

Chapter 26

DO YOU HAVE A PERSONAL TESTIMONY?

The word, "testimony" has become shorthand for one's personal experience of a life change through Christianity. The gospel does change a person's life; however, the person's life does not become the gospel. This is a point of which some Christians seem to be confused. The results of the gospel are not the gospel. For instance, people who view a Christian's changed life cannot be saved by such an observation, and a personal testimony that is based only on life improvement is indeed not the gospel.

It is quite common to hear people give their Christian testimony with little emphasis on the details of the gospel that supposedly saved them. Instead, most of the focus is usually placed on his or her changed behavior. I remember as a teenager hearing a guest speaker share his testimony for about an hour. He told story after story about how he was involved in drugs, alcohol, girls, and breaking the law, but after he got saved, everything changed. There was no gospel account presented. He did not share a single component of the gospel. The emphasis of his testimony was entirely on the changes that he had experienced in his life now that he was "saved." While these changes were good and should accompany true salvation, an improved lifestyle is not the gospel. Shane Rosenthal writes:

Witnessing to others about Christ must be theologically based or it will wind up being testimonial. In other words, if I don't have a solid understanding of the doctrines of Christianity, I will inevitably end up talking about the effects of religion on my life, rather than the objective message of the Gospel itself.[285]

Some Christian's testimonies have a way of promoting personal life change, more than they do the One who has changed them, Jesus Christ. As Michael Horton has written, "While the apostles testified to historical events of which they were eyewitnesses, 'giving your testimony' in evangelical Christianity today typically means talking about one's inner experience and moral transformation."[286] It is wonderful to talk about the new desires that we now have to pursue righteousness and put away sinfulness, but we should not make the effects of the gospel the most important aspect of our story. We must make the gospel the central theme of our testimony; otherwise, the hearer only gets a *feel-good* story but hears nothing about how they can be saved.

Writing about faith and testimony, the great commentator, Charles Hodge wrote:

> If faith, or our persuasion of the truths of the Bible, rests on philosophical grounds, then the door is opened for rationalism; if it rests on feeling, then it is open to mysticism. The only sure and satisfying foundation is the testimony of God, who cannot err, and who will not deceive. Faith may, therefore, be defined to be the persuasion of the truth founded on testimony. The faith of the Christian is the persuasion of the truth of the facts

---

[285] Shane Rosenthal, "When the Method Obscures the Message.," White Horse Inn, August 14, 2007, Theological Training, accessed November 01, 2016, https://www.whitehorseinn.org/.

[286] Michael Scott. Horton, *Christless Christianity: The Alternative Gospel of the American Church* (Grand Rapids, MI: Baker Books, 2008), 50.

and doctrines recorded in the Scriptures on the testimony of God.[287]

Christians must understand that evangelism is not just telling others how they can improve their lives; it is telling them about the One who changed our life by saving us, making us a new creation, and giving us the desire to live a life that glorifies and pleases Him.

Summary: Have you ever shared your testimony? If so, who was the most important person in your testimony? Was it you, or Jesus Christ? Did you share more details about yourself than you did about the gospel? Did you strive to proclaim the gospel in your testimony? Sharing a personal testimony as a method of evangelism can be done well, but only if the testimony includes the gospel. Remember your testimony does not save others, but His testimony most certainly does.

---

[287] Charles Hodge, *Systematic Theology: Vol. 3: Soteriology* (Peabody, MA: Hendrickson Publishers, 1999), 170.

Chapter 27

---※---

DO YOU WANT TO GO TO HEAVEN?

While heaven is a glorious place where all believers will be in the blessed presence of God, asking someone if they would like to go to heaven is not sharing the gospel. If you ask a person if they would rather go to heaven or hell, and they say "Heaven," does that mean that they desire salvation through Jesus Christ, or does it just mean that they like the concept of heaven better than hell? We must be careful with this line of questioning when witnessing because any human in their right mind, will always choose a beautiful place rather than a horrible place to spend eternity.

Jesus comforted his disciples with the concept of heaven when He said, "In my Father's house are many rooms. If it were not so, would I have told you that I go to prepare a place for you? And if I go and prepare a place for you, I will come again and will take you to myself, that where I am you may be also."[288] We are assured by the words of Christ that heaven is a real and wonderful place where all believers will be in the blessed presence of God. However, Jesus never used heaven to entice people to be saved. Instead, it was meant to be a source of comfort to believers. We should keep this in mind as well. Telling people about how glorious heaven is going to be is not witnessing. As Graeme Goldsworthy wrote, "telling people that they can choose either heaven or hell is not telling them the gospel."[289]

---

[288] John 14:2-3
[289] Goldsworthy, *Preaching the Whole Bible as Christian Scripture*, 95.

People are not only prone to invent various ways to get to heaven, but they are also likely to create their own concept of heaven. I can still recall from my childhood, sitting beside a 3rd grade boy named Ricky, in our Children's Sunday School Class who was asked by the teacher, "What do you think heaven will be like?" His reply was humorous, but telling of his ignorance of the matter as he said, "When I get to heaven, I think I'm going to sit on clouds while pretty girls feed me grapes." As childish and whimsical as his answer was, it reveals the selfish way that many people think of heaven. Therefore, asking people if they would like to go to heaven is basically the same as asking them if they want to go to a place where all their dreams come true. Even unsaved God-haters desire to go to their own self-created and self-centered version of heaven.

The unsaved are not interested in heaven, as revealed in Scripture. They do not desire to be in the presence of God and give Him the glory He deserves. They have no desire to spend eternity with "believers" and engage the eternal worship of the Holy One. Their only goal is to avoid the worse destination of hell. In his book, *Gospel Assurance and Warnings*, Paul Washer states:

> All of this demonstrates one powerful and irrefutable truth: everyone wants to go to heaven, but most do not want God to be there... Why would a person who has no desire for worship on earth desire to go to heaven where everything is worship? Why would those who love sin desire a place where sin cannot be found?[290]

Mark records an encounter with just such a man in chapter ten of his Gospel. A man rushed up to Jesus, knelt on the ground, and expressed his desire to go to heaven. The man said, "Good Teacher, what must I do to inherit eternal life?"[291] Since the man desired to go to heaven, then surely he will, right? What would you do if a person ran up to you and said such a thing? Would you assume that

---

[290] Paul Washer, *Gospel Assurance and Warnings* (Grand Rapids: Reformation Heritage Books, 2014), 163.
[291] Mark 10:17

this person is ready to be saved? Would you assure them of their salvation since they desire to go to heaven? Jesus made no such assumption. Jesus saw the man's desire to go to heaven as nothing more than just self-preservation. The man's desire had nothing to do with a love for God. In fact, Jesus exposed the man's soul by demonstrating that even though he wanted to go to heaven, he was unwilling to follow Jesus' directions on how to get there.[292] In the end, this *heaven seeker* was not saved; he desired heaven without the gospel, without belief, and without repentance.

Summary: Heaven is the dwelling place of God, His holy angels, and the eternal home of the truly redeemed. However, the only way to heaven is through Jesus Christ. As Jesus said of Himself, "I am the way, the truth, and the life. No one comes to the Father except through me."[293] While heaven will be unimaginably wonderful, Christians who use it to evangelize the lost sometimes tell of where Christians will spend eternity without telling them about "The Way" to get there. The desire and longing to go to heaven are insufficient to save anyone. It is not enough to convince people that they should desire to go to heaven more than hell, but they must be told of the One who can get them there.

---

[292] Matthew 6:24
[293] John 14:6

Chapter 28

COME TO THE FRONT!

    While this is not necessarily a phrase that Christians use on a day-to-day basis to evangelize, it is most likely something that we have all heard in relation to evangelism. Perhaps, you have listened to this type of language being used at large evangelistic meetings where the evangelist called people to get out of their seats, come to the front of the stage, and be saved. Or, you may even hear this type of language used every Sunday from your pastor at the end of the worship service where he calls for people to come forward and be saved during the time of the Invitation. During such time, soft music is usually played, while the evangelist or pastor stands at the front of the building and cries out something like: "Come to Jesus!", "Come now!", "Come to the front, Jesus is waiting here for you.", "Get up and come quickly!", or "He died for you. The least you can do is take a few steps towards Him."

    This style of evangelistic plea has become the focal point of almost every major evangelistic outreach of our day, and the common end of most Sunday worship services. In fact, it is so common that few people even question the method, and just assume that it has always been an essential part of Christian culture. Few Christians, evangelists, or even pastors seem to be concerned about how the Invitation began or why it is so commonly used. But, as we will see the whole "Come to the front" style of evangelism was unheard of for most of Church History, and did not become popular until recent times.

CHARLES FINNEY AND THE INVITATION.

In the middle of the nineteenth century, Charles Finney, a traveling evangelist with piercing eyes, tremendous personality, mesmerizing communication skills, and very little biblical knowledge, began the time of invitation that would soon come to be practiced at virtually every church in America. Finney became known for his incredible ability to stir up large audiences of people and get them to respond to his messages by beckoning them to come forward during his sermons. To many, it appeared that Finney had found a new method of evangelism that was extremely effective, and with the call to the front, results could be seen immediately.

Finney was successfully drawing massive audiences and seeing thousands of people come to the front for salvation. Surely this must have been a great move of God, right? Sadly, Finney's bigger-than-life personality and his magnetic ability to get people out of their seats to come to the front caused many to overlook the fact that his doctrine was fundamentally flawed.

Finney had distorted the gospel of God, substituted his own version of the gospel and was actually calling on people to believe and respond to "another gospel." Finney did not believe that man was born sinful and required a Savior for the forgiveness of sins. He rejected the biblical truth that we are saved by Christ's righteousness being applied to us. Finney also did not believe in the substitutionary atonement of Jesus Christ, nor did he see any need for it. He believed that it was impossible for Jesus Christ to die for the sins of others.[294] He even went as far as to teach that Jesus Christ's death on the cross was just a great example of selflessness, but in no way brought about salvation.[295] Finney wrote, "It is true, that the atonement, of itself, does not secure the salvation of anyone.[296] He had created a Christ who was nothing more than a moral example for people to follow, but Whose work did not and

---

[294] Charles G. Finney, *Finney's Systematic Theology*, ed. James Harris Fairchild (Grand Rapids: Eerdmans, 1976), 320-322.
[295] Ibid., 209.
[296] Ibid., 217.

could not save anyone. In fact, Christ's righteousness, Finney said, "could do no more than justify himself. It could never be imputed to us . . ."[297]

In a study of the history of American revivalism, historian Bill Leonard summarizes the emergence of the "come-forward method" as such:

> Unknown to evangelical religion before the nineteenth century, the public invitation to 'come forward' and accept Christ began in the frontier camp meetings. Sinners were exhorted to enter the 'anxious pens,' a similar area where those seeking conversion could find support and counsel. Many questioned Finney's actions, fearing that a public response smacked of works done for salvation focusing attention on outward, not inward manifestations...Soon these methods had become linked inseparably to the weekly liturgy of Protestant worship. No service was concluded without an appeal to public decision. So important was this new symbol that evangelical conversion itself is often described in the language of the invitation. Believers speak of conversion as 'walking the aisle' or 'coming forward.'[298]

The altar call has become so popular now that modern Christians just assume that this is the way that it has always been since the time of Christ. However, the new measures put into place to get people to the front of the church is a new concept that does not derive its origin from Christ, the Apostles, or even the early church. However, the invitation system is so prevalent that one would be hard-pressed to find a church that does not use some

---

[297] Charles G. Finney, *Finney's Systematic Theology*, ed. James Harris Fairchild (Grand Rapids: Eerdmans, 1976), 320-322.

[298] Bill J. Leonard, "Evangelism and Contemporary American Life," in *The Study of Evangelism: Exploring a Missional Practice of the Church*, ed. Paul Wesley Chilcote and Laceye C. Warner (Grand Rapids, MI: William B. Eerdmans Publishing Company, 2008), 105.

form of Finney's "altar call" methodology. As Michael Horton writes:

> Sharing roots in Finney's revivalism, perhaps evangelical and liberal Protestantism are not that far apart after all. His 'new measures,' like today's Church Growth Movement, made human choices and emotions the center of the church's ministry, ridiculed theology, and replaced the preaching of Christ with the preaching of conversion.[299]

WHAT'S AT THE FRONT ANYWAY?

So, have you ever wondered what is at the front of the church that is *not* at the back or side of the church for salvation? Truthfully, there is no square footage of a church that someone must go to be saved. God could save a person no matter if they walked to the back, side, front, or even remain seated. Yet, countless pastors and evangelist promote the *front* as the place to come to be saved as if it is a means of salvation. What does walking forward have to do with one believing the gospel of God? Does physical movement somehow aid in salvation? Is there some connection between being saved by Christ and walking forward while music is playing at the end of church service? Regarding the proper response to evangelism, Mark Dever writes:

> Once people have heard the truth about their sin and God's holiness, God's love in Christ, and Christ's death and resurrection for our justification, the message calls out for response. And what is that response? Is it to walk down an aisle? Is it to fill out a card or to lift up a hand? Is it to make an appointment to see the preacher or to decide to be baptized and join the church? While

---

[299] Michael Horton, "Sola Gratia," in *After Darkness, Light Distinctives Of Reformed Theology; Essays In Honor Of R.C. Sproul* (Presbyterian & Reformed Pub, 2004), 125.

any of those things may be involved, none is absolutely necessary. The response to this good news is, as Paul preached, to repent and believe.[300]

It is not just pastors and evangelists who use this terminology. Many professing Christians describe their salvation with such an action as "going to the front," or "walking the aisle" as well. Such Christians often speak of their physical response of "going forward" as if such activity is an essential element of their salvation. For example, it would not be uncommon to hear a testimony like this, "I remember when I was twelve years old at Vacation Bible School. The pastor told all the kids to come forward to receive Christ at Vacation Bible School, and I did. That was the day that I was saved." Though a person using this style of testimony is most likely attempting to share his or her salvation experience genuinely, he or she has failed to emphasize anything about the gospel. If this testimony is analyzed by the words shared, it would be easy for someone to assume that walking forward at church equals salvation.

This is a common mistake of Christians living in a "come to the front" era. In supposedly, telling others about our testimony, we often put the emphasis on the walk forward, instead of the message of the gospel. To an unbeliever, it would be easy for them to assume that "going forward" is what a person does to be saved. We must continually remind ourselves that both the words we use to define the gospel and the words we use to describe the proper response to the gospel are essential. As one of the greatest defenders of the gospel, pastor, and author, James Montgomery Boice wrote:

> When evangelicals think of evangelism, rather than thinking first of the gospel message they are prone to think of a particular response to that message. This perhaps explains why testimonies of saving faith tend to emphasize personal experience rather than the person and work of Jesus Christ... This is not to say that the gospel message does not demand a response. Of course

---

[300] Dever, *The Gospel & Personal Evangelism,* 41.

it does. But that response is not the work of the evangelist; it is the work of God...[301]

IS THE "COME TO THE FRONT" METHOD USED IN THE BIBLE?

While the altar call may be a widespread practice today, there is no scriptural support for such a practice. A quick search of the sermons of Christ and the Apostles shows that the whole "come to the front method" was never used. This methodology is entirely foreign to the Word of God. Many evangelistic sermons are recorded for us in the book of Acts, yet not once is there a call at the end to come to the front. The people are never told to come to the front for salvation; instead, they are told to believe unto salvation.

In his book, *The Invitation System*, Iain Murray presents the following points to consider regarding the high-pressure methodology of the "Invitation" as used in the modern church:

1. The invitation system, because it represents an outward response as connected with 'receiving Christ,' institutes a condition of salvation which Christ never appointed.

2. Because the call to come forward is given as though it were a divine command, those who respond are given reason to believe that they are doing something commendable before God, while those who do not are falsely supposed to be disobeying Him.

3. By treating two distinct issues, 'come to Christ' and 'come to the front' as though they were one, the tendency of the invitation to mislead the unconverted in regard to their duty. The real issue is as stated in John 6:20 'This is the work of God, that ye believe on him who he hath sent.'[302]

---

[301] Boice and Philip Graham Ryken, *The Doctrines of Grace*, 23.
[302] Iain Hamish Murray, *The Invitation System* (Edinburgh: Banner of Truth Trust, 1973), 26.

That being the case, does the "come to the front method" of evangelism add a non-biblical step into salvation? It is difficult to see how the modern emphasis on coming forward would not be seen as contributing in some degree to a person's salvation. In fact, I have commonly heard preachers and evangelists say things like, "If there are 100 steps to your salvation, Jesus will take 99, but you must take the first one.", or "Come now, Jesus is waiting here for you, all you have to do is come Him." It is easy to see how such words could lead to the belief that walking forward is contributing to one's salvation. Could such an invitation be seen as adding to the gospel? Could it even be adding human effort (works) as an essential component of the gospel? Some might not believe that "going forward" is that much work, but if it is contributing in any way even just one percent, how can that not be a mixture of God's grace and human effort?

"OH NO, I WALKED FORWARD! AM I SAVED?"

No one is saved because he or she went forward during an invitation, but some are saved despite their going forward during an invitation. It is possible that some who "come to the front" have genuinely heard the gospel and believed in the gospel for their salvation. Perhaps they understand that walking to the front is not adding to their salvation or required for salvation at all. And maybe they have just followed the speaker's appeal to walk forward now that they are saved. If their faith is in the Jesus Christ of Scripture, then they are saved no matter if they walked forward, backward, or just stayed seated.

However, it is also possible that a person could not have heard the gospel, not believed in the gospel, and still walked forward under the compulsion of the speaker, peer pressure of friends, or an entirely wrong view of what is needed for salvation. Clearly, such a person is not saved; instead, they have just gone for a walk and gotten a bit of exercise. The point is, that genuine salvation and "coming to the front" are not synonymous. It is entirely possible for a person to have one without the other.

As you reflect on your salvation, perhaps you too made a trip down the aisle. However, this does not mean that you are or are not saved. We should never look to a "come forward" event in our lives as proof of our salvation. It is good for professing Christians to, as the Apostle Paul says, "Examine yourselves, to see whether you are in the faith. Test yourselves."[303] Paul was not calling on the Corinthians to reflect on a time when they walked forward as a test of their salvation, but he is calling on them to make sure that they believe in Jesus Christ and what He has done to provide salvation.

SHOULD WE STILL INVITE PEOPLE TO COME TO THE FRONT?

It is possible that invitations, as done by many, should be abandoned altogether for the reasons cited above. However, if church leaders choose to continue to have an invitation, the words they speak during such a time must be carefully selected. The speaker should in no way lead the hearer to think that the act of going forward is an element of their salvation or that walking to the front has been commanded by God. An example of acceptable usage of an altar call might be one in which, following the gospel presentation, the speaker calls upon people to believe in the gospel for salvation. At which time he could address those people in this way:

> Today, if God has revealed your sinfulness to you and has given you a desire to repent, and if you have believed in Jesus Christ for your salvation, then we would love to know about it. As a church, we desire to rejoice with you in your salvation and to talk with you more about what this means in your life. If today you were saved by the grace of God, feel free to come to the front as the music plays. However, you are more than welcome to visit with one of our leaders after church or call the church office to schedule a time to talk, but please let

---

[303] 2 Corinthians 13:5

us know about your salvation and how we can help you to grow in the grace and knowledge of the Lord Jesus Christ.

Such an example serves to demonstrate that a request to come forward can be given without being viewed as a contribution to salvation. The coming forward is not commanded as a requirement for salvation, but it is merely an invitation for a new believer to inform the pastor and the church of their salvation. Does the person have to come to the front? By no means, and in fact, other options were given as to how the person lets the pastor, and the church know of his or her salvation.

Summary: There is no biblical support that a person needs to come forward to be saved. Many preachers and evangelists act as if coming to the front is a biblical command; however, Jesus nor His Apostles ever used such a practice. With such great emphasis placed on the visual act of going forward, many people tend to confuse their physical activity with the spiritual action of salvation. We, as Christians, should keep this in mind when we evangelize or share our testimonies with others. Even if we did walk an aisle, or go to the front, during an invitation, we must be careful that we do not make such an action a part of the gospel that we are proclaiming to others. The gospel's call is not to walk forward but to repent, believe, and walk in obedience to Christ.

Chapter 29

LIFESTYLE EVANGELISM.

Lifestyle evangelism is the belief that Christians can live their lives in such a holy, God-honoring, and Christ-glorifying way that the example of their life becomes a method of evangelization. Perhaps you have heard someone say, "I don't share the gospel, but I do live the gospel." Or, maybe something like, "I have never shared the gospel with anyone, but people can see the gospel by the way that I live." Well, what do you think? Is it possible for one's lifestyle to be an adequate expression of the gospel? Unless one is an excellent mime, and able to portray the person and work of Christ clearly through body gestures, it is impossible to communicate the gospel through lifestyle evangelism. This is because the gospel is a message, and messages are best expressed through words.

No amount of good living can ever lead someone to salvation. As Christians, we know that we are not saved by works and believe the words of the Apostle Paul, "For by grace you have been saved through faith. And this is not your own doing; it is the gift of God, not a result of works, so that no one may boast."[304] However, not only are we not saved by our good works, but our good works, deeds, and lifestyle are inadequate to save anyone else. A Christian's life, no matter how Christlike it may be, is still an inadequate communication of the gospel of God.

---

[304] Ephesians 2:8-9

Now at first, that might sound harsh, but remember that God uses the message of the gospel to bring salvation. Think about it, can someone study your life alone, and understand that Jesus is the promised Messiah, who was God and man, lived a holy life, died on the cross, rose from the dead and ascended into heaven? Of course not, even if you were the best, most morally pure person on the earth, it would still be impossible for onlookers to know the gospel of God just by observing your lifestyle.

No amount of holy living can ever replace clear gospel proclamation. The gospel is news, good news that is made up of essential components about the person and work of Jesus Christ that must be proclaimed for others to hear and believe. As the Apostle Paul says, "how are they to believe in him of whom they have never heard? And how are they to hear without someone preaching?"[305]

Does this mean that our lifestyle does not matter when it comes to evangelism? Certainly not, let's be clear, God does command Christians to live holy lives, "but as he who called you is holy, you also be holy in all your conduct, since it is written, 'You shall be holy, for I am holy.'"[306] However, our holy lives are not a substitute for the gospel. Instead, our holy lives are the outworking of the gospel that we have heard, believed, and have been saved by. As the Apostle Paul writes, "let your manner of life be worthy of the gospel of Christ."[307] Paul would never advocate replacing gospel proclamation with lifestyle evangelism, but he certainly did see that belief in the gospel should have a radical change on a person's behavior.

How we, as Christians live out our lives for unsaved people to see matters. A Christian should be a living example of a life transformed by the gospel. If a professing Christian lives like the unsaved, then they are not living a life worthy of the gospel. Such a lifestyle makes it extremely difficult to witness to others. If the unsaved people that you are around cannot perceive any difference in your supposed "holy" life than their own sinful life,

---

[305] Romans 10:14
[306] 1 Peter 1:15-16
[307] Philippians 1:27

then any attempt to proclaim the gospel to them will most likely not be taken seriously. If you engage in the same sinful ways of speaking, thinking, and behaving that they do, then they will see your supposed salvation and transformation as a joke. The Apostle Peter says, "Keep your conduct among the Gentiles honorable, so that when they speak against you as evildoers, they may see your good deeds and glorify God on the day of visitation."[308] Jesus says, "In the same way, let your light shine before others, so that they may see your good works and give glory to your Father who is in heaven."[309]

The point is that your lifestyle does matter. It matters to God, and it matters to those that you are around every day. How you live not only affects you but those around you as well. Your holy life will never replace the need to communicate the gospel to others, but such a lifestyle does help to create an appropriate platform from which to speak the gospel. There is nothing more powerful than a Christian who is actively pursuing Christ, living a holy life, and who is a bold proclaimer of the gospel.

Is your lifestyle and behavior hindering your ability to witness? If you are acting like the world, then the world is not going to listen to you when you begin to speak about God. They see you as one of them, and no different. If you are a Christian but have not been living a life worthy of the gospel, then confess your sin before God and repent. I would also recommend going to those who know you and admit to them that you have been a poor example of a Christian to them. One of the greatest things for an unbeliever to behold is a Christian confessing and repenting of sin. Most likely, they will see no need for your apology or even your desire to turn from your sin, but you are regaining the platform of a holy life that should be paired with gospel proclamation.

Summary: Your lifestyle is important, and to some degree, it is evangelistic. In so far as the gospel, that has saved should now

---

[308] 1 Peter 2:12
[309] Matthew 5:16

infuse all that you do in life. God has given clear commands about how Christians are to live, and how we are not to live. However, we should never rely on our good deeds to replace gospel proclamation. In fact, if someone truly believed that lifestyle evangelism is the gospel, then he or she would be substituting the gospel of God with another gospel.[310] Gospel proclamation and a Christian lifestyle go together, and we should not focus on only one to the neglect of the other. Your life should be conducted in such a way that the gospel, which has saved you, is expressing a life that reflects the new creation that you are.[311] Your life speaks volumes about what you believe, but make sure that your mouth speaks even louder.

---

[310] Galatians 1:8
[311] 2 Corinthians 5:17

CONCLUSION TO PART III:

Do these widespread statements and questions used to speak about salvation sufficiently proclaim the details of the gospel? Are these modern words of salvation an accurate expression of the "gospel of God."[312] Or do they leave out essential components of the gospel? I think if we are honest, virtually no gospel content is being shared in the popular examples that we have just examined. Instead, various words, distortions of the gospel, and new techniques have been used to replace the gospel. Most of the modern words and phrases used to speak of salvation have become so popular among pastors, churches, and Christians that it is possible that people within our own churches don't know how to express the gospel rightly. Regarding this matter, J. I. Packer in his book *Evangelism And The Sovereignty of God* has written:

> It is right to recognize our responsibility to engage in aggressive evangelism. It is right to desire the conversion of unbelievers. It is right to want one's presentation of the gospel to be as clear and forcible as possible... But it is not right when we take it on us to do more than God has given us to do. It is not right when we regard ourselves as responsible for securing converts, and look to our own enterprise and techniques to accomplish what only God can accomplish. To do this is to intrude ourselves into the office of the Holy Spirit, and to exalt ourselves as the agents of the new birth.[313]

Perhaps, you may not have thought much about the importance of clear gospel communication, but you now realize that there is a disparity between the actual gospel and what is often communicated to be the gospel. This realization can be a shocking realization to Christians who have heard such "evangelism" all of their lives. And it can be even more challenging to face the facts that, perhaps you have even engaged in such inadequate evangelism in the past. If this is you, I pray that such irritation will not

---

[312] Romans 1:1
[313] Packer, *Evangelism and the Sovereignty of God,* 34.

lead to less of a desire to witness, but an intense desire to witness even more by correctly sharing the gospel. By knowing the gospel, and understanding the gospel better, we are then able to communicate it to others more clearly.

In the end, if you have acquired a modern way of speaking about salvation that has no foundation in the Bible, that uses a language that does not emphasize the gospel of God, then what should you do? The answer is simple: return to the gospel presented in Scripture. Study the subject of the gospel: Jesus Christ. The more you know about Him, the easier it will be to present the gospel since He is the source and center of the gospel.

Understanding the gospel also helps to stop calling on people to make responses to the gospel that have no biblical support. As Graeme Goldsworthy writes,

> My concern about evangelism is that sometimes there is a greater emphasis on the need for some kind of response than on the clear exposition of the gospel. Telling people they need to come to Jesus, that they must be born again that they should commit their lives to Christ, and so on, is not preaching the gospel. It is, at best, telling them what they ought to do, or in the case of the new birth, what has happened when they have received the gospel. It is a remarkable thing in Acts 2 that Peter's sermon contained no appeal. The appeal came from the congregation: 'What should we do?' It was the power and clarity of the gospel message that impressed them with the need to do something about it.[314]

We live in a world where few people truly know the gospel, yet so many professing Christians wrongly emphasis a man-made response to the gospel rather than emphasizing the need to repent and believe the gospel. Instead of putting all of the focus on walking the aisle, saying a prayer, or asking Jesus to come into one's heart, we should abandon unbiblical methods and simply rely on God to work through our proclamation of His gospel.

---

[314] Goldsworthy, *Preaching the Whole Bible as Christian Scripture*, 95.

PART IV:

UNPOPULAR, YET BIBLICAL, WORDS USED TO SPEAK OF SALVATION.

Chapter 30

DON'T BE AFRAID TO USE BIBLICAL WORDS.

If you were asked about your religious beliefs, what would you say? Perhaps you would answer by saying, "Well, I am a Christian." How would you respond if you were then asked, "What is a Christian?" Hopefully, you would not immediately give one of the popular Christianese sounding phrases that we evaluated in Part III, like "Christian means that I…" "asked Jesus into my heart," "walked an aisle," "made a decision," or "said the sinner's prayer." Hopefully, by now, you are longing for a way to communicate the truths of God less ambiguously.

However, for some Christians, removing such, so-called, evangelistic phrases, could lead them to wonder, "If not those words, then what words should I use to speak about salvation?" For some believers, those are the only words they have ever heard used to speak of salvation. Now that those phrases have been examined more closely and have been found to be lacking in gospel clarity, many people may feel that they are at a loss for words to communicate their faith.

Coming face to face with one's use of inadequate words, phrases, and methods for evangelism can be quite disheartening. For many, the challenge is to unlearn the incorrect ways we have been speaking about salvation and to be retaught by the Word of God. It is through this process of subtraction and addition that many will step up to the challenge and speak of the gospel and the response to the gospel in a more biblical manner.

So, how can we speak about our salvation in a way that is biblically sound, true, and God-glorifying? Is this where we should get creative and use our imaginations? Should we seek to find terminology that is modern and culturally relevant? No, God has not only defined the gospel for us, but He has also provided the terms which accurately describe salvation. Instead of just repeating the culturally popular (but theologically vacuous), phrases that supposedly describe salvation, we should use the words which God has used in His Word.

Salvation is God's work, and it is only right that He should be the one to define that work. His Word tells us all we need to know about salvation, and His Word is true and sufficient for all things. "All Scripture is breathed out by God and profitable for teaching, for reproof, for correction, and for training in righteousness."[315] If we desire to speak of the gospel of God correctly, then we should proclaim the gospel as it has been delivered to us in God's Word. Likewise, if we desire to speak of the salvation that comes through the gospel, then we should look to God's Word as our example. The words we choose to express the gospel and the words we choose to express our salvation should come from the same source.

It is no surprise that the Bible uses specific words to describe those who have believed in that gospel. In this section, we are going to look at several prominent words taken directly from Scripture that we would do well to put back into our Christian vocabulary. I hope that this study will help you to become clearer in your own expression of the gospel and in your call for others to respond biblically to the gospel.

---

[315] 2 Timothy 3:16

Chapter 31

---✥---

BELIEVED.

What is someone to do upon hearing the gospel? According to the Bible, they should believe. The word *believe* is basic, yet descriptive of what one's response should be upon hearing the gospel. It points to the fact that the gospel must be accepted as presented in Scripture, and to reject that information is to remain a non-believer. The English word b*elieve* is most commonly translated from the Greek word *pisteuó*, which means, "to think to be true, to be persuaded of, to credit, place confidence in."[316] Keeping such a definition in mind helps us to understand what it means to "believe the gospel." As Professor Anthony Hoekema, in his book *Saved by Grace*, has written:

> It is obvious that we cannot have faith in someone of whom we know nothing, or about whom we know the wrong things. ... We must surely have enough knowledge to know in whom we believe, and what Christ has done for us. The Bible clearly teaches that without knowledge there can be no true faith.[317]

Can a person be saved and yet not believe the gospel? No, a person cannot hear the gospel, deny its truth claims, and yet be saved by a message that he or she does not even believe to be true.

---

[316] Joseph Henry Thayer, *Thayer's Greek-English Lexicon of the New Testament* (Baker Book House, 1977), entry for pisteuó.
[317] Hoekema, *Saved by Grace*, 140.

As Paul states, "For I am not ashamed of the gospel for it is the power of God *to everyone who believes*..."[318] Belief in the gospel is mandatory for salvation; therefore, those who proclaim the gospel, call their audience to *believe in the gospel*, and those that do believe in the gospel for salvation are referred to as *believers*.

EXAMPLES OF THE WORD BELIEVE, OR A VERSION OF IT, BEING USED IN THE BIBLE.

But to all who did receive him, who believed in his name, he gave the right to become children of God. (John 1:12)

... whoever believes in him may have eternal life. For God so loved the world, that he gave his only Son, that whoever believes in him should not perish but have eternal life. (John 3:15-16)

Whoever believes in him is not condemned, but whoever does not believe is condemned already, because he has not believed in the name of the only Son of God. (John 3:18)

... these are written so that you may believe that Jesus is the Christ, the Son of God, and that by believing you may have life in his name. (John 20:31)

But many of those who had heard the word believed, and the number of the men came to about five thousand. (Acts 4:4)

Now the full number of those who believed were of one heart and soul . . . (Acts 4:32)

But when they believed Philip as he preached good news about the kingdom of God and the name of Jesus Christ, they were baptized, both men and women. (Acts 8:12)

---

[318] Romans 1:16

... a great number of both Jews and Greeks believed. But the unbelieving Jews stirred up the Gentiles and poisoned their minds against the brothers. (Acts 14:1-2)

For what does the Scripture say? 'Abraham believed God, and it was counted to him as righteousness.' (Rom. 4:3)

Whether then it was I or they, so we preach and so you believed. (1 Cor. 15:11)

For we who have believed enter that rest ... (Heb. 4:3)

I write these things to you who believe in the name of the Son of God, that you may know that you have eternal life. (1 John 5:13)

DOES IT REALLY MATTER WHAT YOU BELIEVE IN FOR SALVATION?

Before calling people to "believe," we must first give them the foundation--or the *Who* and *What*--in which they are to believe. People cannot just believe in anything they wish and be saved by it. The belief must be placed in the right object, or better yet, the right person. Regarding the empty call to "believe" that some Christians were issuing, Charles Spurgeon wrote:

> I have sometimes thought when I have heard addresses from some revival brethren who had kept on saying time after time, 'Believe, believe, believe,' that I should like to have known for myself what it was we were to believe in order to our salvation. There is, I fear a great deal of vagueness and crudeness about this matter.[319]

It is far easier to command people just to believe, but we must never forget that there is a message that must be connected to that belief for true salvation to occur. A call to believe without giving a person what they need to believe is futile. Belief, no matter

---

[319] Murray, *The Invitation System*, 33

how strong it is, in *anything* besides the person and work of Jesus Christ amounts to a faith that is entirely ineffective in bringing about salvation.

God has given us the message which is required of us to believe, and that message is centered on Jesus Christ. The Apostle John is abundantly clear that the gospel is all about Jesus, and it is only belief in Him that saves. For example, in John 3, he writes that "whoever *believes in him* should not perish but have eternal life."[320] He then writes about the condemnation of those who do not believe, "Whoever *believes in him* is not condemned, but whoever *does not believe* is condemned already, because he has not believed in the name of the only Son of God."[321] At the close of his gospel, John summarizes his entire message by stating the purpose of his writing, "these are written so that you may believe that Jesus is the Christ, the Son of God, and that by believing you may have life in his name."[322]

IS AN INTELLECTUAL KNOWLEDGE OF THE GOSPEL ALL THAT IS NEEDED?

The main thrust of this book has been to educate and to equip Christians with the facts of the gospel that have become increasingly lost among modern Christians. While it is important to understand that there must be right belief for salvation, I also want to be careful not to promote a strictly academic belief in the gospel. Saving faith *is more* than just learning and knowing the facts about the historical Jesus; however, it is certainly *not less than* that. Nineteenth-century theologian A. A. Hodge acknowledged that true faith does include an acceptance of the truth expressed in the gospel, but it also involves a personal trust in that truth. Hodge writes:

---

[320] John 3:16
[321] John 3:18
[322] John 20:31

> Generally, knowledge is the apprehension of an object as true, and faith is an assent to its truth. It is obvious, therefore, that in this general sense of the term every exercise of faith includes the knowledge of the object assented to... The apprehension of the moral truthfulness of an object is knowledge, the assent to it, as good and desirable, is faith.[323]

True saving faith means that a person has received the information of the gospel, intellectually believes that it is true, and trusts in the gospel for salvation. This is the right belief in the proper object of salvation. To help understand this, it is sometimes best to think of *right belief* by comparing it to *wrong belief*. For example, can a person be saved without knowing the information contained in the gospel? No. Can a person hear the gospel, believe it to be false, and still be saved by it? No. Can a person receive the information of the gospel, believe it to be true, yet not trust in Christ for their own salvation, and still be saved? No. One must receive the gospel, embrace its truthfulness, and trust in it personally. As Charles Hodge, (the father of A. A. Hodge) wrote:

> When we are commanded to believe in Christ as the Saviour of men, we are not required merely to assent to the proposition that He does save sinners, but also to receive and rest upon Him alone for our own salvation.[324]

Likewise, John Murray, explaining the difference in strictly intellectual belief and a personal, trusting belief, wrote:

> Faith, after all is not belief of propositions of truth respecting the Savior, however essential an ingredient of faith such belief is. Faith is trust in a person, the person of Christ, the Son of God and Savior of the lost. It is

---

[323] Archibald Alexander Hodge, *Outlines of Theology* (London: Banner of Truth Trust, 1972), 467.
[324] Hodge, *Systematic Theology: Vol. 3: Soteriology*, 91.

entrustment of ourselves to him. It is not simply believing him; it is believing in him and on him.[325]

These theologians, as scholarly and studied as they were, fully acknowledged that salvation is not merely an intellectual agreement with the Bible. While it is true that there is something that needs to be believed in for salvation, just knowing the facts about Jesus Christ does not equal salvation.

RIGHT BELIEF IS A SUPERNATURAL GIFT FROM GOD.

Saving faith, which includes belief in the gospel, is a supernatural act that a spiritually dead human cannot achieve by his or her own power. Even if the gospel is proclaimed with utmost clarity and absolute precision, there still must be a supernatural work of God on an individual's spiritually dead soul to bring it to life to believe in the gospel. As Paul writes in Ephesians, "For by grace you have been saved through faith. And this is not your own doing; it is the gift of God, not a result of works, so that no one may boast."[326] "Not your own doing," is hard for us to comprehend, but this is the nature of true salvation by grace. This grace is so wonderful that even our faith is given to us as a gift from God and is not of our own doing. Though we must believe in the gospel, it is God who grants us the ability to even believe and trust in His gospel for salvation.

For instance, after the Apostle Paul proclaimed the gospel, and witnessed many salvations, Luke attributed the cause of their salvation not to themselves, but to God. He wrote, "and when the Gentiles heard this, they began rejoicing and glorifying the word of the Lord, and as many as were appointed to eternal life believed."[327] Likewise, the Apostle John wrote, "But to all who did receive him, who believed in his name, he gave the right to

---

[325] Murray, *Redemption Accomplished and* Applied, 117.
[326] Ephesians 2:8-9.
[327] Acts 13:48

become children of God, who were born, neither of blood nor of the will of the flesh nor of the will of man, but of God."[328] John fully acknowledged that man must believe the gospel, and yet he also affirms that there is more involved than just the will of the person.

We can also hear this teaching in the account where Jesus acknowledges God the Father as the source of Simon Peter's belief: "Simon Peter replied, 'You are the Christ, the Son of the living God.' And Jesus answered him, 'Blessed are you, Simon Bar-Jonah! For flesh and blood has not revealed this to you, but my Father who is in heaven.'"[329] Jesus used this as a teaching moment to reveal His identity, and to show that right belief in Him is a supernatural gift from the Father.

We are to proclaim the gospel so that people can have the knowledge of Christ that is a necessary requirement for salvation, but we must also keep in mind that it is not our job to *make* anyone believe, nor *can* they believe until God supernaturally draws them to Himself.[330] A. W. Pink, commenting on Mark 10:27-28 which says, "with man it is impossible, but not with God. For all things are possible with God," wrote:

> Of himself, the fallen sinner can no more repent evangelically, believe in Christ savingly, come to Him effectually, than he can create a world. 'With men it is impossible' rules out of court all special pleading for the power of man's will. Nothing but a miracle of grace can lead to the saving of any sinner.[331]

Such an acknowledgment of God's role in salvation should not discourage Christian evangelism. Instead, it should empower our evangelistic efforts. It is a relief to know that our role is to present the gospel for belief, but that God, is the one who super-

---

[328] John 1:12-13
[329] Matthew 16:16-17
[330] John 6:65
[331] Pink, *Studies on Saving Faith*, 33.

naturally uses our gospel proclamation to bring people to a saving knowledge of Himself.

Application: The Apostle Paul said, "I believed, and so I spoke,' we also believe, and so we also speak."[332] Paul was clear in his gospel proclamation and in directing the proper response to that gospel. He believed the gospel and spoke the gospel so that others would also believe. What were those who believed in the gospel supposed to do? Repeat the process. They were to speak the gospel so that others would hear and believe the gospel.

How could adding the word *believe* to your vocabulary help in the way you communicate the gospel? What if the next time you are asked about your religious beliefs, you simply said, "I am a believer"? Such a statement almost demands that the listener then ask, "Really, well, what do you believe?" Instead of saying, "Well, I asked Jesus into my heart," you could tell them about the object of your belief—Jesus Christ. By doing so, you are not only correctly speaking about your own personal faith in the Savior, but you are also clearly and biblically communicating the gospel that must be believed in for salvation.

---

[332] 2 Corinthians 4:13

Chapter 32

---✦---

REPENTED.

While the focus of this work has been primarily aimed towards the message of the gospel which is to be believed, we want to make sure to spend some time on another word that is commonly associated with the gospel and with the word *believe*, and that is the word *repent*. Trusted theologian Wayne Grudem defines it this way; "Repentance is a heartfelt sorrow for sin, a renouncing of it, and a sincere commitment to forsake it and walk in obedience to Christ."[333]

In the Bible, the word repent is so closely associated with the word believe that the two are often coupled as the correct way to respond to the gospel. A good example is found in Jesus' first sermon, which contained this exact pairing as He proclaimed, "*repent* and *believe* in the gospel."[334] In this passage, we are given two responses to the gospel that are commanded by Jesus Christ, *both* of which are necessary, as author Dr. Guy Richard writes:

> There is no question that the call of the gospel is to believe in Jesus Christ, which is why our preaching must regularly call people to faith. But if our preaching stops there without ever calling people to repentance, it is dangerously close to presenting a half-truth as though

---

[333] Wayne A. Grudem, *Systematic Theology: An Introduction to Biblical Doctrine* (Leicester, England: Inter-Varsity Press, 1994), 713.
[334] Mark 1:15

it were the whole truth. Repentance and faith are inseparable. They are two sides of the same coin. Faith is the positive side of turning to Christ, and repentance is the negative side of turning away from sin.[335]

It is not enough to only believe the gospel and yet not desire to turn from sin. To present only repentance or only belief is what Dr. Richard warns "is dangerously close to presenting a half-truth as if it were the whole truth." For example, if a person who was being evangelized was directed to repent only, yet the gospel was never presented to them for belief, could that person be saved? On the other side of the coin, what if a person says that he or she believes in Jesus Christ for salvation, yet, he or she has never repented of their sin, could that person be saved? No, as we see, both a right view of sin and desire to turn from it (repentance) and a correct view of oneself and God's provision of salvation (belief) are vital for true conversion

Writing on the inseparable link of these two in true salvation, Wayne Grudem writes:

> Scripture puts repentance and faith together as different aspects of the one act of coming to Christ for salvation. It is not that a person first turns from sin and next trusts in Christ, or first trusts in Christ and then turns from sin, but rather that both occur at the same time. When we turn to Christ for salvation from our sins, we are simultaneously turning away from the sins that we are asking Christ to save us from. If that were not true our turning to Christ for salvation from sin could hardly be a genuine turning to him or trusting in him.[336]

Similarly, trusted author and pastor Mark Dever warns of the dangers of teaching only belief or only repentance:

---

[335] Guy M. Richard, "What Is Faith," *Tabletalk* 39, no. 1 (January 2015): 16.
[336] Grudem, *Systematic Theology*, 714.

> Churches must not err by neglecting either repentance or faith. Without the former, a mental-assent-only faith follows, which is dead (see Jas. 2:17,26). Without the latter, faith and reliance on Christ vanish behind demands of obedience to the law (see Rom. 2-3). A gospel-centered church teaches the need to both turn from sin and turn to Christ. By itself a searching exposition on human sin is not enough. By itself the proclamation of God's love in Christ's atoning death is not enough. Both are necessary. A cross not taken up by repentance or affirmed by faith is a cross that does not save.[337]

As these men have clearly taught, belief and repentance as an either/or proposition leads people to half-truth responses to the gospel which are inadequate to be saved. Yet, this is exactly what we find modern Christians so often doing: focusing on either belief or either repentance when both truths should be proclaimed for you can't truly have one without the other.

EXAMPLES OF THE WORD REPENT, OR A VERSION OF IT, BEING USED IN THE BIBLE.

> Now after John was arrested, Jesus came into Galilee, proclaiming the gospel of God, and saying, "The time is fulfilled, and the kingdom of God is at hand; repent and believe in the gospel. (Mark 1:14-15)

> No, I tell you; but unless you repent, you will all likewise perish. (Luke 13:3)

> Thus it is written, that the Christ should suffer and on the third day rise from the dead, and that repentance for the forgiveness of sins should be proclaimed in his name to all nations, beginning from Jerusalem. (Luke 24:46-47)

---

[337] Dever, *The Church: The Gospel Made Visible*, 26-27.

Now when they heard this they were cut to the heart, and said to Peter and the rest of the apostles, 'Brothers, what shall we do?' And Peter said to them, 'Repent and be baptized every one of you in the name of Jesus Christ for the forgiveness of your sins, and you will receive the gift of the Holy Spirit.' (Acts 2:37-38)

Repent therefore, and turn back, that your sins may be blotted out. (Acts 3:19)

The God of our fathers raised Jesus, whom you killed by hanging him on a tree. God exalted him at his right hand as Leader and Savior, to give repentance to Israel and forgiveness of sins. (Acts 5:30-31)

The times of ignorance God overlooked, but now he commands all people everywhere to repent. . . (Acts 17:30)

Therefore, O King Agrippa, I was not disobedient to the heavenly vision, but declared first to those in Damascus, then in Jerusalem and throughout all the region of Judea, and also to the Gentiles, that they should repent and turn to God, performing deeds in keeping with their repentance. (Acts 26:19-20)

God may perhaps grant them repentance leading to a knowledge of the truth, and they may come to their senses and escape from the snare of the devil, after being captured by him to do his will. (2 Tim. 2:25b-26)

DO WE STILL PREACH REPENTANCE?

There is no doubt that the command to repent was often proclaimed in the New Testament by John the Baptist, Christ, and the Apostles as a proper response to the gospel. What about our day? Is the command to repent still commonly proclaimed in evangelism? Or, do we remove the word "repentance" to make way for easier means of evangelism? Pastor J. D. Greear warns:

> I have begun to wonder if both problems, needless doubting and false assurance, are exacerbated by the clichéd ways in which we (as evangelicals) speak about the gospel. Evangelical shorthand for the gospel is to 'ask Jesus into your heart,' or 'accept Jesus as Lord and Savior,' or 'give your heart to Jesus.' These phrases may not be wrong in themselves, but the Bible never tells us, specifically, to seek salvation in those ways. The biblical summation of a saving response toward Christ is 'repentance' and 'belief' in the gospel.[338]

Greear's point is simple—Christians are creating responses to the gospel that have no biblical precedent. We should not substitute alternate responses to the gospel which are not prescribed by God. Instead, we should return to the responses that are commanded in Scripture to "repent and believe."

Charles Spurgeon warned of the teaching used in the revivals of his day which failed to deal with sinfulness and repentance (which has equal application to much of the teaching of our day) by writing:

> Sometimes we are inclined to think that a great portion of modern revivalism has been more a curse than a blessing because it has led thousands to a kind of peace before they have known their misery; restoring the prodigal to the Father's house, and never making him say, 'Father, I have sinned.' How can he be healed who is not sick?[339]

Spurgeon, not known as one to skirt an issue, called the revivalism of his day "a curse." How could revivalism, closely related

---

[338] J. D. Greear, *Stop Asking Jesus into Your Heart: How to Know for Sure You Are Saved*, 7.
[339] Murray, *The Invitation System*, 34

to evangelism, become a curse? According to Spurgeon, it happens when the issue of sin is never addressed. If people do not acknowledge their sinfulness, then there is really no perceived need for the Savior. But many preachers in his day were utterly avoiding the issues of sin, confession, and repentance yet still proclaiming people to be saved. Such people were becoming Christians by name only, but were actually still in their sin, unrepentant, and still under the curse of sin.

J. C. Ryle, well known for his clarity of gospel proclamation and the requirement of those who believe in Christ to repent of their sin to be saved, was appalled by those who claimed to love Christ, yet there was no change in their pursuit of sin. He wrote:

> Let no man ever persuade you that any religion deserves to be called *the* gospel, in which repentance toward God has not a most prominent place. *A* gospel, indeed! That is no gospel in which repentance is not a principal thing. *A* gospel! It is the gospel of man, but not of God. *A* gospel! It comes from earth, but not from heaven. *A* gospel! It is not *the* gospel at all. … You have as yet no part or lot in Christ. So long as you do not repent of sin, the gospel of our Lord Jesus Christ is no gospel to your soul.[340]

It seems that what Ryle warned of, has become the standard means of evangelism in our times. Many people seem to acknowledge a belief in the gospel, and yet they go on sinning and never repent. Ryle exposes that individual as one who does not genuinely have the gospel, for if they did, they would both believe and repent.

Wayne Grudem has also warned of the danger of creating false converts when a "believe only" gospel is proclaimed without any call to repentance. He writes:

---

[340] J. C. Ryle, "The Necessity of Repentance," Chapellibrary.org, Section C, accessed November 16, 2016, http://www.chapellibrary.org/files/ebooks/ggog/index_split_043.html.

> When we realize that genuine saving faith must be accompanied by genuine repentance for sin, it helps us to understand why some preaching of the gospel has such inadequate results today... But this watered-down version of the gospel does not ask for a wholehearted commitment to Christ—commitment to Christ, if genuine, must include a commitment to turn from sin. Preaching the need for faith without repentance is preaching only half of the gospel. It will result in many people being deceived...[341]

Grudem is convinced that people must not only hear, know, and believe the gospel, but they also must be told of their sinfulness and their need to turn from it. To do otherwise is to lead people into being deceived about their salvation.

Application: *Sin* is a word that has all but disappeared in our society and, consequently, the biblical teaching of *repenting of our sin* has disappeared as well. If nothing is viewed as a sin, then there is no need for repentance. In a time of ever-increasing moral relativism, it is controversial to call any behavior sinful, and it is viewed as disdainful to call anyone to repent from his or her sin. However, until people see themselves as sinners who need to repent, they will never see the need to be saved from their sins by God's one and only Savior. As Tim Keller has preached:

> You don't actually get that salvation into your life through your strength; it is only for those who admit they are weak. And if you cannot admit that you are a hopeless moral failure and a sinner and that you are absolutely lost and have no hope apart from the sheer grace of God, then you are not weak enough for...the great salvation that God has brought into the world.[342]

---

[341] Grudem, *Systematic Theology*, 716.
[342] Timothy J. Keller, *Heralds of the King: Christ-centered Sermons in the Tradition of Edmund P. Clowney*, ed. Dennis E. Johnson (Wheaton, IL: Crossway Books, 2009), 70.

It can be tempting, in our evangelistic efforts as Christians, to speak around sin and repentance to get to salvation, but if there is no acknowledgment of sin, then there will be no perceived need for salvation. If the problem is sin, and yet the problem is never addressed, then people will never see the need for Jesus paying the price for their sins so that they could be forgiven. We must resist the tendency to think that we have found a new and improved way to evangelize by not speaking about repentance. If repentance from sin was common to the teachings of Jesus Christ, God in the flesh, and the Apostles that He trained, then we are clearly not in line with biblical evangelism if we remove repentance from our witness. As John MacArthur writes:

> The Bible is clear: Repentance is at the heart of the gospel call. Unless we are preaching repentance we are not preaching the gospel our Lord has charged us to preach. If we fail to call people to turn from their sins, we are not communicating the same gospel the apostles proclaimed.[343]

To clearly articulate the full, and correct response to the gospel, belief, and repentance must be proclaimed. Repentance is a crucial aspect of evangelism that continues to lose its place in modern evangelism. However, Christians who do not want to come across as offensive by speaking about sin and the need to repent from sin, have created a gospel that allows people to remain in their sin. Such a gospel is not the gospel, and non-repentance is certainly not the appropriate response to the gospel. Jesus called people to repent, the Apostles called people to repent, and so should we.

---

[343] MacArthur, *The Gospel According to the Apostles*, 74.

Chapter 33

SAVED.

My daughter, concerned about a fellow third-grader, witnessed to him by asking, "Have you ever been saved?" After thinking about it for a moment, the boy replied, "Yes," but he then went on to say, "One time I was drowning in a pool, about to die, and my dad jumped in and saved me." While that was not the type of "saved" my daughter had in mind, the boy did at least understand the term to mean a dangerous situation from which he had been rescued. Like the young boy's example of being saved, people are often rescued from various calamities, diseases, and dangers, but what did my daughter, and we as Christians mean when we say something like, "I am saved," or "Are you saved?" From exactly what kind of danger have we been rescued? What kind of danger are we warning others to be rescued from?

In his book, *Saved from What,* R. C. Sproul tells the story of being asked by a stranger if he was saved. Sproul, in turn, asked him, "Saved from what?" To which the man did not have an answer. Of the man, Sproul said:

> . . . it was clear that, though this man had a zeal for salvation, he had little understanding of what salvation is. He was using Christian jargon. The words fell from his lips without being processed by his mind. As a result, his words were empty of content. Clearly, the man had a love for Christ and a concern for people . . . But sadly,

he had little understanding of what he was so zealously trying to communicate.[344]

Dr. Sproul had exposed the fact, that even though the man was using an excellent biblical word, he did not know how it related to being a Christian. While the word "saved" is one of the most commonly used words to describe a person in a right relationship with God, if we do not know what we have been saved from then we could easily find ourselves in the same shoes as the man in Dr. Sproul's account. The man in the story did not understand what he was saved from, which hindered his evangelistic efforts to tell others of the danger which they need to be rescued from as well. This man is not alone, many professing Christians would have found themselves equally dumbfounded to be asked such a question, "Saved, saved from what?"

Soon after the Apostle Paul proclaimed the "gospel of God" in the opening of Romans he wrote, "For I am not ashamed of the gospel for it is the power of God for salvation to everyone who believes..."[345] Paul let the reader know that God had provided the method of rescue: the gospel. However, by just reading this verse by itself, someone might be confused and would wonder, "Why do I need to be saved?" Paul gave the answer in the verses that immediately follow, "For the wrath of God is revealed from heaven against all ungodliness and unrighteousness of men."[346]

The greatest need of any human is to be saved from God and, specifically, God's wrath against "all ungodliness and unrighteousness" because by nature we, as humans, are unrighteous and justly deserve the wrath of God. Just a little further in his letter to the Romans, Paul elaborates on the need of every man to be saved from God when he wrote:

> But because of your hard and impenitent heart you are storing up wrath for yourself on the day of wrath when God's righteous judgment will be revealed . . . but for

---

[344] R. C. Sproul, *Saved from What?* (Wheaton, IL: Crossway Books, 2002), 1.
[345] Romans 1:16
[346] Romans 1:18

those who are self-seeking and do not obey the truth, but obey unrighteousness, there will be wrath and fury. There will be tribulation and distress for every human being who does evil ... (Rom. 2:5, 8-9)

Unrepentant sinners will face God's wrath and fury! Now here is indeed something to be saved from. More than any dangerous situation that we could ever imagine, is our need to be saved from the wrath of God. It is not just *some* people who need to be saved, but it is universal. As Paul writes, "all have sinned and fall short of the glory of God" and deserve to be punished.[347] However, the God who will punish sinners in wrath and fury is the same God who has given us the good news of rescue. There is hope, and there is salvation from the wrath of God through the gospel of God. Salvation does not come from our own hands, but it is a gift given to us directly by God Himself.

As Paul continues to expound the gospel in the book of Romans, he writes, ". . . but God shows his love for us in that while we were still sinners, Christ died for us. Since, therefore, we have now been justified by his blood, much more shall we be saved by him from the wrath of God."[348] The good news is that the God we need to be saved from is the God who provides our salvation through His Savior. Dr. Sproul went on to write in his book *Saved from What*:

> We have seen that the grand paradox or supreme irony of the Christian faith is that we are saved both *by* God and *from* God. The God of perfect holiness, who demands satisfaction of His justice and who will not wink at sin, has from all eternity decreed that He himself should provide salvation to those people who, by their sin, are exposed to His wrath and judgment. The means *by* which God accomplishes this great salvation

---

[347] Romans 3:23
[348] Romans 5:8-9

may be described as the most crucial aspect of the work of Christ.[349]

This is a critical theological truth that we as believers need to understand so that we will not be like the man in Dr. Sproul's account; not knowing what we are even saved from.

EXAMPLES OF THE WORD SAVED, OR A VERSION OF IT, BEING USED IN THE BIBLE.

> . . . praising God and having favor with all the people. And the Lord added to their number day by day those who were being saved. (Acts 2:47)

> This Jesus is the stone that was rejected by you, the builders, which has become the cornerstone. And there is salvation in no one else, for there is no other name under heaven given among men by which we must be saved. (Acts 4:11-12)

> But we believe that we will be saved through the grace of the Lord Jesus, just as they will. (Acts 15:11)

> For 'everyone who calls on the name of the Lord will be saved.' How then will they call on him in whom they have not believed? And how are they to believe in him of whom they have never heard? And how are they to hear without someone preaching? (Rom. 10:13-14)

> For since, in the wisdom of God, the world did not know God through wisdom, it pleased God through the folly of what we preach to save those who believe. (1 Cor. 1:21)

---

[349] Sproul, *Saved from What?*, 41.

In him you also, when you heard the word of truth, the gospel of your salvation, and believed in him, were sealed with the promised Holy Spirit. (Eph. 1:13)

For by grace you have been saved through faith. And this is not your own doing; it is the gift of God, not a result of works, so that no one may boast. (Eph. 2:8-9)

But when the goodness and loving kindness of God our Savior appeared, he saved us, not because of works done by us in righteousness, but according to his own mercy, by the washing of regeneration and renewal of the Holy Spirit, whom he poured out on us richly through Jesus Christ our Savior. (Titus 3:4-6)

Consequently, he is able to save to the uttermost those who draw near to God through him, since he always lives to make intercession for them. (Heb. 7:25)

To those who have obtained a faith of equal standing with ours by the righteousness of our God and Savior Jesus Christ. (2 Peter 1:1)

Application: There could be nothing scarier and nothing worse than facing God as a sinner and receiving the eternal wrath that is justly due. By far the greatest need of humanity is to be saved from God's wrath, and the best news that could ever be given to mankind is that the one whose wrath we deserve has also sent the One to save us from it. We, as people who have been saved by the Savior, should not try to hide the unimaginable danger that mankind needs to be saved from by using evangelism techniques that never get to the real problem (sin), the consequence of their sin (the judgment and punishment of God), and the real solution for their sin (the gospel of Jesus Christ).

The word "saved," like the words "believe" and "repent," can easily be added to the Christian vocabulary. For instance, if you were asked about your religious views, or maybe how you became a Christian, instead of saying, "I made a decision for Christ," which carries virtually no meaning or gospel significance, you might say, "I am saved. How about you? Have you been saved, or are you still in danger?" To which the hearer could naturally respond, "What are you talking about? I'm in no danger. What do I need to be saved from?" "Well," you might reply, "let me tell you about the danger that you are in and about the only One that can save you. You see, we are naturally under the wrath of God because we have sinned. Therefore, we will face the judgment and eternal punishment of God for our sins. However, the good news is that God has sent His Savior to rescue us from our sin . . ." Notice how easy it is to explain the bad news of sin and the good news of the gospel when the word "saved" is used to witness. You will find that incorporating these biblical words back into your common Christian vocabulary will not make sharing the gospel more difficult, but they will make it much easier for you to communicate the real gospel.

Chapter 34

JUSTIFIED.

Justification can be defined as, "Man's acceptance with God, or his being regarded and treated as righteous in His sight—as the object of His favour, and not of His wrath; of His blessing, and not of His curse."[350] However, as wonderful as the doctrine of justification is, the word *justified,* or *justification,* is rarely used among Christians today. For instance, when is the last time you have heard someone say, "Praise God, I've been justified!"? Odds are you haven't because not only has this word but the doctrine that it represents has been underemphasized for a very long time. There is a desperate need for the word justification to be brought back to the minds and mouths of today's Christians.

There was certainly a time in Church History where the word justification was commonly spoken. In fact, it could be said that this was *the* word that the Protestant Reformation was fought over, and it was over the definition of justification that countless lives were lost in its defense. Compare the current sentiment toward justification to the great reformer Martin Luther's view of the doctrine, and you will see a vast difference:

> The article of justification is the master and prince, the lord, the ruler, and the judge over all kinds of doctrines;

---

[350] James Buchanan, *The Doctrine of Justification: An Outline of Its History in the Church and of Its Exposition from Scripture* (Birmingham, Ala.: Solid Ground Christian Books, 2006), 100.

> it preserves and governs all church doctrine and raises up our conscience before God. Without this article the world is utter death and darkness.[351]

> Whoever departs from the article of justification does not know God and is an idolater . . . For when this article has been taken away, nothing remains but error, hypocrisy, godlessness, and idolatry, although it may seem to be the height of truth . . .[352]

One thing is clear: Luther believed justification to be of utmost importance. Luther was a man obsessed with ridding himself of his sin and his guilty status before God. During his life, he immersed himself into the Roman Catholic system of works to make himself right with God, but even as he plunged to the deepest depths of that religion, he only became more miserable as he realized that there was no hope to be found in his own ability to right himself before God. However, as Luther began to immerse himself in Scripture, he discovered a word and a doctrine that brought his anguished soul an inexpressible peace as he came to understand it is God who justifies man through the atoning work of Christ.

Justification became *the* source of peace to Luther's soul and went on to become *the* watchword of the Reformation, but what exactly does "justification" mean? Some Christians equate the term "justification" to mean the same thing as the word "forgiveness." Perhaps you might have even heard someone say something like, "Justified means just if I'd never sinned." While justification does have to do with sins being forgiven, that is only part of the definition. Professor Guy Waters, who has spent much time writing and teaching on the doctrine of justification, has explained justification as:

---

[351] Martin Luther and Ewald M. Plass, *What Luther Says, an Anthology* (Saint Louis: Concordia Pub. House, 1959), 2:703.
[352] Ibid., 703.

> ... a legal declaration in which God pardons the sinner of all his sins and accepts and accounts the sinner as righteous in His sight. God declares the sinner righteous at the moment that the sinner puts his trust in Jesus Christ (Rom. 3:21-26, 5:16; 2 Cor. 5:21). ... God justifies the sinner solely on the basis of the obedience and death of His Son, our representative, Jesus Christ. Christ's perfect obedience and full satisfaction for sin are the only ground upon which God declares the sinner righteous (Rom. 5:18-19; Gal. 3:13; Eph. 1:7; Phil. 2:8). We are not justified by our own works; we are justified solely on the basis of Christ's work on our behalf. This righteousness is imputed to the sinner. In other words, in justification, God puts the righteousness of His Son onto the sinner's account. Just as my sins were transferred to, or laid upon, Christ at the cross, so also His righteousness is reckoned to me (2 Cor. 5:21).[353]

The Apostle Paul summarizes the dire need of humankind to be made right in the eyes of God, and stresses our absolute inability to do so by writing, "None is righteous, no, not one; no one understands; no one seeks for God. All have turned aside; together they have become worthless; no one does good, not even one."[354] We have sinned, and we deserve God's wrath, but how can we escape the punishment that we are rightly due for breaking God's law? Is there something that we can do to fix the problem? Do we just try harder? No, as Paul goes on to write, "For by works of the law no human being will be justified in his sight."[355]

Immediately following a series of dreadful passages which describe humanity's guilty position before God, Paul presents the wonderful news of how God has provided the way for the guilty status of humanity to be removed and to be replaced by the bless-

---

[353] Guy Waters, "What Are Justification and Sanctification?" *Tabletalk* 39, no. 1 (January 2015): 2.
[354] Romans 3:10-12
[355] Romans 3:19

ing of being credited with the righteous status of the Son of God Himself. Paul writes:

> —the righteousness of God through faith in Jesus Christ for all who believe. For there is no distinction: for all have sinned and fall short of the glory of God, and are justified by his grace as a gift, through the redemption that is in Christ Jesus, whom God put forward as a propitiation by his blood, to be received by faith. This was to show God's righteousness, because in his divine forbearance he had passed over former sins. It was to show his righteousness at the present time, so that he might be just and the justifier of the one who has faith in Jesus. (Rom. 3:22-26)

This is the absolute best news humanity could ever receive. The record of our sin is removed and replaced with the record of Jesus Christ's life of perfect obedience. Justification is a legal declaration by God that is both instantaneous and permanent for all believers. Take a moment to reflect on the implications of this marvelous truth. Believers receive the righteous life of Christ instead of our account of sinfulness, and this legal declaration by God will never change. Amazing! One of the most thought-provoking summaries of this doctrine is found in Dr. Martyn Lloyd-Jones' classic book, *The Cross*:

> And by him all who believe, you included, are at this moment justified entirely and completely from everything you have ever done—if you believe that this is the Lord Jesus Christ, the Son of God, and that he died there on the cross, for your sins and to bear your punishment. If you believe that, and thank him for it, and rely utterly only upon him and what he has done, I tell you, in the name of God, all your sins are blotted out completely, as if you had never sinned in your life, and his righteous-

ness is put on you and God sees you perfect in his son. That is the message of the cross . . . [356]

Justification is the sole work of God by which he removes our sins, places them on His Son, Jesus Christ and then credits us with the righteousness of Christ. There is absolutely nothing we contribute to this legal declaration by God. As the seventeenth-century pastor of Geneva Switzerland, Francis Turretin, wrote in his masterful work on justification:

> The gospel teaches that what could not be found in us and was to be sought in another, could be found nowhere else than in Christ, the God-man; who taking upon himself the office of surety most fully satisfied the justice of God by his perfect obedience and thus brought to us an everlasting righteousness by which alone we can be justified before God.[357]

How can a sinful person be made right before God? Only by the justification that is found in Jesus Christ. We are all guilty sinners, who can do nothing to right ourselves or remove our own sin. But praise be to God that He has provided the solution by sending the God-man to live a life of perfection in our place. Justification is based wholly on Christ's life and death, and by the grace of God, it is applied to all of those who by grace, through faith, in Jesus Christ are saved.

Application: Since our justification by Christ is the foundational element of our salvation, it would serve us well to know more about it to understand it, and to make it a part of our gospel communication to others. Understanding justification not only helps us to understand our salvation better but in turn, understanding

---

[356] Lloyd-Jones and Christopher Catherwood, *The Cross: God's Way of Salvation*, 36.

[357] François Turrettini, George Musgrave. Giger, and James T. Dennison, *Justification* (Phillipsburg, NJ: P & R Publications, 2004), 29.

our salvation better helps us to be better equipped as we explain salvation to others.

The gospel is made up of who Christ is, what He has done, and what His accomplishment means for us. Justification concerns all three of these elements. It defines who Jesus is, tells us what He did, and lets us know what this means for us. Christ, the Son of God and descendant of David was born of a virgin, lived a perfect, sinless life, fulfilled all righteousness, died on the cross and took the sins of all believers on Himself. On the cross, our sin is placed on Him. He takes our record, receives full punishment for it, and gives us His record of righteousness. Now that is good news!

Chapter 35

ATONED.

The word *atoned*, or *atonement* has to do with the satisfaction or appeasement of a party that has been offended by another. For example, in times past if a king had somehow angered another king, then he could try to make atonement by sending a gift to appease the other king's wrath and to make peace between the two parties. Biblically, we see this idea of the atonement taught in the fact that we have angered the King of Kings, God Himself with our sin, and as sinners, we rightfully deserve His wrath. However, Jesus Christ, the God-man died on the cross to make atonement on behalf of His people. Jesus satisfied the wrath of God by paying the price for our sin and makes peace between God and us. As the late Professor J. Gresham Machen wrote:

> The atoning death of Christ, and that alone, has presented sinners as righteous in God's sight; the Lord Jesus has paid the full penalty of their sins, and clothed them with His perfect righteousness before the judgment seat of God. It never could have been predicted, for sin deserves naught but eternal death. But God triumphed over sin through the grace of our Lord Jesus Christ.[358]

---

[358] J. Gresham Machen, "The Atonement," in *Christianity and Liberalism* (New York: Macmillan Company, 1923), http://www.westminsterconfession.org/introduction-to-the-christian-faith/the-atonement.php.

On the cross, Jesus took our sin upon Himself and was punished in our place. Satisfaction was made on our behalf, and God is no longer angry with those who have had their sins atoned for by Jesus Christ. Jesus fully satisfied the just demands of God's Law. This substitutionary atonement of Jesus on our behalf is taught in many places, but here are three to begin with:

> He himself bore our sins in his body on the tree, that we might die to sin and live to righteousness. By his wounds you have been healed. (1 Peter 2:24)

> For our sake he made him to be sin who knew no sin, so that in him we might become the righteousness of God. (2 Cor. 5:21)

> Christ redeemed us from the curse of the law by becoming a curse for us—for it is written, 'Cursed is everyone who is hanged on a tree.' (Gal. 3:13)

Christ has taken the place of sinners who deserved the punishment of God. He bore our sins for us, became sin for us, and became a curse on our behalf. Otherwise, we could never be at peace with God and would have to face the full wrath of God one day. In his work *The Atonement*, the great Scottish Pastor, and Westminster Theologian, John Murray wrote:

> Sin is the contradiction of God and he must react against it with holy wrath. Wherever sin is, the wrath of God rests upon it (*cf.* Rom. 1:18). Otherwise God would be denying Himself, particularly His holiness, justice, and truth. But wrath must be removed if we are to enjoy the favor of God which salvation implies. And the only provision for the removal of wrath is propitiation.[359]

---

[359] John Murray, "The Atonement," in *Encyclopedia of Christianity*, Vol. 1 (Evansville: Sovereign Grace Publishers, 1976), http://www.the-highway.com/atonement_murray.html.

The biblical truth of God being angered by sin and the need for atonement is not only found in the New Testament but also throughout the Bible. In Genesis, we see that the first sin of Adam and Eve angered and deserved immediate death, yet God displays mercy by allowing them to live but killing animals to cover their nakedness.[360] Not that the death of the animals truly atoned for sin, but it did lay the foundation for sin, wrath, and blood atonement.[361]

In Exodus, God gave directions for the Israelites to sacrifice a lamb (the Passover Lamb) so that God's wrath would pass over their homes.[362] Later, in the book of Leviticus, as the nation of Israel was established God instituted the annual Day of Atonement that was a clear example of the sinfulness of man, the holiness of God, and the need for appeasement to be made.[363] These and many other Old Testament examples point to the fact that humanity's sin angers God, humanity deserves to be punished, and the satisfaction of God's justice must be met. The examples of atonement that took place in the Old Testament were meant to point to (a type or shadow) the ultimate source of atonement that would be sent from God, once and for all, to satisfy His wrath. Jesus Christ, the Son of God, is the one who died in our place and "entered once for all into the holy places, not by means of the blood of goats and calves but by means of his own blood, thus securing an eternal redemption."[364]

OTHER EXAMPLES OF THE DOCTRINE OF ATONEMENT BEING EXPRESSED IN THE BIBLE.

> Jesus Christ, whom God put forward as a propitiation by his blood, to be received by faith. This was to show

---

[360] Genesis 3:20
[361] Hebrews 9:12
[362] Exodus 12:23
[363] Leviticus 16:34
[364] Hebrews 9:12

God's righteousness, because in his divine forbearance he had passed over former sins. (Rom. 3:24-25)

...but God shows his love for us in that while we were still sinners, Christ died for us. (Rom. 5:8)

He who did not spare his own Son, but gave him up for us all—how will he not also, along with him, graciously give us all things? Who will bring any charge against those whom God has chosen? It is God who justifies. (Rom. 8:32-33)

Pay careful attention to yourselves and to all the flock, in which the Holy Spirit has made you overseers, to care for the church of God, which he obtained with his own blood. (Acts 20:28)

For Christ, our Passover lamb, has been sacrificed. (1 Cor. 5:7)

Therefore, if anyone is in Christ, he is a new creation. The old has passed away; behold, the new has come. All this is from God, who through Christ reconciled us to himself and gave us the ministry of reconciliation; that is, in Christ God was reconciling the world to himself, not counting their trespasses against them, and entrusting to us the message of reconciliation. (2 Cor. 5:17-19)

Christ loved us and gave himself up for us, a fragrant offering and sacrifice to God. (Eph. 5:2)

... and to wait for his Son from heaven, whom he raised from the dead, Jesus who delivers us from the wrath to come. (1 Thess. 1:10)

In this is love, not that we have loved God but that he loved us and sent his Son to be the propitiation for our sins. (1 John 4:10)

> Therefore he had to be made like his brothers in every respect, so that he might become a merciful and faithful high priest in the service of God, to make propitiation for the sins of the people. (Heb. 2:17)

Application: Though the actual word atonement is not used often in the New Testament, the concept of God's righteous anger against sinners being satisfied by Christ is a fundamental and often repeated truth. Sadly, the atonement of Christ is not as a familiar teaching in churches as it once was. This means that it may take a little more study on your part to become comfortable enough to speak to others about it, but it will be worth it. And as you share about the atonement, don't think of it as such a lofty topic that is beyond you or your audience. Take, for example, this brief summary of atonement by R. C. Sproul, "A Substitute has appeared in space and time, appointed by God Himself, to bear the weight and the burden of our transgressions, to make expiation for our guilt, and to propitiate the wrath of God on our behalf. This is the gospel."[365]

---

[365] Sproul, *The Truth of the Cross*, 81.

Chapter 36

---✛---

REDEEMED.

Redeemed, or *redemption* is a financial term that means "to purchase or to buy." What does this economic term have to do with the gospel, Jesus, or salvation? Are we in debt to God? Yes, all people have sinned and are in moral debt to God. How can we ever pay God back for breaking His Law? What can we give Him in exchange for our souls?[366] Truth be told, we have absolutely nothing of worth to give Him.

God operates in the currency of righteousness, and the bad news is that we have no righteousness in and of ourselves. Even the best, most righteous acts that we can think of are still useless in the transaction of paying off our sin debt. In fact, our best efforts to be good are nothing but filth compared to God's righteous requirement of us.[367] Long story short, we do not even possess the currency needed to pay the price for our sins. Neither can we obtain such currency on our own. Our pockets are empty before God, and there is no hope of ever working or acquiring the payment that is needed to pay for our sin debt.

Some people get into such deep financial debt with cars, homes, credit cards, and so on that, a stringent financial plan must be put into place to help them pay their debts off over time. However, God offers no such payoff plan for our debt to Him. Some people get into such extreme financial debt that they cannot

---

[366] Matthew 16:26
[367] See Isaiah 64:6

ever pay for their debt and even must file bankruptcy. In some situations, these debtors receive a full pardon for their debts even though they never repaid what they owed. God does not offer a bankruptcy plan. God is perfectly holy and just; therefore, every sin must be paid for entirely, or entirely punished by God. The good news is that even though we cannot ever pay the price for our sin debt to God (no long-term payment plan is offered), and God cannot just act as if we have no sin debt (as in the case of financial bankruptcy), He does have the solution to our problem. He, the One we owe, paid the price for our debt. The transaction was made on the cross. Jesus Christ, God in the flesh, paid the price that we could never pay. As A. W. Pink writes:

> They who were under the law could be 'redeemed' only by Another fulfilling its requirements and suffering its curse. Our sins could be 'taken away' only by their being blotted out by the precious blood of Christ. The demands of Justice must be met: the requirements of God's Holiness must be satisfied: the awful debt we incurred must be paid. And on the Cross this was done; done by none less than the Son of God; done perfectly; done once for all.[368]

Jesus paid the price for the sin of all those who are His, released us from the bondage of sin, and purchased us for Himself. Those who are saved by Christ go from being slaves with no way to pay for their own freedom, to being bought by the Most High God. As Pink points out, this is a "once for all" transaction. This is why Jesus can, and does, utter "It is finished" as he dies on the cross.[369] The debt had been paid. He had done all the work needed to secure our redemption.

---

[368] Arthur W. Pink, *The Seven Sayings of the Saviour on the Cross* (Grand Rapids: Baker Book House, 1958), 112.
[369] John 19:30

EXAMPLES OF THE DOCTRINE OF REDEMPTION BEING EXPRESSED IN THE BIBLE.

Pay careful attention to yourselves and to all the flock, in which the Holy Spirit has made you overseers, to care for the church of God, which he obtained with his own blood. (Acts 20:28)

…for all have sinned and fall short of the glory of God, and are justified by his grace as a gift, through the redemption that is in Christ Jesus. (Rom. 3:22-23)

And because of him you are in Christ Jesus, who became to us wisdom from God, righteousness and sanctification and redemption. (1 Cor. 1:30)

…You are not your own, for you were bought with a price. (1 Cor. 6:19)

Christ redeemed us from the curse of the law by becoming a curse for us—for it is written "Cursed is everyone who is hanged on a tree." (Gal. 3:13)

In him we have redemption through his blood, the forgiveness of our trespasses, according to the riches of his grace. (Eph. 1:7)

He has delivered us from the domain of darkness and transferred us to the kingdom of his beloved Son, in whom we have redemption, the forgiveness of sins. (Col. 1:13-14)

Therefore he is the mediator of a new covenant, so that those who are called may receive the promised eternal inheritance, since a death has occurred that redeems them from the transgressions committed under the first covenant. (Heb. 9:15)

Application: A good understanding of the term *redeemed* helps Christians to understand better why the gospel is such good news. It can also serve as another word to help explain the saving work of Jesus Christ to others. If you are a believer, then you have been redeemed. Your sins are paid for by God Himself. There was nothing that you could ever have done to earn your own redemption. However, for His own good pleasure, out of the abundance of His grace and riches, Jesus paid the price for your sins and for your purchase. Jesus Christ is your Redeemer, and you are His Redeemed.

B. B. Warfield believed that the work of Christ as our Redeemer is one of the most underused, yet most awe-inspiring aspects of our salvation. He writes:

> There is no one of the titles of Christ which is more precious to Christian hearts than 'Redeemer.' There are others, it is true, which are more often on the lips of Christians. The acknowledgment of our submission to Christ as our Lord, the recognition of what we owe to Him as our Saviour, - these things, naturally, are most frequently expressed in the names we call Him by. 'Redeemer,' however, is a title of more intimate revelation than either 'Lord' or 'Saviour.' It gives expression not merely to our sense that we have received salvation from Him, but also to our appreciation of what it cost Him to procure this salvation for us. It is the name specifically of the Christ of the cross. Whenever we pronounce it, the cross is placarded before our eyes and our hearts are filled with loving remembrance not only that Christ has given us salvation, but that He paid a mighty price for it.[370]

---

[370] Benjamin B. Warfield, "Redeemer and Redemption," Monergism.com, Intro., accessed December 30, 2016, https://www.monergism.com/threshold/sdg/warfield/warfield_redeemer.html.

CONCLUSION TO PART IV:

Believed, repented, saved, justification, atonement, and redeemed are some excellent examples of biblical words that speak of salvation in a God-approved manner. And there are even more biblical terms that could be considered, such as: adopted-to be brought permanently into the family of God,[371] sanctified-to be made holy by God,[372] and regenerated-to be made new, born again.[373] The point is, words are important because they are used to communicate meaning. As Christians, one of our chief duties is to convey the message and meaning of the gospel to others.[374] In teaching on the need for Christians to maintain the common usage of biblical words to describe salvation, B. B. Warfield wrote:

> I think you will agree with me that it is a sad thing to see words like these die like this. And I hope you will determine that, God helping you, you will not let them die thus, if any care on your part can preserve them in life and vigor. But the dying of the words is not the saddest thing which we see here. The saddest thing is the dying out of the hearts of men of the things for which the words stand. As ministers of Christ it will be your function to keep the things alive. If you can do that, the words which express the things will take care of themselves. Either they will abide in vigor; or other good words . . . will press in to take the place left vacant by them.[375]

In your opinion, are we communicating the gospel in the same way that it was communicated in the Bible? Are preachers and teachers doing a good job of not letting such words die? What

---

[371] Romans 8:14,23; Galatians 3:26; 4:5-6
[372] John 17:17; 1 Corinthians 1:2; Hebrews 9:13-14
[373] John 3:3; 1 Peter 1:3,23; Titus 3:5
[374] Romans 10:14-15
[375] B. B. Warfield, "Redeemer and Redemption" Monergism.com, accessed December 20, 2016, https://www.monergism.com/thethreshold/sdg/warfield/warfield_redeemer.html.

about you? Have you been speaking words that speak of salvation correctly, or have you been relying on the more popular words and phrases that have little or nothing to do with the Bible?

Perhaps, it may have been brought to your attention that your own Christian vocabulary may need some adjusting. Honestly, evaluate how you have shared the gospel in the past and what words you have used to speak of salvation. If you find that you have been using a lot of unbiblical words and phrases in your attempts to communicate salvation to others, then start trying to remove that terminology and replace them with God approved terms that correctly express salvation. We must understand that we cannot create better words than the Holy Spirit, who inspired the biblical authors. Let us use the gospel, the response, and the terms that God has given us to rightly speak of the wonders of salvation.

FINAL THOUGHTS

Jesus Christ, our Savior, is *the* apex of God's revelation to humanity. The most important subject for any Christian to know is Jesus. He is the incarnation of the second person of the Trinity. He is the only One who is both God and man. He is the Christ who the prophets of God proclaimed would come. He has fulfilled the prophecies and the exact lineage of which God said He would come. He lived a holy sinless life, died on the cross for the sins of all whom the Father has given him. He rose from the dead, ascended into heaven, and will be the final judge of all mankind. He and He alone is the Way, the Truth, the Life, any other belief that does not lead to heaven, is a lie, and leads to eternal death.[376] He is the chief cornerstone, and without Him, nothing of value shall be built.[377]

We must *not* assume that the world, or even professing Christians, know this message automatically. Instead, we would do better to assume that people *do not* know the gospel and that it is our duty, honor, and privilege to inform them of God's message of salvation. Paul made it clear that the gospel "is the power of God for salvation to everyone who believes," but he also wrote of the importance of informing others of the gospel so that they can be saved as well. He writes, "How then will they call on him in whom they have not believed? And how are they to believe in him of whom they have never heard? And how are they to hear without

---

[376] See John 14:6
[377] Mark 12:10; Ephesians 2:20-22

someone preaching? As it is written, 'How beautiful are the feet of those who preach the good news!'"[378] People must believe the gospel to be saved, and those who have been saved by it, are the ones that are called upon to boldly and clearly proclaiming the saving message of Jesus Christ to them. It is our feet which are to be beautiful, for we run with the most important message that can ever be heard, to a people who are perishing without it.

The need to proclaim the gospel is obvious; however, many professing Christians are unfamiliar with the very message that they are to proclaim. Knowing and understanding salvation through Jesus Christ should be a consuming desire for every Christian. However, this does not seem to be the case with much of modern Christianity. There is a dire need to re-educate, even professing Christians, on the gospel. Much liberty has, wrongly, been taken with this message from God. Professing Christians have added, subtracted, softened, and twisted the gospel to the point that creative license with the gospel seems to be the norm, not the anomaly. Unless there is an intentional effort to equip believers with the knowledge and understanding of the gospel, there will be a steady departure from *the* core belief of Christianity: the gospel of God.

Everything about Christianity hinges on the gospel. It is the axis on which everything in Christianity rotates. It is the "power of God for salvation." If we cannot accurately transmit this message to others, then how can a person be saved? Therefore, knowing and understanding the gospel personally, and desiring to communicate the gospel to others should be the great Christian obsession.

Witnessing is already difficult for most, but witnessing when you don't even know the message, that you are supposedly a witness to, can lead not only to frustration but a false witness as well. Without proper knowledge and understanding of the authentic gospel, it is easy for a distorted gospel to be spread. As Shane Rosenthal, writes of his salvation, yet lack of discipleship in the gospel:

---

[378] Romans 1:16; 10:14,15

> There I was, brand new to the faith, and within a year I had street witnessed, gone door to door, answered phones for the Billy Graham Crusade hotline, helped out teaching Sunday School to children in juvenile hall, and even considered becoming an overseas missionary. The only problem was, I didn't know what the Gospel was. My experience is not unique. I have met a number of folks with similar stories to tell, some who are no longer Christians. This problem occurs when we push evangelism from our pulpits rather than *the Evangel*. I can honestly say that during the first two years of my Christian walk I had never heard of the doctrine of justification by grace alone through faith alone, but I sure had it drilled into my head that I needed to be a witness for Jesus. The problem was, I knew that I was to be a witness, but I didn't quite understand what it was I was to witness about."[379]

Rosenthal does not seem to be alone in this. Instead of spending time teaching believers about the gospel, the mistake of assuming that people know the gospel is repeated over and over. Paul tells Timothy to "Keep a close watch on yourself and on the teaching. Persist in this, for by doing you will save both yourself and your hearers."[380] Sound gospel belief is no little matter. It is not only essential for our own salvation but the salvation of those to whom we are witnessing as well.

Paul severely warned the Galatian believers about the false teachers that were distorting the gospel. They were creating a different message than the one originally passed down to Paul from God and that Paul had passed on to them. Paul realized that distorting the gospel could be catastrophic, and we should recognize the danger as well. A false gospel produces false converts, and false converts become false witnesses who continue to make other

---

[379] Shane Rosenthal, "When the Message Obscures the Message," Reformation Ink, 1995, Introduction, accessed February 20, 2012, http://homepage.mac.com/rosenthal/reformationink/classic.htm

[380] 1 Timothy 4:16

false converts and who often go on to become false members of local churches. When the authentic gospel is changed, everything that Christianity holds true falls. In the words of J. I. Packer,

> There is no doubt that evangelicalism today is in a state of perplexity and unsettlement. ...there is evidence of widespread dissatisfaction with things as they are and or equally widespread uncertainty as to the road ahead. This is a complex phenomenon, to which many factors have contributed; but, if we go to the root of the matter, we shall find that these perplexities are all ultimately due to our having lost our grip on the biblical gospel. Without realizing it, we have during the past century bartered that gospel for a substitute product which, though it looks similar enough in points of detail, is as a whole a decidedly different thing. Hence our troubles; for the substitute product does not answer the ends for which the authentic gospel has in past days proved itself so mighty.[381]

There is no doubt that the gospel is being reduced, changed, and distorted by professing Christians. Some create their own gospel message from a desire to be less offensive. Others create a different gospel out of a lack of understanding the gospel themselves. Sadly, this lack of gospel clarity has caused a dangerous drifting away from the true, biblical gospel. And like a ship with no anchor, professing Christians, frequently not even realizing it, are drifting further and further away from the foundation of the faith that they claim to possess.

My hope is for all who read this work to be further grounded in the knowledge and understanding of the gospel of God, and that by knowing and understanding the gospel better you will be better equipped to communicate the gospel to others rightly. Only the real gospel can lead to real salvation, and only the real gospel

---

[381] J. I. Packer, introduction, in *The Death of Death in the Death of Christ*, by John Owen (Edinburgh: Banner of Truth Trust, 1983), http://www.the-highway.com/Death.html.

can change people's lives and eternal destinations. This is the gospel that we must believe and the gospel that we must continue to proclaim.

Bibliography

Alexander, T. Desmond. *Exodus*. London: Apollos, 2017.

"Baptist Confession of Faith of 1689 with Scriptural Proofs." Historic Church Documents at Reformed. org. Accessed November 25, 2016. http://www.reformed.org/documents/index.html.

Barrs, Jerram. *The Heart of Evangelism*. Wheaton, IL: Crossway Books, 2001.

Begg, Alistair, and Sinclair B. Ferguson. *Name above All Names*. Wheaton, IL: Crossway, 2013.

Berkhof, Louis. *Systematic Theology*. Grand Rapids, MI: W.B. Eerdmans Pub. Co., 1996.

Boice, James Montgomery, and Philip Graham Ryken. *The Doctrines of Grace: Rediscovering the Evangelical Gospel*. Wheaton, IL: Crossway Books, 2002.

Boyce, James P. *Abstract of Systematic Theology*. Cape Coral, FL: Founders Press, 2006.

Buchanan, James. *The Doctrine of Justification: An Outline of Its History in the Church and of Its Exposition from Scripture*. Birmingham, AL: Solid Ground Christian Books, 2006.

Chantry, Walter J. *Today's Gospel: Authentic or Synthetic?* London: Banner of Truth Trust, 1970.

Cheeseman, John. *The Grace of God in the Gospel.* London: Banner of Truth Trust, 1972.

Comfort, Ray. *God Has a Wonderful Plan for Your Life: The Myth of the Modern Message.* Bellflower, CA: Living Waters Publications, 2010.

Dever, Mark, and Paul Alexander. *The Deliberate Church: Building Your Ministry on the Gospel.* Wheaton, IL: Crossway Books, 2005.

Dever, Mark. *The Church: The Gospel Made Visible.* Nashville, TN: B & H Academic, 2012.

Dever, Mark. *The Gospel & Personal Evangelism.* Wheaton, IL: Crossway Books, 2007.

Dodd, C H. "The Apostolic Preaching and Its Developments." The Apostolic Preaching and Its Developments. Religion Online. Accessed December 7, 2015. http://www.religion-online.org/showbook.asp?title=539.

Edwards, Jonathan. "Select Sermons." - Christian Classics Ethereal Library. Accessed October 19, 2016. http.//www.ccel.org/ccel/edwards/sermons.sinners.html.

Erickson, Millard J. *Christian Theology.* Grand Rapids, MI: Baker Book House, 1998.

Ferguson, Sinclair B., and Derek Thomas. *Ichthus: Jesus Christ, God's Son, the Saviour.* Edinburgh: The Banner of Truth Trust, 2015.

Finney, Charles G. *Finney's Systematic Theology*. Edited by James Harris Fairchild. Grand Rapids, MI: Eerdmans Pub., 1976.

Finney, Charles G. *Memoirs of Rev. Charles G. Finney*. New York, NY: A.S. Barnes & Company, 1903.

"Form of Presbyterian Church-Government According to the Westminster Standards." A Puritan's Mind » Form of Presbyterian Church Government. Accessed November 26, 2016. http://www.apuritansmind.com/westminster-standards/form-of-presbyterian-church-government/#Of the Church.

Gilbert, Greg. *What Is the Gospel?* Wheaton, IL: Crossway, 2010.

Goldsworthy, Graeme. *Preaching the Whole Bible as Christian Scripture: The Application of Biblical Theology to Expository Preaching*. Grand Rapids, MI: W.B. Eerdmans, 2000.

Greear, J. D. *Stop Asking Jesus into Your Heart: How to Know for Sure You Are Saved*. Nashville, TN: B&H Publishing Group, 2013.

Green, Michael. *Evangelism in the Early Church*. Grand Rapids, MI: W.B. Eerdmans Pub., 2004.

Greidanus, Sidney. *Preaching Christ from the Old Testament: A Contemporary Hermeneutical Method*. Grand Rapids, MI: W.B. Eerdmans Pub., 1999.

Grudem, Wayne A. *Systematic Theology: An Introduction to Biblical Doctrine*. Leicester, England: Inter-Varsity Press, 1994.

Hendriksen, William, and Simon Kistemaker. "1 John." In *New Testament Commentary*, Vol. James, Epistles of John, Peter, and Jude. Grand Rapids, MI: Baker Book House, 2007.

Hodge, Archibald Alexander. *Outlines of Theology*. Edinburgh: Banner of Truth Trust, 1972.

Hodge, Archibald Alexander. *Outlines of Theology*. London: Banner of Truth Trust, 1972.

Hodge, Charles. *Commentary on the Epistle to the Romans*. Grand Rapids, MI: Wm. B. Eerdmans Pub., 1950.

Hodge, Charles. *Systematic Theology: Volume 3: Soteriology*. Peabody, MA: Hendrickson Publishers, 1999.

Hoekema, Anthony A. *Saved by Grace*. Grand Rapids, MI: W.B. Eerdmans Pub. Co., 1989.

Horton, Michael Scott. *Christless Christianity: The Alternative Gospel of the American Church*. Grand Rapids, MI: Baker Books, 2008.

Horton, Michael. "Sola Gratia." Essay. In *After Darkness, Light Distinctives Of Reformed Theology; Essays In Honor Of R.C. Sproul*. Phillipsburg, NJ: P & R Pub., 2004.

Johnson, Dennis E. *Him We Proclaim: Preaching Christ from All the Scriptures*. Phillipsburg, NJ: P & R Pub., 2007.

Keil, Carl Friedrich, and Franz Delitzsch. *Commentary on the Old Testament*. Vol. 2. Joshua, Judges, Ruth, 1 and 2 Samuel. Peabody, MA: Hendrickson Publishers, 2011.

Keil, Carl, and Franz Delitzsch. "1 & 2 Samuel." In *Commentary on the Old Testament*. Peabody, MA: Hendrickson Publishers, 2011.

Keller, Timothy J. *Heralds of the King: Christ-Centered Sermons in the Tradition of Edmund P. Clowney*. Edited by Dennis E. Johnson. Wheaton, IL: Crossway Books, 2009.

Kistler, Don, R C Sproul, Eric Alexander, and Albert Mohler. *Feed My Sheep: A Passionate Plea for Preaching*. Orlando, FL: Reformation Trust Pub., 2008.

Leonard, Bill J. "Evangelism and Contemporary American Life." Essay. In *The Study of Evangelism: Exploring a Missional Practice of the Church*, edited by Paul Wesley Chilcote and Laceye C. Warner. Grand Rapids, MI: William B. Eerdmans Publishing Company, 2008.

Lloyd-Jones, Martyn., and Christopher Catherwood. *The Cross: God's Way of Salvation*. Westchester, IL: Crossway Books, 1986.

Lloyd-Jones, Martyn. *The Plight of Man and the Power of God*. Ross-shire: Christian Focus Publications, 2009.

Luther, Martin, Alessandro Gavazzi, and James Kerr. *Sermons: by Martin Luther; with Preface by Alessandro Gavazzi; Edited, with Life of Luther, by James Kerr*. Edinburgh: Lyon and Gemmell, 1875.

Luther, Martin, and Ewald M. Plass. *What Luther Says, an Anthology*. Vol. 2. Saint Louis, MO: Concordia Pub. House, 1959.

Luther, Martin. *Commentary on Romans*. Edited by John Theodore Mueller. Grand Rapids, MI: Kregel Classics, 1976.

Luther, Martin. *Galatians*. Edited by Alister McGrath and J. I. Packer. Wheaton, IL: Crossway Books, 1998.

Luther, Martin. *Luther's Works*. Edited by Jaroslav
    Pelikan and Helmut T Lehman. Vol. 40.
    Philadelphia, PA: Fortress, 1965.

MacArthur, John. *Ashamed of the Gospel:
    When the Church Becomes like the World*.
    Wheaton, IL: Crossway Books, 1993.

MacArthur, John. *The Gospel According to God:
    Rediscovering the Most Remarkable Chapter in the
    Old Testament*. Wheaton, IL: Crossway, 2018.

MacArthur, John. *The Gospel According to the
    Apostles: The Role of Works in the Life of
    Faith*. Nashville, TN: Word Pub., 2000.

MacArthur, John. *The Jesus You Can't Ignore: What
    You Must Learn from the Bold Confrontations of
    Christ*. Nashville, TN: Thomas Nelson, 2008.

MacArthur, John. *Why One Way?: Defending an Exclusive Claim
    in an Inclusive World*. Nashville: W Pub. Group, 2002.

Machen, J. Gresham. "The Atonement." In *Christianity
    and Liberalism*. New York: Macmillan Company,
    1923. http://www.westminsterconfession.org/intro-
    duction-to-the-christian-faith/the-atonement.php.

Machen, J. Gresham. *What Is Faith?* Edinburgh:
    Banner of Truth Trust, 1991.

Metzger, Will. *Tell the Truth: The Whole Gospel to
    the Whole Person by Whole People: A Training
    Manual on the Message and Method of God-
    Centered Witnessing to a Grace-Centered Gospel*.
    Downers Grove, IL: InterVarsity Press, 2002.

Mohler, Albert R. "The Scandal of Biblical Illiteracy: It's Our Problem." Christianity - Faith in God, Jesus Christ - Christian Living, Trivia. Accessed December 3, 2016. http://www.christianity.com/.

Mohler, R. Albert, Don Kistler, R. C. Sproul, and Eric Alexander. *Feed My Sheep: A Passionate Plea for Preaching*. Orlando, FL: Reformation Trust Pub., 2008.

Murray, Iain Hamish. *Revival and Revivalism: The Making and Marring of American Evangelicalism 1750-1858*. Edinburgh: Banner of Truth Trust, 1994.

Murray, Ian H. *The Invitation: New Testament*. Nashville, TN: Holman Bible Publishers, 2006.

Murray, John. *Redemption Accomplished and Applied*. William B. Eerdmans Publishing Company, 2015.

Murray, John. "The Atonement." In *Encyclopedia of Christianity*, Vol. 1. Evansville: Sovereign Grace Publishers, 1976. http://www.the-highway.com/atonement_murray.html.

Nichols, Stephen J. *For Us and for Our Salvation: The Doctrine of Christ in the Early Church*. Wheaton, IL: Crossway Books, 2007.

Owen, John, and J. I. Packer. "The Death of Death in the Death of Christ." Introduction. In *The Death of Death in the Death of Christ*. Edinburgh: Banner of Truth Trust, 1983. http://www.the-highway.com/Death.html.

Packer, J. I. *Evangelism and the Sovereignty of God*. Downers Grove, IL: IVP Books, 2012.

Packer, J. I., and Gary A. Parrett. *Grounded in the Gospel: Building Believers the Old-Fashioned Way*. Grand Rapids, MI: Baker Books, 2010.

Parsons, Burk. "What Is the Gospel?" *Tabletalk* 39, no. 1 (January 2015): 2.

Pickard, Stephen K. "Evangelism and the Character of Christian Theology." In *The Study of Evangelism: Exploring a Missional Practice of the Church*, edited by Paul Wesley Chilcote and Laceye C. Warner. Grand Rapids: William B. Eerdmans Publishing Company, 2008.

Pink, Arthur W. *Studies on Saving Faith*. Memphis, TN: Bottom Of The Hill Publishing, 2011.

Pink, Arthur W. *The Attributes of God*. Grand Rapids: Baker Book House, 1975.

Pink, Arthur W. *The Seven Sayings of the Saviour on the Cross*. Grand Rapids: Baker Book House, 1958.

Pink, Arthur W. *The Sovereignty of God*. Carlisle, Penn.: Banner of Truth Trust, 1976.

Platt, David. *Radical: Taking Back Your Faith from the American Dream*. Colorado Springs, CO: Multnomah Books, 2010.

Richard, Guy M. "What Is Faith." *Tabletalk* 39, no. 1 (January 2015): 16.

Rosenthal, Shane. "When the Method Obscures the Message." White Horse Inn, August 14, 2007. https://www.whitehorseinn.org/.

Ryle, J. C. "The Necessity of Repentance." Chapellibrary. org. Accessed November 16, 2016. http://www.chapellibrary.org/files/ebooks/ggog/index_split_043.html.

Schreiner, Thomas R. *Commentary on Hebrews*. Edited by Köstenberger Andreas J. and T. Desmond Alexander. Nashville, TN: B & H Publishing Group, 2015.

Slick, Matt. "Apollinarianism." CARM Christian Apologetics & Research Ministry. Accessed April 24, 2017. https://carm.org/.

Slick, Matt. "Jehovah's Witness' Beliefs." CARM Christian Apologetics & Research Ministry, September 22, 2016. https://carm.org/jehovahs-witnesses-beliefs.

Slick, Matt. "Mormon Beliefs, Are They Christian?" CARM Christian Apologetics & Research Ministry. October 10, 2016. Accessed November 15, 2016. https://carm.org/mormon-beliefs.

Smith, Joseph F. *Family Home Evening Manual*. Salt Lake City, UT: Church of Jesus Christ of Latter-day Saints, 1972.

Sproul, R. C. *Defending Your Faith: An Introduction to Apologetics*. Wheaton, IL: Crossway Books, 2003.

Sproul, R. C. *Everyone's a Theologian: An Introduction to Systematic Theology*. Orlando, FL: Reformation Trust, a division of Ligonier Ministries, 2014.

Sproul, R. C. *Getting the Gospel Right: The Tie That Binds Evangelicals Together*. Grand Rapids, MI: Baker Book House, 2017.

Sproul, R. C. "Is Jesus Knocking at the Heart of the Unbeliever?" Ligonier Ministries, February 10, 2017. http://www.ligonier.org/blog/jesus-knocking-heart-unbeliever/.

Sproul, R. C. *Renewing Your Mind: Basic Christian Beliefs You Need to Know*. Grand Rapids, MI: Baker Books, 1998.

Sproul, R. C. *Saved from What?* Wheaton, IL: Crossway Books, 2002.

Sproul, R. C. *The Holiness of God*. Wheaton, IL: Tyndale House Publishers, 1985.

Sproul, R. C. *The Truth of the Cross*. Lake Mary, FL: Reformation Trust Pub., 2007.

Sproul, R. C. *The Work of Christ: What the Events of Jesus' Life Mean for You*. Colorado Springs, CO: David C Cook, 2012.

Sproul, R. C., ed. *The Reformation Study Bible: English Standard Version*. Orlando, FL: Reformation Trust, 2015.

Spurgeon, Charles A. *All of Grace*. New York: Cosimo, 2008.

Spurgeon, Charles. "Sermon No. 3084 Paul's Parenthesis," March 1908, 2.

Stott, John R. W. *The Message of Galatians: Only One Way*. Leicester, England: Inter-Varsity Press, 1986.

Terry, John Mark. *Evangelism: A Concise History*. Nashville, TN: Broadman & Holman, 1994.

"The Heidelberg Catechism." The Heidelberg Catechism. Accessed December 7, 2015. http://reformed.org/documents/heidelberg.html.

"The Second Helvetic Confession." Historic Church Documents at Reformed.org. Accessed November 26, 2016. http://reformed.org/documents/index.html.

The Watchtower Bible and Tract Society. "Who Is Jesus Christ? Is Jesus God or God's Son? | Bible Teach." JW.ORG. Accessed April 24, 2017. https://www.jw.org/en/publications/books/bible-teach/who-is-jesus-christ/.

Tozer, A. W. *That Incredible Christian*. Harrisburg, PA: Christian Publications, 1964.

Tripp, Paul D. "One Thing - Mark 10:17-34." SermonAudio, 2011. http://www.sermonaudio.com/.

Turretin, Françis. George Musgrave. Giger, and James T. Dennison. *Justification*. Phillipsburg, NJ: P & R Publications, 2004.

Warfield, Benjamin B. "Redeemer and Redemption." Monergism.com. Accessed December 30, 2016. https://www.monergism.com/thethreshold/sdg/warfield/warfield_redeemer.html.

Warfield, Benjamin B. "Redeemer and Redemption." Monergism.com. Accessed December 20, 2016. https://www.monergism.com/thethreshold/sdg/warfield/warfield_redeemer.html.

Warfield, Benjamin B. *The Works of Benjamin B. Warfield*. Vol. 2. Grand Rapids, MI: Baker Book House, 1981.

Washer, Paul. *Gospel Assurance and Warnings*. Grand Rapids: Reformation Heritage Books, 2014.

Washer, Paul. *The Gospel Call and True Conversion*. Grand Rapids, MI: Reformation Heritage Books, 2013.

Washer, Paul. *The Gospel's Power and Message*. Grand Rapids, MI: Reformation Heritage Books, 2012.

Watch Tower Bible and Tract Society of Pennsylvania. *The Watchtower*, May 15, 1963, 307.

Watch Tower Staff. *Reasoning from the Scriptures*. New York: Watchtower Bible and Tract Society of New York, 1985.

Waters, Guy Prentiss. *The Life and Theology of Paul*. Reformation Trust Publishing, 2018.

"Westminster Confession of Faith." Westminster Confession of Faith. Accessed December 7, 2015. http://www.reformed.org/documents/wcf_with_proofs/.

Young, Brigham. *Journal of Discourses by Brigham Young ... His Two Counsellors, the Twelve Apostles and Others*. Vol. 3. Liverpool: Orson Pratt, 1856.

Zaspel, Fred G. *The Theology of B.B. Warfield: A Systematic Summary*. Wheaton, IL: Crossway, 2010.

Made in the USA
Middletown, DE
22 January 2020